ACUA
Underwater Archaeology
Proceedings
2017

edited by
John Albertson and Frederick Hanselmann

AN ADVISORY COUNCIL ON UNDERWATER ARCHAEOLOGY PUBLICATION

2017 © Advisory Council on Underwater Archaeology

Library of Congress Control Number: 2017951831

Made possible in part through the support of
the Society for Historical Archaeology.

Cover Image: Stockfleth, Julius, Circa 1898 Harbor Scene. (Courtesy of the Rosenberg Library Galveston, TX: Collection Number 70.54)

Contents

Foreword..vi

Contributed Papers

Managing Missteps: Complications with Marine Magnetometer Surveys and Data Interpretation 7
    DANIEL HADDOCK

The Investigation of the Anniversary Wreck, a Colonial Period Shipwreck off St. Augustine, Florida: Results of the First Excavation Season 12
    CHUCK MEIDE

Guns in the Potomac: Collaborative Research on Several Historic Shipwrecks Undertaken in the Spring of 2016..21
    P. BRENDAN BURKE

The 450th Anniversary Shipwreck Survey: Applying Updated Methodologies to the Search for Historic Shipwrecks in the Nation's Oldest Port..30
    OLIVIA MCDANIEL, P. BRENDAN BURKE, CHUCK MEIDE

The Dish Ran Away with the Spoon: Revisiting Unprovenienced Food Ways Artifacts from the Spanish Fleet Wrecks of Eighteenth Century Florida..39
    OLIVIA THOMAS

A Preliminary Autopsy on Coffin's Beach, Gloucester, Massachusetts...........................45
    LELAND S. CRAWFORD, VICTOR MASTONE

In Every Grain of Sand, There is a Story: The 19th Century Sand Schooner, ADA K DAMON, as a Case Study in Fostering Maritime Archaeological Heritage and Education in Massachusetts...51
    CALVIN MIRES

A Lot Harder Than It Looks: Conservation of a Worst Case Scenario...........................60
    CHRISTOPHER P. MORRIS, ANDREW FEARON

The Goodwin Sands: Patterns of Burial and Updating the Wreck Record.....................69
    ELIZABETH KRUEGER, JUSTIN DIX

The Pirates of the Pamlico: A Maritime Cultural Landscape Investigation of the Pirates of Colonial North Carolina and their Place in the State's Cultural Memory.....................78
    ALLYSON ROPP

Loss of British Tanker *Mirlo* Revisited: New Considerations Regarding the Vessel's Loss of the North Carolina Coast during the First World War..88
  JOHN BRIGHT

Carpeted with Ammunition: Investigations of the *Florence D* shipwreck, Northern Territory, Australia..98
  JASON T. RAUPP, DAVID STEINBERG

Shipwrecks, Doghole Ports, and the Lumber Trade: Maritime Cultural Landscape Survey of California's Sonoma Coast...105
  TRICIA DODDS

Second Campaign of Excavation on the Saintes Bay's Wreck, Guadeloupe, FWI........111
  JEAN-SÉBASTIEN GUIBERT, FRANCK BIGOT, MAGALI LACHÈVRE, MARINE SADANIA, NOÉMIE TOMADINI

Foreword

The Once and Future Past

Archaeology informs us that maritime activity has been a part of our human experience since long before the inception of recorded human thought. For most people throughout time, the waters of the world have been a mirror-- a boundary, a reflection, a stopping place for the land. In the case of the underwater archaeological community, however, and increasingly for the general public, the maritime cultural landscape does not stop at the waterline, at the end of the pier or wharf, nor at the deceptively reflective surface of the sea. Our global maritime cultural landscape continues unchanged, beneath the wind and lapping waves, becoming a liminal world of water and light. These waters are volumes, not surfaces; three-dimensional spaces rather than planes. Through courage and innovation, the underwater archaeological community is revealing the knowledge they guard beneath their timeless reflections: our heritage preserved in the depths.

The Society for Historical Archaeology celebrated its 50th anniversary in 2017 in Fort Worth, Texas. Participants in the Annual Conference on Historical and Underwater Archaeology submitted 610 abstract submissions; 482 terrestrial papers and 128 underwater or maritime papers. The conference hosted 36 sponsored symposia (7 of which were specific to underwater archaeology), 24 general sessions (7 which were maritime focused), and 10 forums. On this historic anniversary, we would like to give special thanks to the PAST foundation, which for the last ten years has provided expert leadership in facilitating the publication of these valuable ACUA proceedings.

The following volume highlights the complexity and intricacy of underwater cultural heritage and our efforts in its study, management, and preservation. The authors' papers attest to the continuing importance of the Society for Historical Archaeology on its 50th anniversary and demonstrate why archaeology remains increasingly critical to sustaining a symbiotic connection with our collective past.

JOHN ALBERTSON

ACUA
Underwater Archaeology
Proceedings
2017

Managing Missteps: Complications with Marine Magnetometer Surveys and Data Interpretation

Daniel Haddock

Many survey companies operating in the oil and gas industry rely heavily on a single magnetometer, which if not utilized properly can create multiple problems for archaeologists. Magnetic data with outside interference, bottom strikes, or collected during geomagnetic storms will create data artifacts that look like real magnetic anomalies. Several shallow water surveys from 2015 are provided as examples of poorly collected data, which show how the data can inhibit archaeologists' recommendations to operators. Marine Archaeologists are responsible for showing our clients the value in gradiometers over a single marine magnetometer, especially in surveys that may potentially identify shipwrecks or in areas with the potential for unexploded ordinance (UXO). Even though gradiometers have been in use for marine surveys for over 60 years (Wow and Cooper 1989), they are rarely used for marine surveys, especially in the oil and gas industry.

Introduction

An archaeologist's primary job is to protect cultural resources. The first step in protecting cultural resources is to locate and define the archaeological site boundaries. For a long time, archaeologists were viewed within the oil and gas industry as obstructions due to their avoidances preventing or delaying development. However, these avoidances protect our collective human history. The cultural resources located within the Gulf of Mexico span thousands of years. Shipwrecks, specifically, represent a time in human history of great technological and economic advancement during which European countries explored and settled the Americas followed by the birth and expansion of the United States of America.

The collection of human history in the Gulf of Mexico must be protected while allowing the oil and gas industry to develop new fields and infrastructure. This balance is best achieved when the collected geophysical data is clean and precise allowing the archaeologists to present the best recommendations and avoidances. The magnetometer is one of the most useful tools in identifying potential buried archeological sites and seafloor hazards in water depths less than 200 m.

Archaeologists use side-scan sonar, subbottom profiler, magnetometer, and multibeam or singlebeam bathymetry to assess the archaeological conditions on and beneath the seafloor. Using all these instruments together creates a complete picture at and below the seafloor to identify cultural material and modern debris. The side-scan sonar, subbottom profiler, and multibeam bathymetry all provide imagery of the seafloor and subseafloor using sound. The magnetometer measures the localized fluctuations in Earth's magnetic field, called anomalies, which are generated by ferrous material either on the seafloor or buried beneath it. The anomalies create monopoles and dipoles of various intensity and duration that stand out from the ambient magnetic field.

The marine magnetometer has limited ability to identify cultural resources. The magnetometer only measures Earth's magnetic field at the location of the sensor, therefore, the interpreter does not know the direction from the sensor that the ferrous object is located. Smaller line spacing may be necessary for the same anomaly to be visible on adjoining lines, narrowing the possible location of the object. Even with this drawback, the magnetometer is a necessary tool for identifying potential cultural resources with its ability to record very small variations in Earth's magnetic field.

The magnetometer, however, is not the most effective remote sensing tool at locating magnetic anomalies. The gradiometer is capable of collecting clean magnetic data where the magnetometer cannot, especially during geomagnetic storms. While the gradiometer has been used for decades (Fraser-Smith 1983) especially on land, surveyors operating in the Gulf of Mexico have not adopted this alternative equipment.

Gradiometers are simply an array of two or more marine magnetometers. Each magnetometer in the array is aligned to a different plane so that temporal variations in Earth's magnetic field will not be recorded. Archaeologists can identify smaller anomalies from gradiometer data without the worry of external interference from geomagnetic storms or other external sources that would affect a single magnetometer. Gradiometers can be more effective at identifying older shipwrecks due to the small magnetic signature produced by the artifact assemblage and ship construction (Catsambis et al 2011). A sample of magnetometer data collected in the Gulf of Mexico in 2015 will show how difficult it can be for an archaeologist to interpret magnetometer data.

Without an archaeologist onboard to provide QA/QC during data collection, there is a risk that the data will not comply with the Bureau of Ocean Energy Management (BOEM) Notice to Lessees (NTLs). Bottom strikes and processing errors can prevent the magnetometer data from being accepted for an Exploration Plan. If it became common practice to have an archaeologist QA/QC a survey with the use of a gradiometer, then many common mistakes would be avoided and any avoidances recommended by the interpreter would be more reliable.

Statement of Theory and Definitions

More value needs to be placed on magnetometer data collection and interpretation. Errors occur during fieldwork and during processing. Magnetometers are very sensitive instruments that are not as well understood in the survey industry as side-scan sonar, subbottom profilers, or multibeam echosounders. Magnetometers measure Earth's ambient magnetic field using two units: nanoteslas (nT) or gammas. Archaeologists analyze the data for magnetic anomalies that stand out from the ambient magnetic field in the form of monopoles and dipoles (Figure 1). Magnetic anomalies that occur parallel on adjoining lines likely represent a common ferrous object located between the survey lines.

A magnetometer is omni directional so magnetic anomalies must be strong enough to be measured on adjoining survey lines to be considered for avoidance. The magnetic signature of an anomaly is directly related to its size and distance from the instrument. It is common for primary survey lines to be spaced at 50 m in geophysical surveys in less than 200 m of water depth. At this distance, magnetic anomalies must be large in size to be measured on multiple lines. Many hazards or wooden shipwrecks may only measure in the tens of gammas (nT), which may not be strong enough to be identified at 50-m line spacing.

BOEM's 2005-GO7 NTL stipulates the guidelines for archaeological survey and reporting. Two of the main guidelines for archaeological surveys using magnetometers are related to background noise and altitude. Background noise cannot exceed three gammas, and the altitude of the magnetometer cannot exceed six m from the seafloor. These two parameters ensure the data collected is clean and consistent. While the altitude of the magnetometer can be controlled with diligent monitoring, excessive background noise is sometimes uncontrollable.

Geomagnetic storms are one of the biggest threats to marine magnetometer surveys. Geomagnetic storms are caused by solar winds from coronal mass ejections impacting the earth's magnetic field. These solar winds contain approximately a billon tons of plasma and can take from several days to just 18 hours to reach earth from the sun. The magnetic disturbances generated by the storms typically last one to two days.

While geomagnetic storms are a known threat in higher latitudes where interference is stronger, their effects are not as well known in the Gulf of Mexico. The effects of these storms at higher latitudes on magnetometer surveys have been recently studied and shown to shown to affect collected data (Carrier et al. 2016). Ongoing investigations by the authors have shown that these storms still cause interference on surveys in lower latitudes (Carrier and Heinz 2017). Geomagnetic storms are categorized on a scale of 1-9 Kp or K index. Any storms greater than 5 Kp are strong

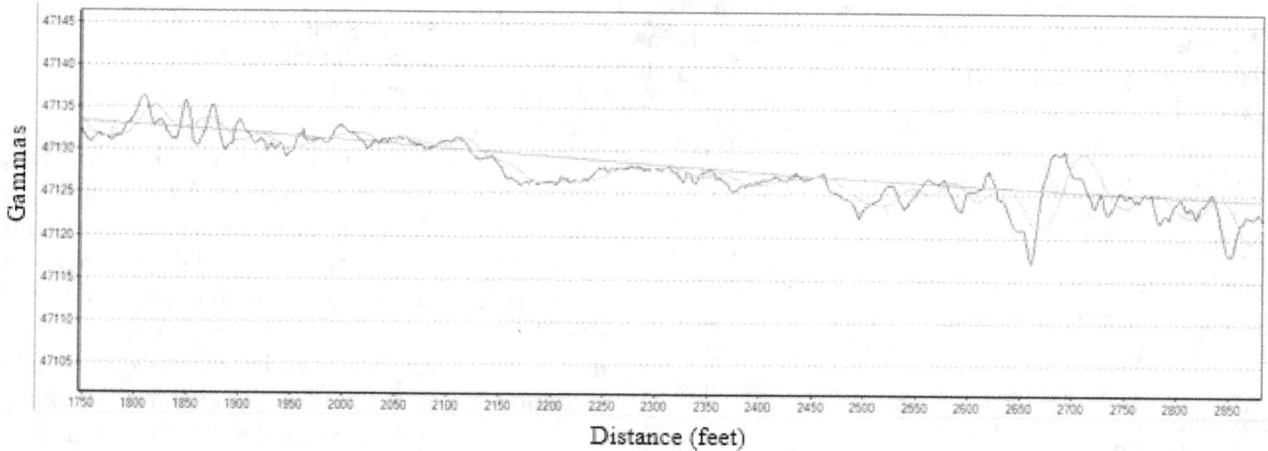

Figure 1. Example of clean magnetometer data. The blue line represents the raw data, the green line is smoothed, and the grey line is the ambient trend. Magnetic anomalies representing ferrous material is represented by peaks and troughs that are greater than five gammas (Author, 2016).

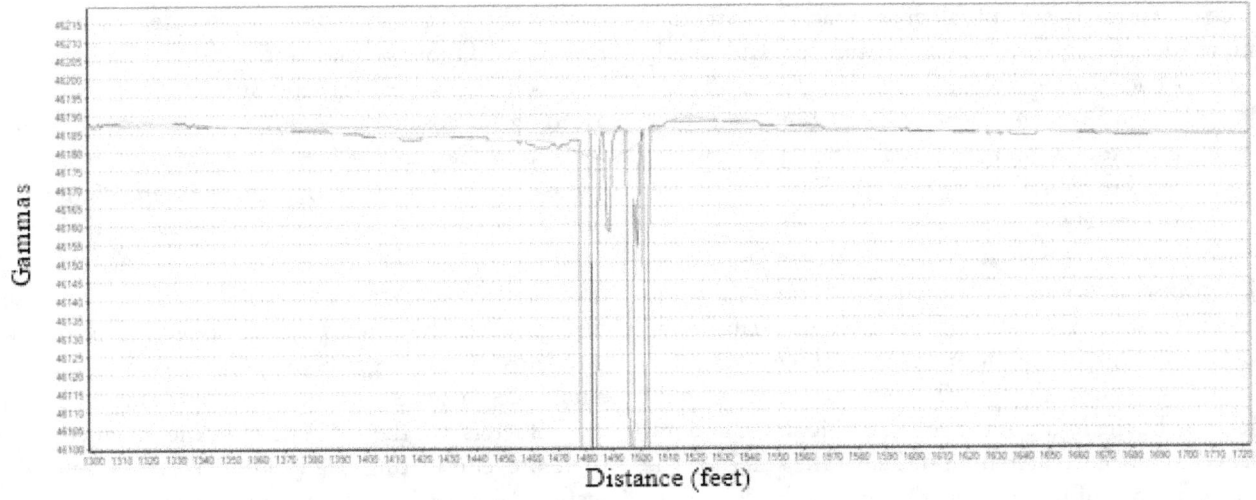

Figure 2. Magnetometer bottom strike. Note the right angle at which this anomaly turns away from the line. This particular strike resulted in a 5,000 gamma reading (Author, 2016).

enough to interfere with magnetometers and cause false anomalies within the data.

Methods

Four magnetometer surveys collected between June and October 2015 in the Gulf of Mexico were used to study the consistency and interpretative value of each survey. All the magnetic data were delivered fully processed and were later interpreted in SonarWiz 5 to complete archaeological assessments. Data quality was compared between the surveys to identify issues with collection and processing. Altitude, background noise, and consistency were used to determine the quality of each dataset. The times the surveys occurred were correlated to the Space Weather Prediction Center's 2015 geomagnetic storm observations.

Results

Two of the four data sets revealed poorly collected magnetic data or poorly processed data. The magnetometer for Survey A failed to maintain consistent altitude. The magnetometer not only exceeded 6 m in altitude but also impacted the bottom several times resulting in false anomalies (Figure 2). Bottom strikes are usually obvious and can be removed from the data once interpretation begins, however, if multiple strikes are present on a survey line, data validity cannot be assured.

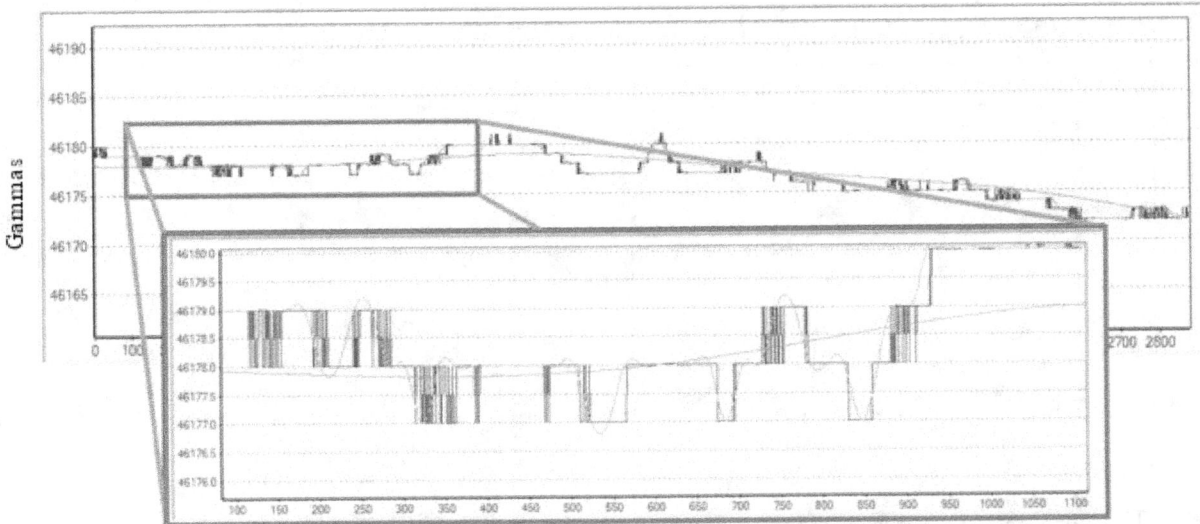

Figure 3. Magnetic data that was poorly processed. The presence of right angles in the data is not consistent with good quality data. Good quality data will have upward and downward slopes (Author, 2016).

The data set collected in July was delivered with processing errors that made all of the magnetometer data uninterpretable (Figure 3). Magnetometer data should have low background noise and sinuous data unlike the blocky data in Figure 3. The poor data set meant it could not be used for an archaeological assessment and the operator had to gain a waiver from BOEM.

Unfortunately, all data sets were collected during geomagnetic storms graded 5 Kp or higher (Figure 4). Because each data set was collected during a storm strong enough to create interference, the data could not be interpreted with high confidence. Magnetic anomalies with a five to ten gamma reading could therefore be the result of the geomagnetic storm and not related to ferrous material on or below the seafloor. The interpretations of these magnetic data sets likely created more identified magnetic anomalies and avoidances compared to if they had been collected in the absence of a strong geomagnetic storm.

Conclusions

Marine magnetometer data is very sensitive to external variations. Many errors that occur during a survey can be easily avoided by having an archaeologist onboard to QA/QC. The archaeologist will know what the data should look like and can monitor the magnetometer in real time, allowing for bad lines to be identified immediately and be re-surveyed in the field. Open communication with the field crew and the processing team is critical to ensure that the delivered data is the best quality that is possible, resulting in a timelier and more accurate interpretation and report.

Avoiding a geomagnetic storm is just as easy as avoiding atmospheric weather. The Space Weather Prediction Center provides 27 and 3-day forecasts for geomagnetic storms. Although these predictions are not very accurate until the storm has passed through an orbiting satellite, they can give surveyors a general idea if geomagnetic storms are expected during their fieldwork.

The best way, however, to avoid most of these problems is to use a gradiometer for collecting magnetic data. Geomagnetic storms do not interfere with gradiometers as they do with single magnetometers therefore eliminating many anomalies not related to seafloor objects. In addition, a gradiometer will be able to identify smaller magnetic anomalies as well as provide direction from the survey line. This is especially useful for marine surveys that have line spacing less than 20m and are looking for small magnetic anomalies. While gradiometers can be more expensive to use in the field, time and resources will be saved by avoiding stand-down time for space weather or having to recollect new data for archaeological assessments.

Acknowledgments

The author would like to acknowledge Kimberly L. Faulk for her support during the interpretation of the magnetometer data and for this paper. This paper would

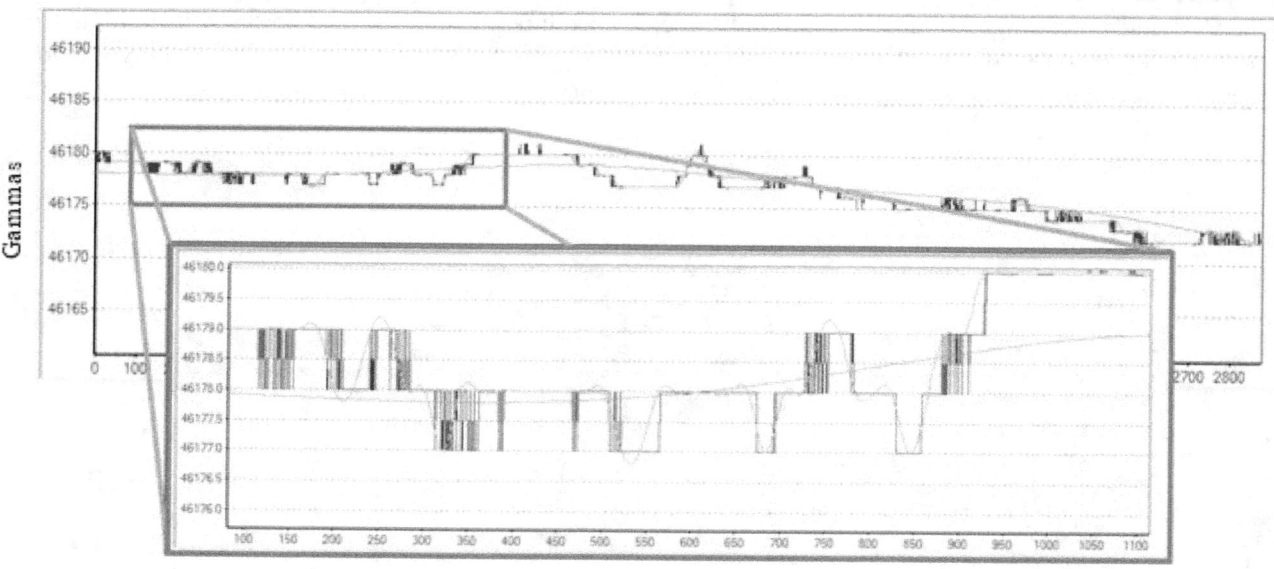

Figure 4. Timeline showing when geomagnetic storms of 5 Kp or greater occurring during 2015. The color lines represent the survey dates the magnetometer data was collected in the Gulf of Mexico with the lightning bolts represent geomagnetic storms of a Kp of five or higher (Author, 2016).

have also not been possible without the work of Brandi Carrier of BOEM with her research and presentations on the effects of geomagnetic storms on magnetometer surveys.

References

CARRIER, BRANDI, ANTTI PULKKINEN, AND MICHAEL HEINZ
2016   Recognizing Geomagnetic Storms in Marine Magnetometer Data: Toward Improved Archaeological Resource Identification Practices. Science and Technology of Archaeological Research, 2:1.

CARRIER, BRANDI, ANTTI PULKKINEN, AND MICHAEL HEINZ
2017   *Geomagnetic Storms in Marine Magnetometer Data at Low Latitudes.* Paper presented at OTC, Houston, 1-4 May. OTC-27801-MS

FRASER-SMITH, A.C.
1983   *The Magnetic Field Gradiometer.* Stanford Electronics Laboratory, Stanford University

CATSAMBIS, ALEXIS, BEN FORD, AND DONNY LEON HAMILTON
2011   *The Oxford Handbook of Maritime Archaeology.* Oxford, Oxford University Press

WOW, RICHARD J., COOPER ALAN K.
1989   *The Marine Magnetic Gradiometer – A Tool for the Seismic Interpreter.* Geophysics: The Leading Edge of Exploration. August 27th

Daniel Haddock
10619 Whispering Meadows Trail
Houston, Texas 77064
(w) 281-994-3373
(c) 850-449-1791
dhaddock0324@gmail.com

The Investigation of the Anniversary Wreck, a Colonial Period Shipwreck off St. Augustine, Florida: Results of the First Excavation Season

Chuck Meide

In July 2015, a buried shipwreck was discovered off St. Augustine, Florida by the Lighthouse Archaeological Maritime Program (LAMP), the research arm of the St. Augustine Lighthouse & Maritime Museum. Testing revealed a remarkable amount of material, dating to 1750-1800 and suggesting Spanish or British national origins. In summer 2016, researchers returned to the site and excavated a 4 x 3 m area, unearthing concreted barrels, a variety of ceramic sherds, pewter plates, brass shoe buckles, dressed stone blocks, and as many as 28 cast-iron cauldrons. This paper summarizes the results of the first excavation season on the Anniversary Wreck.

Introduction

The colonial shipwreck site known as the Anniversary Wreck (8SJ6461) was discovered by LAMP archaeologists in 2015 when testing targets originally defined during a 2009 remote sensing survey (Meide et al. 2016; McDaniel et al. this volume). The magnetic target was initially designated "Silver Surfer," but upon identification as a historic shipwreck the site was named in honor of the 450th anniversary of the founding of the city being celebrated that year. The Anniversary Wreck is located only about 0.7 km from the coast, and around 2.7 km from St. Augustine's other two known 18th-century shipwrecks, *Industry* and the Storm Wreck (Meide 2015). It is situated in about 5.79 to 7.01 m of water, depending on the tide.

The physical nature of the site can be described as a very dense scatter of buried concretions and other artifacts covering an area of unknown extent, but at least around 7 ×

4 m. Hydraulic probing conducted in 2015 suggests the scatter becomes more sporadic further away from the currently perceived center of the site. Probing was curtailed, however, to avoid potentially damaging fragile material, and much about the extent of the site remains unknown. Every unit excavated, comprising a total area measuring 3 × 4 m, contained an abundance of artifacts, typically so closely positioned that many have concreted together into large masses. This material culture is relatively deeply buried, covered by between 0.6 and 1.2 or more meters of sand.

No articulated hull remains have been encountered to date, though a few individual fragments of well-preserved wood have been unearthed. When first discovered, all wreckage was buried and there were no signs that divers had ever visited the site before, though some modern beverage cans have been encountered among the historic material.

Conditions on this wreck can be adverse, with sudden storms threatening daily operations while divers face heavy surge and frequent poor visibility. Despite these challenges fieldwork in the initial 2016 summer season was productive. During 22 days of diving between July and September, excavators logged a total of 342 dives for a total of 276 hours and

40 minutes of bottom time. Twelve 1 × 1 m units were excavated, including Units 1 and 2 which had been first excavated the season before during the target testing phase. A total of 184 field specimens were collected and catalogued in 2016, including 39 sediment samples which will be analyzed for microscopic organic remains (Shidner 2016). The 2016 excavation was carried out in conjunction with LAMP's tenth annual field school with the 31 ft. vessel *Empire Defender* and the 29 ft. *Mombo*.

The archaeological data collected to date has led to the tentative identification of this shipwreck as a merchant vessel loaded with cargo that wrecked while attempting to enter St. Augustine sometime between 1750 and 1800. This paper presents an overview of the methodology and results of fieldwork conducted on the Anniversary Wreck since its discovery.

Methodology

Horizontal and Vertical Control

A grid system was established on the site in July 2015 for test excavation, and expanded in 2016. At the start of the 2016 season, two baselines were deployed to provide a physical reference for the grid system. They were secured with large steel screw anchors which served as locational datums. Each of the 12 units excavated can be referred to by an identifying number (Units 1-12) or by their specific grid coordinates.

Excavation grids were fashioned of PVC piping in 1 × 1 m or 1 × 2 m sizes, marked at 10 cm intervals with tape discernable by touch, and pinned to the seafloor

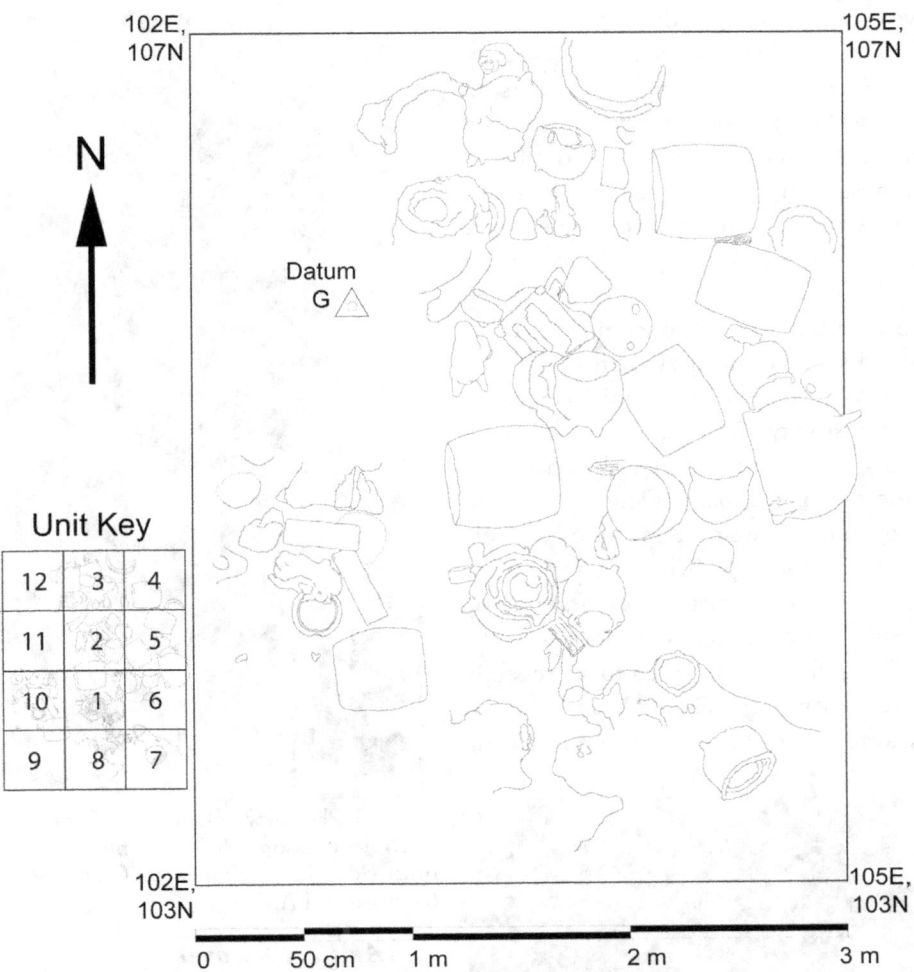

Figure 1. The Anniversary Wreck main excavation area site plan, 2016 (by Chuck Meide, vectorized by Tim Jackson, courtesy of LAMP).

using fiberglass rods. The initial grid, a 2 × 1 m rectangle, had been deployed in 2015 for target testing at Units 1 and 2. It was left in place and was subsequently buried by natural processes. When re-exposed by dredging in July 2016, it was used as a reference to deploy grids for Units 3-12. These were left in place at the end of the 2016 field season and will likely remain buried through summer 2017.

A vertical datum (Datum B) was established during 2015 testing by driving a 4.57 m long steel pipe into the seafloor using the hydraulic probing system. It provided a secure anchor for the datum. A loop was fixed to the upper portion of the pipe and designated zero, so that a level line could be extended from there and vertical measurements taken below that point could be expressed as cmbd (cm below datum). In 2016 an additional vertical datum (G) was deployed in the excavation area, in Unit 11, for ease of use by divers and to serve as a backup.

Excavation and Recording

Two handheld, 10.2 cm diameter dredges, powered by water pumps, were used for excavation. They were operated simultaneously by two teams to excavate two units at a time. The exhaust end of each dredge hose was left on the seafloor downcurrent from the site (to the northwest), and all dredge spoil was filtered through attached doubled mesh bags. Dredge spoil, consisting primarily of shell hash, was later sorted by laboratory volunteers.

Divers excavated in arbitrary levels. Before the start of excavation, elevation measurements (in cmbd) were recorded, usually in all four corners and the center of the unit. After an excavation dive, divers recorded closing elevations, and the volume excavated was treated as a single provenience. The site is characterized by deep deposits of shifting sand with little if any discernable sediment stratigraphy. Clay deposits have been observed around some concretions, and in some cases divers have encountered dark layers of more organic sediment.

These are believed to represent mud deposits brought by outgoing tides from estuarine rivers which have filled scoured voids (either from natural events or previous archaeological excavation). Excavated areas left untouched for more than a day or two tend to fill with slumping sand from surrounding areas so that backfilling is rarely required. A more thorough discussion of site formation processes on St. Augustine shipwrecks is presented by Burke (2016).

When such excavation revealed concretions or other artifacts, detailed 1:5 scaled drawings were made of each unit. Multi-day delays occurred between initial exposure and a period of visibility adequate for recording, sometimes requiring re-excavation to re-expose artifacts. In addition to the drawn site plan (Figure 1), GoPro underwater video cameras were used to extensively record all exposed excavation areas. This footage was then processed using Agisoft PhotoScan photogrammetric software to generate a three dimensional model of the excavation area. This technique was used to successfully model the 2015 test excavation (Figure 2) and most of the expanded excavation area (Units 1-8) the following year (Figure 3).

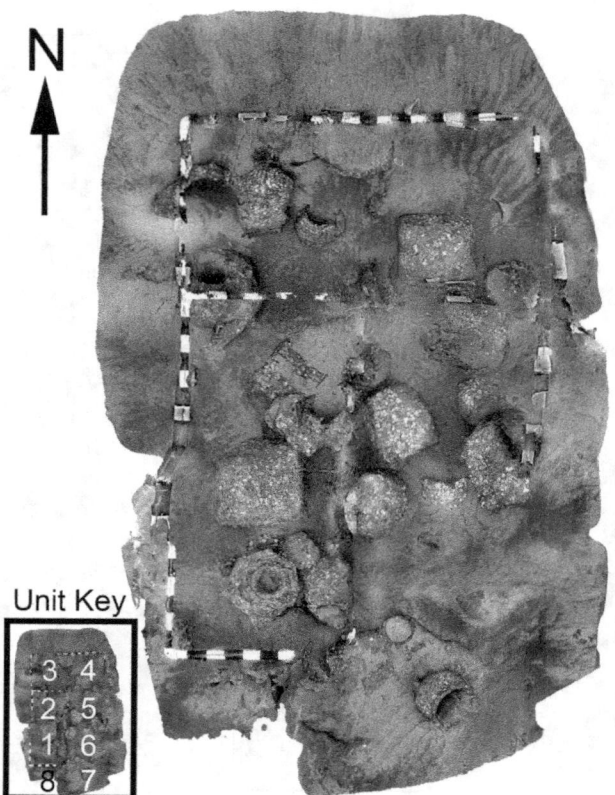

Figure 3. Plan view of Units 1-8 after twelve days of excavation, 2016 field season. Photogrammetric model by Eric J. Wilson from video footage taken by Chuck Meide on 29 July 2016 (courtesy of LAMP).

Artifact Recovery

Once recorded, artifacts were recovered by hand, usually being brought to the surface in sturdy plastic baskets lined with window screen, preventing the loss of even tiny objects. Archaeologists were somewhat discriminatory in what they recovered, so as not to overtask the conservation laboratory still processing material from six years of excavation on the Storm Wreck. Large objects concreted together, including casks and cauldrons, were left in place while smaller, loose finds were typically recovered.

Summary of 2016 Fieldwork

The 2016 excavation of the Anniversary Wreck lasted the entire month of July and most of the first week of August. The investigation began with a pre-disturbance sidescan sonar and magnetometer survey of the site. Diving commenced immediately afterwards, initially focusing on establishing the grid, datum, and mooring systems. Once Units 1 and 2 were re-exposed, after three days of excavation, the grids for Units 3-8 were installed and excavation continued until this 2 × 4 m area was adequately exposed for recording. This

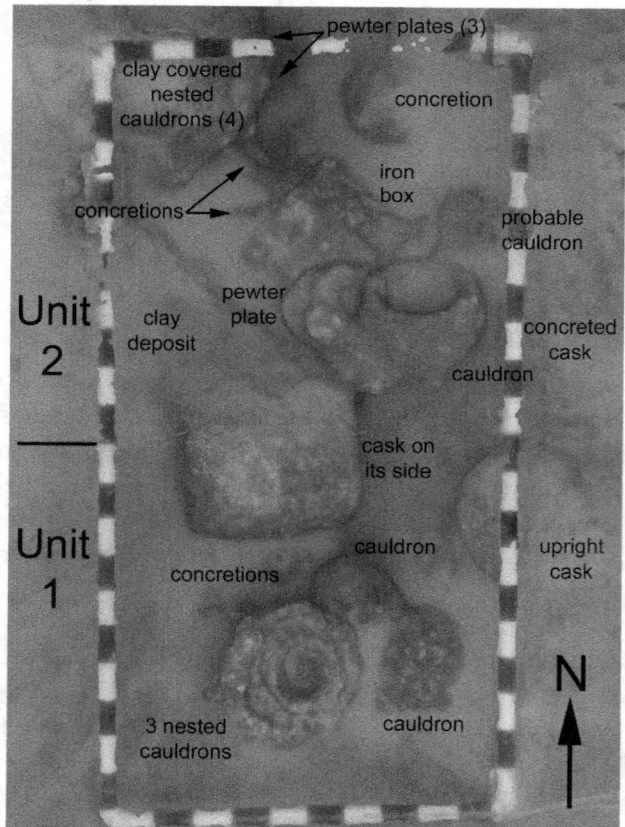

Figure 2. Plan view of Units 1 and 2 after 2015 target testing. Photogrammetric model by Nick Budsberg from video footage taken by Chuck Meide on 24 July 2015 (courtesy of LAMP).

process entailed dredging in at least two and as many as four units each day, alternating between units so that no one was excavated significantly deeper than the others, in an attempt to remove sand from the entire area relatively evenly. It took nine days of excavation before enough sand had been removed to prevent constant sand slumping. Once Units 1-8 were relatively stable (in terms of sand slumping), the area was recorded by hand drawing and digital video on a day of particularly good visibility, 29 July.

With the initial 2 × 4 m excavation area recorded, four new units (9-12) were established on its western border. Excavation began in these new units but was curtailed after only two days due to foul weather. In that limited time, divers were able to expose, record, and recover the artifacts in Unit 10, but did not have the time to complete Units 9, 11, and 12. This is why these units appear blank in the site plan (Figure 1), even though limited excavation did reveal the uppermost portions of barrels and other objects. Work will continue in these units in the 2017 field season.

The remainder of the field season was dedicated to continued testing at a number of other potential shipwreck targets. Only four additional days were spent at the Anniversary Wreck, to recover equipment and clean up the site, and to test another magnetic anomaly located only 90 m away, which was believed to potentially represent another component of the shipwreck site. No buried remains were detected, however, despite 124 hydraulic probe tests.

Artifacts

Cauldrons

By far the artifact type found in greatest numbers on the Anniversary Wreck is the cast-iron cauldron or cooking pot. As many as 28 individual cauldrons were observed in the excavation area, most of them apparently intact. They were distributed across Units 1-7 but did not appear in Units 8-12 on the western and southwestern portion of the excavation area. It is clear that this ship was carrying a cargo of cauldrons, and in several cases two, three, and four cauldrons were found stacked or nested inside each other. Others were found individually, and likely were originally nested for shipment, but fell apart during or after the wrecking process.

All of the cauldrons were heavily concreted, and in many cases they were concreted to each other or other surrounding objects. Because of the problematic logistical and conservation challenges this situation presents, no cauldrons were separated from adjacent objects or recovered during the 2016 season. While it is desirable to collect a representative sample which could help develop a cauldron typology, this may be done in future seasons.

All of the observed specimens appear to be of identical form, that of the classic round-bodied and round-bellied pot which narrows at the top before flaring out at the rim (Noël Hume 1969:175-177; Neumann 1984:176; Eveleigh 1997:15). They all have three legs, enabling them to stand stably in a fire, a characteristic common by the middle ages and lasting into the 19th century until iron hobs and kitchen ranges required flat bottomed cookware (Eveleigh 1997:17). Each cauldron also displays opposing pairs of "ears" on its rim, from which an arched wrought-iron handle or bail was once placed, so as to hang the vessel over a hearth or fire. The ears in all cases appear to be pointed or squared, a style that predates the rounded ears introduced in the 19th century (Neumann 1984:176). Casting seams and other surface details are not visible due to concretion.

Concretion also prevented entirely accurate measurements, but the largest example (straddling Units 5 and 6) measured 61 cm at its maximum diameter, 54 cm across the rim, and 46 cm in height (not including its 11 cm long legs). Nested inside that pot were three others measuring around 40 cm, 35 cm, and 21 cm across their rims. These four seem to represent typical sizes in the assemblage. Another cauldron (in the southeast corner of Unit 1) measuring 21 cm at the rim was 29 cm maximum diameter and 25 cm tall (not including legs). The pot centered in Unit 7 was 32 cm maximum diameter, 31 cm across the rim, and 24 cm in height. Inside it was a smaller one measuring 20.5 cm across the rim. The smallest example was in the southwest corner of Unit 6, and measured about 19 cm across the rim, 24 cm maximum diameter, and 20 cm in height. The largest of these is considerably larger than the biggest Storm Wreck cauldron, while the smallest is still somewhat larger than the smallest Storm Wreck cauldron (Meide et al. 2011:Table 9).

The Anniversary Wreck cauldrons display a rounded rather than oval shape, which according to Neumann (1984:175-177) suggests a date range of 1740-1780. This should be considered a general temporal range, as cauldrons of this older form were still used after the newer styles were introduced in the 19th century, especially in more rural or remote kitchens (Everleigh 1997:17). Likewise, Noël Hume (1969:175) notes that neither cauldrons nor skillets "can be dated at all closely,

Provenience of Cask	Overall length	Diameter at booge	Diameter at head
Straddling U1 and U2	48	45	39
Upright straddling U1 and U6	not recorded	not recorded	34.5
U4, southwest quadrant	40	42	38
U5, northern half	47	40	33
U5, southwest quadrant	43	38	33
Straddling U9 and U10	42	35	30
Possible cask in U9	not recorded	not recorded	not recorded
U12 in center	not recorded	not recorded	not recorded
All measurements in cm			

Table 1. Dimensions of the casks or barrels in the 2016 Anniversary Wreck excavation area (all measurements in cm).

as traditional shapes continued to be made in a great many places over a long period of time."

These cauldrons are identical or very close in form to the nine recovered from the Storm Wreck, which wrecked trying to enter St. Augustine in December 1782 (Meide et al. 2011:118-126; Carter 2014, 2016). They are also very similar to a cauldron recovered on the nearby *Industry* lost in 1764 (Meide 2015).

Barrels or Casks

At least seven and possibly eight barrels or casks were encountered in the excavation area. While most were recorded, none were recovered. In all cases it appears that the wooden staves and head pieces have completely deteriorated, leaving the extant contents concreted in the shape of a cask. This phenomenon has been observed before on three St. Augustine shipwrecks, including the Storm Wreck, where two concreted casks were determined to have originally contained wrought iron nails. It is probable that the Anniversary Wreck casks also contained nails or some other iron hardware or tools, most likely cargo intended for the St. Augustine market.

All of the Anniversary Wreck casks are somewhat similar in size. Table 1 presents the dimensions of the casks as recorded in situ.

Pewter Plates

A total of seven pewter plates were encountered in the excavation area. Two were in Unit 2, three more were in Unit 3 at the border with Unit 2, and two more were in Unit 10. Four of these were recovered. The others were concreted to massive objects and could not be easily removed. All were found relatively close to each other, and the three in Unit 3 were overlapping each other and appear to have originally been stacked together. All but one are about the same size, 23.2 to 23.5 cm in diameter. The exception is a larger plate or charger which, while deteriorated, originally would have been somewhat greater than 33 cm in diameter.

Pewter flatware was commonly used throughout the 17th and 18th centuries, and declined in popularity in the early 19th century. The rim styles discernable on several of the plates are temporally diagnostic. In the first decades of 18th century, multiple-reeded brims which had been popular in the late 17th century gave way to single-reeded brims and smooth-edged brims. Both single-reed and smooth-edged brims are present in the Anniversary Wreck assemblage. These styles both date to ca. 1720-1800 (Neumann 1984:276-277).

The recovered pewterware has not yet been cleaned or conserved. After this process is complete, it may be possible to discern maker's marks which could better identify the date and nationality of these artifacts.

Shoe Buckles

Eleven shoe buckle frames (seven whole and four partial) were recovered by excavators, along with another fragment found in dredge spoil. All are missing their chapes, are brass, and appear identical in form. They were also all located in a very confined area, around the border between Units 1, 8, and 9. Their spatial proximity and stylistic uniformity both suggest they were cargo items rather than personal possessions. This is in contrast to those found on the Storm Wreck, a refugee vessel with many passengers, where shoe buckles varied in material, style, and distribution across the site.

These buckles are devoid of decoration with a simple frame shape that could be described as somewhat more ovoid than rectangular with rounded edges (Figure 4). The frames are convex or curved to fit the top of the foot, are flat in cross-section, and feature a Type 1 pin terminal (White 2005:34). Each frame flares or widens noticeably in the center of its upper and lower portions, but not on the sides. They appear similar in shape to one of the 1782 Storm Wreck buckles, though they are slightly more rounded or ovoid in shape. They are also similar to some of the brass buckles found on the 1785 British wreck *General Carleton*, which were noted as having become popular by 1730 and common throughout most of the 18th century (Wróblewska 2008:205-206,209). They are also similar, if again somewhat more rounded, to Spanish buckles that Powell (2008) has dated to ca. 1740-1785. The Anniversary Wreck buckles measure 5.8 × 4.8 cm. This is smaller than the famously flamboyant Artois buckles popular between 1775 and 1790, and could date to the last two decades of the 18th century when buckles were made plainer and smaller (White 2005:41).

Ceramics

Twenty-one ceramic pieces were recovered from the shipwreck, including 10 stoneware sherds, 6 course earthenware sherds, 3 tile or brick fragments, and 1 refined earthenware sherd. They were more or less evenly distributed across the excavation area, typically found in low and narrow crannies between large objects like cauldrons or casks.

The most common type was British brown salt-glazed stoneware (Figure 4). The manufacture of salt-glazed stoneware, which was more vitrified, waterproof, and durable than delft or other English earthenwares, was a monopoly dominated by Rhenish potters until the process was perfected by Fulham ceramicists in the 1670s. Copying and competing with imported bellarmine bottles, the industry was booming by the start of the 18th century, and brown stoneware tankards, mugs, and utilitarian storage vessels were immensely popular through that and the following century (Green 1999).

Ten sherds of brown stoneware from at least two vessels are present in the assemblage but have not yet been extensively analyzed. They generally feature a rich brown exterior color, typically achieved with an iron or manganese wash, and a buff or gray interior. Two of these are base sherds, likely from large, jug-like storage containers common on other 18th-century shipwrecks (Johnson and Meide 1998:82). There is also a handle fragment. It is particularly interesting, because it is

Figure 4. Diver showing recovered shoe buckle and British brown stoneware body sherds. Unit 1 is visible in the immediate background. Photograph by Brendan Burke (courtesy of LAMP).

asymmetrical (thicker on one side) with non-parallel sides. Initially believed to represent a vertical handle on a jug or tankard, it may be a horizontal or angled strap handle (Noël Hume 2001:180). While brown stoneware is typically assigned a broad date range of 1600-1900, it does not generally appear in St. Augustine archaeological assemblages until around 1750 (Carl Halbirt 2015, pers. comm.). These could therefore date to St. Augustine's late First Spanish, British, or Second Spanish periods.

The single example of refined earthenware is a white-glazed rim sherd, perhaps from a jar or small container. The course earthenware sherds tend to be reddish in color, thick-bodied, and feature an interior glaze. The four tile or brick fragments are orange-red in color, and are between 2.58-3.5 cm thick. The most intact example is 13.9 cm wide, and would have been at least 18.6 cm long. They could represent flat Spanish bricks known as *ladrillos*, though one specimen displays a rounded edge which may not be consistent with that identification. Further analysis may shed more light on these pieces.

Glass

One bottle base fragment was recovered from Unit 5, likely from an English 18th-century liquor bottle. Its cylindrical shape became the norm by the 1730s. Often referred to as wine bottles, the form was also used for beer, cider, and other beverages, and was the dominant container for such liquids until around 1820 (Jones 1986). Their remains are commonly found in North American colonial assemblages. While this specimen has not yet been carefully analyzed, a cursory examination of the push up shape suggests it is similar to examples dated by Noël Hume (1969:68) to 1788 and 1798. More thorough analysis using methods pioneered by Jones (1986) could provide a more accurate date.

Other glass fragments were found scattered throughout the excavation area, but all appeared to be modern and intrusive.

Cut Stone

Three oblong blocks of dressed or cut stone were unearthed in Unit 10, two of which were recovered. The examples collected measured 37.5 ×10.5 × 5.6 cm and 39.5 × 11 × 5.7 cm, respectively. The third block was not fully excavated from its surrounding clay matrix but its dimensions seemed similar to the others. While a geological analysis has not yet been conducted, they appear to be comprised of sandstone. These were likely intended as building material to be sold in St. Augustine, and could have been used to make a threshold, sill, or some other architectural feature. There is no natural source of building stone in northeast Florida other than coquina, a sedimentary rock formed of bivalve shell fragments, so such an import would have been valued in St. Augustine.

Brass Tacks and Pins

Three small brass tacks were recovered from the shipwreck, including two from Unit 2 dredge spoil and one still in a thin strip of wood found in Unit 3. In addition, two brass straight pins were recovered. Pins were used for sewing or other crafts, and as wig or clothing fasteners. They were manufactured from the 16th century onwards by cutting and filing a piece of brass wire, and then wrapping a second wire around one end and stamping it to form the head. They are common finds on terrestrial and shipwreck sites, and have been encountered on both the Storm Wreck and *Industry* (McCarron 2016:172-173).

Knife Handle

A single knife handle slab or scale was found when sorting dredge spoil from Unit 8. It is carved from wood and is relatively small, only about 5.7 cm long. It features two small holes for pins or rivets which would have been used to fasten it through the knife tang and to the other scale. Its outer surface displays a series of intricate carvings in a cross-hatch pattern. This may be decorative, or functional to provide a better grip, or both. As only one has been encountered, it may be that this is a personal item rather than cargo.

Lead Shot

Numerous tiny lead pellets or birdshot in the 2.5 to 5 mm size range were recovered from the site, mainly collected from dredge spoil. These tiny lead shot were found in every excavated unit except for Units 6 and 7 to the southeast, and Unit 12 at the northwest, but they appear to be most concentrated in Units 10 and 2. Similar lead pellets have been found on other colonial shipwrecks including *Belle* (1686), *Queen Anne's Revenge* (1718), *Machault* (1760), and the Storm Wreck (1782) (Meide et al. 2011:127). Known as Rupert shot after their alleged inventor, Prince Rupert of the Rhine, they were first publicized in 1665, and thereafter used throughout the colonial period. They display an ovoid shape with a slight dimple, characteristic features which are by-products of the manufacturing process. A more sophisticated method of producing spherical pellets was patented in 1782, but the simple Rupert shot process continued well into the 19th century (Meide et al. 2011:128). The shot encountered on the wreck could have either been intended for self-defense while at sea or as a cargo item.

Coal

Three pieces of coal were recovered, including two from Units 3 and 4 and a third, smaller fragment from Unit 8 dredge spoil. Coal found in such small amounts likely represents fuel used on board the vessel for heating or cooking, rather than a cargo item for St. Augustine, where firewood was plentiful.

Other Artifacts

Other artifacts recovered include numerous concretions, mostly rather small in size, which have not yet been x-rayed or cleaned, and also a number of well-preserved wood fragments, at least one with an apparent fastener hole.

Conclusion

A significant amount of data has been amassed after only one full season of excavation, and a better understanding of the Anniversary Wreck is coming to light. Excavation has revealed a vast and dense deposit of material culture buried deep beneath the sand, and further excavation promises even more material. The great quantity of cauldrons, barrels, plates, and buckles, and their stylistic homogeneity, indicate that this ship was a merchant vessel loaded with cargo, making its way towards St. Augustine when it ran aground and likely broke up on the bar. All of these objects, along with the building stone and ceramics, were imports that would have been valued in St. Augustine's markets, and could have been acquired in no other way than by ship.

It appears that most of the diagnostic artifacts are of British origins. This does not necessarily mean that the ship was British, as an early American vessel might be plying similar wares, or a Spanish vessel might have been trading illegally with British colonies (Deagan 2007). A strong possibility remains, however, that this ship was English. Many of the artifacts are datable, and suggest with a good degree of certainty a date range of 1750-1800. Some artifacts may indicate the ship was lost later in this period, perhaps in its final two decades; but much of this analysis is in a preliminary stage, and the date range cannot yet be narrowed with confidence. This 50-year span was a period of cultural transformation in St. Augustine, as it shifted from Spanish to British and then back to Spanish control. As of yet we do not know the cultural context in which this ship once played its now-forgotten role.

What is known is that this shipwreck has immense archaeological potential. This is the first colonial-era merchant vessel that has been discovered in the waters of America's oldest port, and it features a wealth of material culture. Further excavation will lead to a better understanding of not only the physical nature and extent of the wreckage, but also of its cultural milieu. Once the date of loss and ship's nationality are refined, then researchers can bring the cargo items into sharp focus to better understand this ship's participation in the dawning global capitalist system. The continued archaeology of the Anniversary Wreck will allow us to ask meaningful questions and to explore 18th-century consumerism and the wants and needs of St. Augustine's colonial population during a time of great social change.

Acknowledgments

The 2015-2016 seasons were funded by field school fees and with grants from the Bureau of Historic Preservation, Division of Historical Resources, Florida Department of State with the Florida Historical Commission. Dave Howe, Mike Potter and Kevin Carrigan have provided working vessels, and the Hutcherson family dock space, to support our research. The project's success ultimately lies with the team of LAMP and the St. Augustine Lighthouse & Maritime Museum staff, students, and volunteers who have given time, talent, and passion to this shipwreck. There are too many to name, but thanks to all of you.

References

Burke, Brendan P.
2016   Hidden in Plain Sight: Monitoring Shipwrecks in the Atlantic Waters of St. Augustine, Florida. In *ACUA Underwater Archaeology Proceedings 2016*, Paul F. Johnston, editor, pp. 25-34. Advisory Council on Underwater Archaeology, Washington, D.C.

Carter, Annie E
2016   An Archaeological Examination of Cookware from the Storm Wreck, 8SJ5459. In *ACUA Underwater Archaeology Proceedings 2016*, Paul F. Johnston, editor, pp. 177-181, Advisory Council on Underwater Archaeology, Washington, D.C.

2014   A Wreck of a Site: An Archaeological Examination of Cauldrons from the Storm Wreck, 8SJ5459. Bachelor's Thesis, New College of Florida, Sarasota, FL.

Deagan, Kathleen
2007   Eliciting Contraband through Archaeology: Illicit Trade in Eighteenth-Century St. Augustine. *Historical Archaeology* 41(4):98-116.

Eveleigh, David J.
1997   *Old Cooking Utensils*. Shire Album No. 177. Shire Publications Ltd, Buckinghamshire.

GREEN, CHRIS
1999   *John Dwight's Fulham Pottery: Excavations 1971-79*. Archaeological Report No. 6. English Heritage, London.

JOHNSON, DAVID A. AND CHUCK MEIDE
1998   In Soufrerie's Shadow: An Introduction to an Historic Shipwreck in Kingstown Harbour, St. Vincent and the Grenadines. In *Underwater Archaeology*, Lawrence E. Babits, Catherine Fach and Ryan Harris, editors, pp. 79-87. Advisory Council on Underwater Archaeology, Atlanta, GA.

JONES, OLIVE R.
1986   *Cylindrical English Wine and Beer Bottles 1735-1850*. Studies in Archaeology, Architecture and History. Parks Canada, Ottawa.

MCCARRON, CHRISTOPHER
2016   Household Artifacts from the Storm Wreck. In *ACUA Underwater Archaeology Proceedings 2016*, Paul F. Johnston, editor, pp. 169-176. Advisory Council on Underwater Archaeology, Washington, D.C.

MEIDE, CHUCK
2015   "Cast Away off the Bar": The Archaeological Investigation of British Period Shipwrecks in St. Augustine. *Florida Historical Quarterly* 93(3):355-387.

MEIDE, CHUCK, OLIVIA MCDANIEL, P. BRENDAN BURKE AND SAMUEL P. TURNER
2016   450th Anniversary Shipwreck Survey: Report on Archaeological Investigations. Lighthouse Archaeological Maritime Program, St. Augustine, FL

MEIDE, CHUCK, SAMUEL P. TURNER, P. BRENDAN BURKE AND STARR COX
2011   First Coast Maritime Archaeology Project 2010: Report on Archaeological Investigations. Lighthouse Archaeological Maritime Program, St. Augustine, FL.

NEUMANN, GEORGE C.
1984   *Early American Antique Country Furnishings: Northeastern America, 1650-1800*. McGraw-Hill, NY.

NOËL HUME, IVOR
1969   *A Guide to Artifacts of Colonial America*. University of Pennsylvania Press, Philadelphia.

2001   *If These Pots Could Talk : Collecting 2,000 Years of British Household Pottery*. Chipstone Foundation, Milwaukee, WI.

POWELL, JOHN T.
2008   Spanish Military Buckles of the Floridas and Louisiana, 1700-1821. St. Augustine, FL www.artifacts.org/Bucklepage Accessed 01 March 2017.

SHIDNER, JACOB D.
2016   Life Among the Wind and Waves: Examining Living Conditions on Sailing Vessels Through the Use of Microscopic Remains. In *ACUA Underwater Archaeology Proceedings 2016*, Paul F. Johnston, editor, pp. 202-208. Advisory Council on Underwater Archaeology, Washington, D.C.

WHITE, CAROLYN L.
2005   *American Artifacts of Personal Adornment, 1680-1820: A Guide to Identification and Interpretation*. AltaMira Press, Lanham, MD.

WROBLEWSKA, ELŻBIETA
2008   Buckles from Shoes and Clothing. In *The General Carleton Shipwreck,1785*, Waldemar Ossowski, editor, pp. 199-212. Polish Maritime Museum, Gdansk, Poland.

Chuck Meide
Lighthouse Archaeological Maritime
    Program (LAMP)
81 Lighthouse Avenue
St Augustine, FL 32080
cmeide@staugustinelighthouse.org

Guns in the Potomac: Collaborative Research on Several Historic Shipwrecks Undertaken in the Spring of 2016

P. Brendan Burke

The Institute of Maritime History (IMH) and the Lighthouse Archaeological Maritime Program (LAMP) partnered for a research initiative in the Potomac River from 12-20 May, 2016. The multi-phase project investigated several sites including a 19th century centerboard sailing vessel, the 1864 wreck of USS Tulip, *a possible canal boat scuttled during the Civil War containing heavy ordnance, and the schooner* Favorite. *Acoustic imagery and magnetic data were gathered on each site and diver investigation was undertaken at one site. This paper includes preliminary findings from the survey as part of IMH's continued dedication to research, preservation, and education. Since 1995, the Institute of Maritime History (IMH) has supported maritime research and fieldwork throughout the east coast. From the Submerged Historical Inventory Project (SHIP) in the mid-Atlantic to recordation of a 19th century wreck at Seal Cove, Maine, to excavation of an 18th century French wreck in St. Vincent and the Grenadines, IMH has worked closely with state and national governments to assist in the management of submerged cultural resources. During the spring of 2016, IMH undertook a survey in the Potomac River to explore several wreck sites that have particular regional historic relevance. The results of that survey are presented here.*

Methodology

To gather comparable data across multiple sites, a consistent survey methodology was designed to standardize lane orientation and spacing, sensor altitude, and speed. Survey lanes were spaced 15.24 m (50 ft.) and north/south lanes were aligned with magnetic north. Survey boundaries were planned with sufficient area to capture the complete magnetic signatures of each target. East/west lanes were run perpendicular to north south lanes to generate high-density sampling throughout survey boundaries. All survey lanes were run in the same direction. When magnetic contours exceeded survey boundaries, additional survey lanes or lane extensions were added.

Survey speed ranged from a minimum of 3 knots to 4.5 knots. Positioning was provided by a Trimble DSM-232 DGPS operated with an HDOP of <1.1 to ensure sub-meter accuracy. Sidescan sonar instrumentation was a Klein 3900 Search & Recovery set to 900kHz. The project magnetometer was a Marine Magnetics Explorer utilizing an Overhauser sensor capable of an absolute accuracy of 0.1 gamma (g). Sensor height was maintained at less than 6 m (20 ft.) when possible and sidescan range was set to 30 m (98.42 ft.). Survey data were backed up daily and reviewed to ensure complete coverage. Magnetic data were collected with Hypack, also used for survey navigation and monitoring GPS HDOP accuracy. Sidescan sonar data was collected using SonarPro, which was also used to control towfish settings during survey.

Magnetic data were post-processed in Hypack and corrected to ambient field, removing background gradient. Data were filtered to ignore deviations from ambient field with a value of <3 g. Edited survey files were used to create a triangulated irregular network (TIN) model for contouring and 3D representation purposes. Change in field strength was indicated by a change in color, red hues for positive, blue hues for negative. Color intensity mimicked value and each site received a custom palette respective of the total field strength. Magnetic moments were calculated for each site as a comparative dataset for research undertaken by LAMP in northeast Florida (McDaniel et al, this volume). A primary goal for this undertaking was to gather magnetic data from a series of shipwreck sites with known features while keeping as many variables constant (vessel, type of sensor, survey orientation, etc.). Sidescan sonar data were processed using SonarMAP, software capable of making corrections to poor bottom tracking, gain adjustments, and mosaicking processed files.

Riverview Wreck (18CH800)

During a 2010 transit from Tall Timbers, Maryland to Mount Vernon, IMH was provided a list of submerged acoustic targets to ground truth en route. The target list was generated in 2007 during a NOAA underwater hazard avoidance survey. This survey cleared the channel for safe navigation of the *Thomas Jefferson* up the Potomac River to Washington D.C., where the research vessel participated in NOAA's bicentennial commemoration. The target list was provided to the Maryland Historical Trust (MHT), steward of submerged cultural resources within state waters. In order to begin the assessment process, MHT requested IMH investigate the targets.

Since three years had passed between the initial survey and the Mount Vernon project, IMH decided to scan each target with a low-frequency sonar to verify presence and revisit the targets on the return trip with a higher resolution sonar. A Klein 3900 Search & Recovery sidescan sonar was deployed on each target appearing on the low resolution survey. One particular target, located off of Riverside, Maryland appeared as a submerged vessel with extant hull remains and a centerboard trunk. On May 12, 2016 IMH returned to the site for a more intensive remote sensing survey. A survey border encompassing 5.79 acres was established, centered on the wreckage. Magnetic data revealed a large dipolar anomaly approximately 56 m (183.7 ft.) east/west by 32 m (104.9 ft.) with a magnetic moment of 343° M. The dipole contained a maximum positive deflection of 95.9nT, a negative deflection of -21.6nT, and a total amplitude of *117*.5nT.

Depicted in Figure 1, sidescan imagery shows intact hull structure with a maximum length of approximately 20 m (65.61 ft.) and a width of 7.46 m (24.47 ft.). Scouring around the wreck was most evident on the eastern (downstream) side. Frame heads are also visible, especially along the northern edge of the hull. The centerboard trunk, likely still connected to the hull, indicates and a vessel orientation of 72.8°T. Measurements taken from the sidescan record indicate a frame spacing of approximately 27-38 cm (10.63-14.96 in.). A similar wreck, located near Poplar Island, Maryland, was identified as a type of oyster dredge, perhaps the remains of a bugeye or skipjack (Turner et al 2006: iii). Frame spacing for that vessel averaged about 30 cm (11.81 in.) and the centerboard trunk measured 5.05 m (16.57 ft.) (Turner et al: 2006: 27). The length of the Riverside Wreck centerboard trunk, taken from the 2016 sonograph, appears to be 4.33 m (14.21 ft.)

Attributes of the Riverside Wreck corroborate an interpretation of this wreck as an oyster dredge. The length/width ratio of approximately 3:1 is typical of Chesapeake sail-powered oyster dredgers recorded in the Historic American Merchant Marine Survey. Similarly, the centerboard trunk, frame spacing, and shape of the hull are consistent with an oyster-fishing craft. Chowning (2007: 28) indicates Maryland builders built more, and larger, sail-powered fishing craft as a response to prohibitions on engine-powered dredging, a practice regularly used by Virginia fishermen. Tilp (1978: 18) recorded sail-powered fishing craft, such as bugeyes, trading as far upriver as Washington D.C., carrying oysters, herring, and shad. The location of the wreck at

Figure 1. The outline of the Riverside Wreck (18CH800) can be easily seen here, including some shadowing of frame heads and the centerboard trunk. In the right-hand portion of the sonograph, portions of the bow remain intact. The inset image depicts the magnetic contour (negative-pole is on the upper side) with a shaded representing the extant remains of the vessel.

Riverside coincides with the upper reaches of Potomac oyster grounds and so it is plausible that the wreck came to rest in its native fishing waters.

By the end of the Civil War, siltation from tobacco monoculture impacted draft throughout much of the Potomac watershed and vessel design took on a beamier, shallower hull incorporating a centerboard to offset the loss of hull depth. The bugeye, a ketch-rigged answer to shoal water fisheries, replaced the venerable pungy schooner, a vestige from the early 19th century. Fifty-nine bugeyes appear in 1902 under Potomac registry, many as fishing craft but a few as freight haulers. By the 1880s, the sloop-rigged skipjack joined the fishing fleet and edged aside the pungy by the early 20th century. The popular and iconic skipjacks were commonly built as late as the 1960s. In addition, hundreds of schooners transited the Potomac, adapted to fishing vessels and engaging in freighting. (Tilp 1978: 33-39).

The wreck at Riverside is a prime candidate for further study. Of the sailing craft that have plied the Potomac, few remain. Diver investigation of the site may reveal mast steps to indicate an original sailing rig, an attribute which may indicate type or purpose. Additionally, we may learn if the vessel was abandoned and left to slip beneath the waters, or if it sank while engaged in trade and may bear part of its cargo, a time capsule from a Potomac of long ago.

USS *Tulip*

Originally built in New York as the *Chih Kiang* for service in China, Tulip never made it farther than the nation's capital. Purchased by the U.S. Navy in 1863 and armed with two 24-pounder guns and one 20-pounder Parrot rifle, Tulip was a formidable contribution to the Potomac River Flotilla. *Tulip*'s tonnage moved U.S. Army troops in support of the Bristoe Campaign, led by Major General George Meade during the fall of 1863. During the first half of 1864, the vessel was engaged again as a transport, moving men across the Potomac River and into Virginia. By late summer, *Tulip* suffered from a defect in the starboard boiler and by November, was ordered by Commander Foxhall Parker Jr. to the Washington Navy Yard for repairs. Departing St. Inigoes, Maryland, *Tulip* steamed on port boiler alone down the St. Mary's River. At its confluence with the Potomac, the vessel turned upstream and for reasons unexplained, brought up steam in the starboard boiler. In less than ten miles, with Ragged Point abeam the port side, an explosion rocked the vessel. Tearing through framing, planks, decks, and men, steam and shrapnel from the starboard boiler instantly killed 47 sailors. Within minutes *Tulip* came to rest on the river bottom. Ten men were rescued, of whom only eight survived.

Today, *Tulip*'s remains are silent monument to the single largest loss of life in the U.S. Navy during the Civil War. During the 1960s, the site was looted by scuba divers, including the removal of human remains. Until efforts were made to alert the public to the illegality of removing artifacts from an archaeological site and a war grave protected by the Sunken Military Craft Act of 2005 removal of artifacts as diving trophies continued. In 1995, a study of the site was undertaken by the Maryland Historic Trust (MHT) for the Naval History and Heritage Command (NHHC) (Thompson 1998).

The 1998 study included magnetic, acoustic, and diver investigation of the site and surrounding river bottom. Thompson noted (1998: 62) that the site was found to have almost 3 m (9.84 ft.) of relief in 1995 but almost completely covered during diver inspection in 1996, including a covering of trees and debris deposited on the site presumably during winter storms.

In March of 2016, staff from the NHHC and Phoenix International joined IMH to deploy a Seaeye Falcon ROV and Iver-3-580-3037 AUV to assess the condition of the wreck. AUV operations were successful and recorded the site with its onboard sidescan sonar. ROV operations were less successful due to high levels of turbidity which prevented safe navigation of the ROV around extant wreckage. It was decided to return to *Tulip* during the May 2016 survey and record updated magnetic data from the site.

On May 24, 2.57 lane miles of survey were completed within a survey boundary encompassing 8.70 acres. Survey lanes were run north/south as well as east/west at a lane spacing of 15.24 m (50.0 ft.) Magnetic data recorded during the survey revealed a large dipolar anomaly with a total amplitude of 2,762 g (+2381.4/-381.0) and a magnetic moment of 348° M. Numerous smaller monopoles and dipoles surround the primary signature. A secondary dipole was located 45 m (147.64 ft.) from the southern end of the hull at a bearing of 154°T. The 1995 survey recorded a maximum amplitude of 640 g (Thompson 1998: 55), indicating a sensor altitude of approximately 10.66 m (35 ft.). Water depth over the site, observed during the 2016 survey, was approximately 12.19 m (40 ft.)

Sidescan imagery revealed extant frames with a maximum height above the river bottom of 1.5 m (4.92 ft.) Amidships, on the port side, a large acoustic target was visible, likely remains of the port boiler. Frame heads clearly outlined the hull, including damage to the starboard side where a break in the extant remains was noted, Figure 2.

Imagery gathered during the two spring 2016 surveys differed from the 1998 data, principally due to increased resolution of digital sidescan sonar. Positioning is now more accurate, and magnetic data on the site is denser and likely gathered closer to the target. While no remote sensing fully replaces diver inspection it does offer large-scale site assessment – often accomplished in the same time or less than it would take to deploy and recover the multiple dive teams needed for a full inspection – and is less subject to adverse conditions such as current and turbidity. For resource managers such as NHHC and MHT, this type of survey can offer a baseline or baseline+ data from which a site may be studied, monitored, and protected.

Shipping Point Wreck

Almost immediately after war was declared in 1861, a struggle erupted between U.S. and Confederate forces to control strategic points throughout the Chesapeake Bay and its tributaries. Confederate Commander C. H. Kennedy reconnoitered the Potomac River near Quantico Creek and noting high bluffs at Shipping Point, reported to Captain Barron, Officer of Ordnance in Richmond, "9-inch guns [placed upon the bluff] will command the channel, and with the aid of one rifled 12-pounder close the river by day time." (Rush and Woods 1896: 776). On 30 June, 1861 General Robert E. Lee requested three 9-inch "columbiads" (sic) sent to General Theophilus Holmes, charged with the formation of batteries at Shipping Point (Moody et al 1880: 961). By the late summer of 1861, batteries were emplaced at Shipping Point, Possum Point, Freestone Point, and Cockpit Point. Each battery contained formidable firepower and could deliver a 'pill' handily across the river.

Washington was cut off by water, and the Navy from one of its most important naval yards. Strategic isolation and embarrassment spurred the U.S. Navy into action. Assaults were immediately launched against Confederate batteries. In September of 1861 Freestone Point was engaged by the screw sloop *Seminole* and gunboat *Jacob Bell*, but to no effect. In January of 1862, a second assault was led by *Anacostia* and *Yankee* on Cockpit Point. Largely inconclusive, a ball passed through *Yankee*'s hull and wounded a sailor. By March 1862, the Potomac Blockade entered its seventh month. *Anacostia* and *Yankee* once again attacked, but this time armed with a landing party. At the time, Confederate General Joseph E. Johnston busied himself by withdrawing the Army

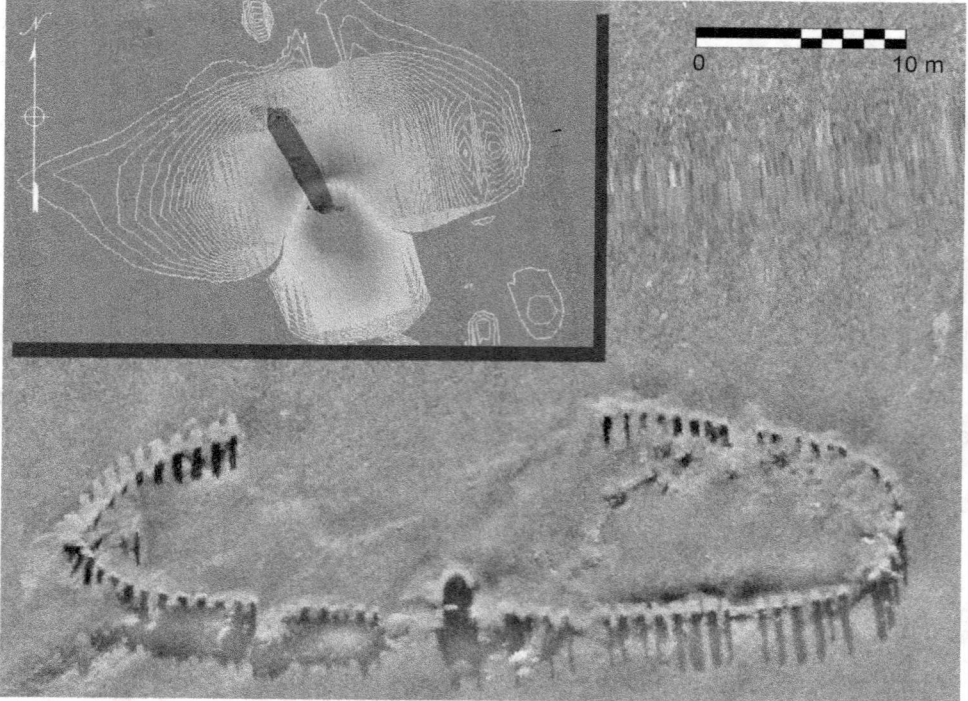

Figure 2. In this sonograph of USS Tulip, a discontinuity in extant frames indicates where a boiler explosion on 11 November, 1864 caused the sinking of the vessel and the largest loss of sailors in a single incident during the Civil War. The inset image depicts a shaded area, representing the hull, superimposed on the magnetic contour of the wreck. The negative pole is on the upper (north) side.

of Northern Virginia south to defend Richmond from pending assault by U.S. General George McClellan. Confederate batteries along the Potomac were no longer tenable and Johnston ordered their abandonment. U.S. soldiers sent ashore by *Anacostia* and *Yankee* landed unopposed. John Thomas Scharf, artillerist with the 1st Maryland Artillery said of the withdrawal:

> Before we left we heard rumors of the Army about to fall back and we volunteered to save the heavy guns in the batteries. We commenced the work like fine fellows and dismounted two large Dahlgreens (sic) and put them in a large scow, preparatory to sending them to Acquia (sic) Creek Railroad on the river. The boat was to leave with them the night we evacuated, but they would not stop to save them and we then took the boat and sunk it in the river with the guns. Before we evacuated we destroyed some very fine guns some of which were saved by the army (Kelley 1992: 9-10).

During a 2011 research project undertaken to locate and record the remains of the CSS *City of Richmond* (ex-ferry *George Page*), sidescan sonar revealed an unanticipated shipwreck near the mouth of Quantico Creek. At the time it was believed the second wreck might be Scharf's scow (Watts 2016, pers. comm.). IMH and LAMP returned to the site on 13 May 2016 and completed a total of 3.119 k (1.68 nm) of survey lanes over the site.

This survey deviated from the planned methodology regarding altitude of the sonar and magnetometer. The site rests in about 12.80 m (42 ft.) of water adjacent to a steep bank where depths quickly shoal to 2 m (6.56 ft.) in less than 60 m (196.85 ft.) Local knowledge of the river indicated the possibility of submerged debris along the bank. Therefore, the sonar and magnetometer were maintained at an altitude of between 8-11 m (26.24-36.08 ft.) Strong river currents were observed during the survey, requiring slowing vessel speed to between 2-3 knots (3.3-5.0 fps.) to maintain desired altitude of the towed array. A test lane in deeper water with the vessel running with the current proved to be too fast with increased cross-track error. Tie lines were run from east to west, towards the riverbank, and were terminated as soon as the magnetic signature returned to ambient field for ten seconds, or shoal water prevented safe navigation. Cross track error was maintained at 2 m (6.5 ft.) or less.

Magnetic data revealed a simple dipolar anomaly with an amplitude of 53.2 g. Oriented north/south with a magnetic moment of approximately 26° M. The dipole measured approximately 44 m (144.36 ft.) north/south by 38 m (124.67 ft.) east/west. Adjusted for altitude (to 6 m [19.68 ft.]) the total amplitude for the dipole is 176.2 g, a value curiously low considering the mass of iron within the site. Sonar imagery, Figure 3, depicted a remarkably intact hull structure with associated debris around the site.

Diver investigation of the wreck site on 14 and 15 May revealed remarkable preservation of hull remains and remnant cargo. Divers experienced complete blackout conditions. Using powerful lights, visibility was never more than 30 cm (1.0 ft.) and often clouded by suspended particulates. Diving operations were only conducted during slack water. The downline was attached to a mushroom anchor placed just off the wreck, but within arm's reach of a long portion of cap rail wrenched at a right angle from its original position on the gunnel. Still through-bolted, this timber led divers to the hull by touch.

Exploring the starboard side of the vessel, divers found the hull largely intact. Resting on an even keel the hull is partially buried within plough mud. Numerous transverse beams were encountered inside the hull, likely thwarts and providing a structure on which to place tarpaulins for covering cargo.

While exploring the inside of the vessel, a large iron mass was identified as a type IX Dahlgren resting upside down. The gun's starboard trunnion is located approximately 7.92 m (26 ft.) aft of the stem and 76 cm (2.5 ft.) inboard from the outer edge of the gunwale. Developed during the early 1850s as shell guns, Dahlgrens were labelled according to their bore diameter and found use throughout coastal defenses, aboard warships, and in limited field applications. Over 1,100 type IX Dahlgren tubes were cast, the most popular size in the Dahlgren line (Swain 2011). The gun within the wreck was identified based on several attributes including trunnion measurements of 20.32 cm (8 in.) long by 19.05 cm (7.5 in.) in diameter. Additionally, the breech was rounded according to Dahlgren's style and terminated in a slightly-flared cascabel vertically pierced for an elevation screw and horizontally pierced for breeching tackle. From the trunnion forward, the breech narrowed in the style known as a 'soda bottle'.

Columbiad and Rodman guns were cast without cascabels and are easily distinguished. Parrot and Brooke rifles were manufactured with wrought iron breech reinforces, differentiating them from the smooth lines of Dahlgren's heavy ordnance. When survey disclosed

Figure 3. Seen here from a sonar image captured on 13 May, 2016 the intact remains of a scow or canal boat rest on, and in, the bottom of the Potomac River. Frame heads indicate where the gunwhale has been damaged from modern anchoring and fishing, including linear debris around the wreck that has been torn away. The inset image depicts a shaded area of the vessel overlaying the magnetic contour. The negative pole is up (north).

the guns, IMH suspended diving operations and immediately informed MHT and NHHC.

After clearance from MHT and NHHC, IMH returned to the site from 15-18 October. The second expedition's reconnaissance recorded scantlings and construction details, and fully circumnavigated the wreck. The hull was found to have an overall length of 25.30 m (83 ft.) with a beam of 4.27 m (14 ft.) The cap rail measured 30.48 cm (12 in.) wide by 7.62 cm (3 in.) thick. Two courses of planks comprised the cap rail, with overlapping scarph joints. Hull planking was measured as 5.08 cm (2 in.) molded by 25.4 cm (10 in.) sided. Ceiling planking rose from the bilge to within one strake of the cap rail, allowing access to frames and measured 3.81 cm (1.5 in.) molded by 30.48 cm (12 in.) sided. Frames measured 7.62 cm (3 in.) molded by 12.7 cm (5 in.) sided, on 40.64 cm (16 in.) centers. Measurements taken on deck beams/thwarts were 10.16 cm (4 in.) molded by 12.7 cm (5 in.) sided. The stem measured 22.86 cm (9 in.) molded by 15.24 cm (6 in.). The adjoining apron measured 7.62 cm (3 in.) square. An exposed timber at the stern of the vessel measured 10.16 cm (4 in.) square, centered on the outer face of the transom, and may be the sternpost.

While exploring the exterior of the hull, divers encountered a second gun. Resting within one meter of the port side, its muzzle and a trunnion were exposed. Trunnion dimensions were identical to the first gun, and the bore diameter was recorded as 22.86 cm (9 in.). The second gun brings the total known ferromagnetic mass of the wreck to a minimum of 8,346 kg (18,400 lbs). The relatively low amplitude for the site (176.2 g @ 6 m altitude) is surprising when compared to other similar sites with a known ferromagnetic mass such as the Industry (1764) site off St. Augustine, Florida. Consisting of five six-pounder cannon, two mooring anchors, and miscellaneous iron bar stock, at least 5,400 kg (12,000 lbs.) of iron can be accounted for. A 2009 survey of the site revealed a total amplitude of approximately 369.5 g (Meide et al 2016: 54).

While much is left to document, this discovery supports the statement made by Jonathan Scharf regarding the sinking of two Dahlgren guns in March of 1862. Lee's 1861 order to ship three 9-inch Columbiads to Battery No. 1 was impossible to execute. Columbiads were manufactured with eight and ten inch bores, not nine. Most likely, Lee used common parlance of the era by referring to any large gun as a 'Columbiad'. Ironically, it was the placement of Dahlgren guns at Shipping Point that bottled up the Washington Navy

Yard with its commanding officer and 'father of modern naval ordnance' John A. Dahlgren.

Favorite

As illustrated in the previous section, the Potomac River was a contested landscape during the first months of the Civil War. Until the U.S. Navy was able to exert its authority along the extent of the river and Chesapeake Bay, ports on the Virginia bank plied a vigorous trade in contraband. Towns such as Kinsale maintained trade with sympathetic or opportunistic merchants in southern Maryland. In order to pacify the Virginia shore, the U.S. Navy undertook routine patrols of the shore, including port towns. Tonnage useful to the Confederate cause would either be seized or destroyed. On 14 July, 1861 USS *Yankee* steamed into Kinsale and cut the schooner *Favorite* from her mooring. Towed across the Potomac, *Favorite* was moored off a U.S. Navy coaling station at Piney Point, Maryland. Only four days later, *Favorite* suspiciously sank during the night with her cargo intact (Thompson 2004: 1-2).

When captured, *Favorite* was loaded with anthracite, a hard coal popular in steam-powered shipping. While no official cause was given for its sinking, the schooner was without crew or watchman at the time it settled. Causes for the sinking range from intentional scuttling by departing crew to the vessel being hit by river traffic at night and damaged to the point of sinking. Nonetheless, *Favorite* was forgotten until 1994 when archaeologists with MHT located the wreck while conducting a remote sensing survey. Initially known as the Swan Cove Wreck (18ST643), the site was investigated by divers between 1999 and 2002. Extant remains of the wreck include two large iron-stock anchors, a large coal pile, bow and stern hull components, framing, and a centerboard trunk (Thompson 2004).

Like other sites in this paper, the goal for gathering sidescan sonar and magnetic data was to form a comparative dataset for magnetic interpretation of features such as moment orientation and pole discrimination (Gearhart 2011). *Favorite* is an exemplary target for comparison since much is known about the wreck, including its original size and cargo. However, results of the magnetic survey differed more on the east/west transects than the north/south transects, an anomaly witnessed at this site. East/west transects defined a large dipole approximately 104 m (341.21 ft.) east/west by 73 m (239.50 ft.) north/south, an area that encompasses approximately 3,900 m² (0.96 acres). The total amplitude for the east/west transects was 48.3 g (+40.7/-7.6). Results of the north/south transects defined a much smaller dipolar anomaly with a north/south extent of 44 m (144.35 ft.), an east/west extent of 57 m (187 ft.) and an area of

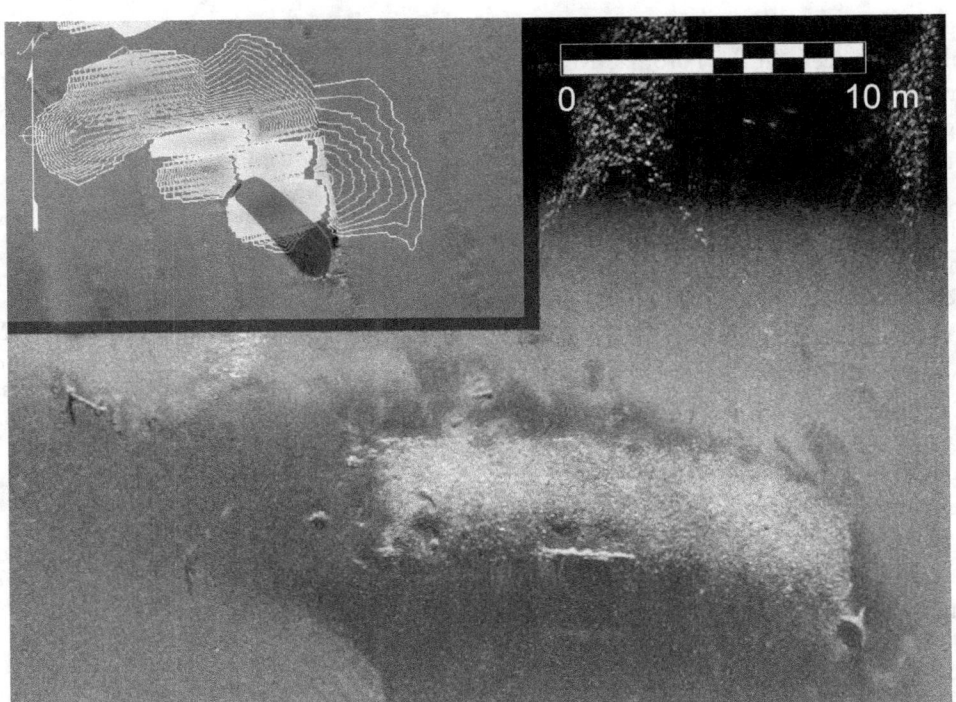

Figure 4. Sunk on 18 April, 1861, Favorite was loaded with a cargo of anthracite while moored near a coaling depot at Piney Point, Maryland. Her cargo is still visible, with a stern anchor and centerboard trunk exposed from the coal. A bow anchor is visible in the left-hand portion of the sonograph. The inset depicts a shaded area of the wreck superimposed on the magnetic contour. The negative pole is up (north).

approximately 1,853m² (.46 acres). The total amplitude for north/south survey lanes was 28.7 g (+23.6/-5.1). The difference in amplitude of the two survey directions results in a 168% increase in amplitude value for the east/west lanes and a 210% increase in area. Data has been analyzed by two separate labs and no conclusive answer explains the difference. Heading shift is unlikely as instrumentation proximity to the vessel and each other was sufficiently distant.

While magnetic data for Favorite resulted in more inconsistencies than in other sites surveyed during the project, magnetic data nonetheless aligns with wreckage and produces a typical signature for the wreck. Magnetic signatures on the edges of the survey were noted, particularly on the northern and western extent. Sonar imagery depicted the central coal pile with centerboard trunk visible. Some frames were also visible, as were the bow and stern anchors. Linear anomalies, some in excess of 50 m (164 ft.), were also identified more than 40 m (131.23 ft.) away from the wreck. These linear targets may be the source, or part of the source for magnetic anomalies detected to the north and west of the wreck. More research into these anomalies is warranted, including diver investigation, and may help explain the differential in survey values based on direction.

Conclusion

The spring 2016 survey revealed new data about known and unknown wrecks in the Potomac River and spurred further research during October of the same year at the Shipping Point site. IMH has been able to make contributions to maritime history through partnership with MHT, LAMP, and NHHC. A central objective of this work is to continue gathering public interest and investment into submerged cultural resources of the Potomac River. Arguably, shared public interest in historic resources can garner protection and support. IMH has the unique ability to work across the public/private gap to bring volunteers directly into contact with archaeological sites and still meet the needs of public resource managers and site security. Continuing this work, other projects include an ongoing survey for Lord Dunmore's 'floating city' of 1776, recordation of shipwrecks relating to the Mallows Bay Complex, continued monitoring of the *U-1105* (*Black Panther*) site, and work with NHHC involving Navy plane wrecks in the Patuxent River and Chesapeake Bay. This work has, and will continue, to involve avocational and professional archaeologists to pursue the Institute's mission of research, preservation, and education in nautical archaeology and maritime history.

Acknowledgments

The author wishes to thank Dr. Susan Langley, of the Maryland Historic Trust. Susan has been a long-time supporter of the Institute. Joshua Daniel, of Daniel Archaeological Consulting LLC, provided valuable assistance in the second phase of fieldwork at the Shipping Point site. IMH volunteers Charlie Reid, Dan Lynberg, Bill Isbell, Todd Hutchings, Earl Hemminger, Vinny Mallardi, and Lee Nelson, Silas Dean, Polaris Luu, Carolin McManus, and Bill Utley all donated their time and expertise during both fieldwork phases of the Shipping Point project. Rick Meatyard and Carol Samson provide the wonderful home for research that is Tall Timbers Marina. Additionally, Dr. George Schwarz of the Naval History and Heritage Command deserves special thanks for his leadership in the USS *Tulip* survey. Jim Sanborn and Jae Ko graciously opened their home in support of the Dunmore survey. My colleagues at the St. Augustine Lighthouse & Maritime Museum have energetically supported archaeological field work and research since 1999, a commendable dedication. Finally, thanks to Dr. Gordon Watts for sharing data from the 2011 survey of the *George Page*.

References

CASPER, JULIA A.
2009   "Navy Restores Rare Artifact From Looted Civil War Vessel". *America's Navy*. Naval History and Heritage Command, Department of the Navy. Washington D.C.

CHOWNING, LARRY S.
2007   Deadrise and Cross-planked. Tidewater. Centerville, MD.

GEARHART, ROBERT
2011   Archaeological Interpretation of Marine Magnetic Data. In *The Oxford Handbook of Maritime Archaeology*, edited by Alexis Catsambis, Ben Ford and Donny Leon Hamilton, pp.90-113. Oxford University Press, Oxford and New York.

KELLEY, THOMAS
1992   *The Personal Memoirs of Jonathan Thomas Scharf of the First Maryland Artillery*. Butternut and Blue. Baltimore, MD.

McDaniel, Olivia, P. Brendan Burke, and Chuck Meide
2017 The 450th Anniversary Shipwreck Survey: Applying Updated Methodologies to the Search for Historic Shipwrecks in the Nation's Oldest Port. In *ACUA Underwater Archaeology Proceedings 2017*, John Albertson and Fritz Hanselmann, editors, pp. XXX-XXX. Advisory Council on Underwater Archaeology, Washington, D.C.

Moody, John Sheldon, Calvin Duvall Cowles, Frederick Caryton Ainsworth, Robert N. Scott, Henry Martyn Lazelle, George Breckenridge Davis, Leslie J. Perry, and Joseph William Kirkley
1880 *The War of the Rebellion: A Compilation of the Official Records of the Union and Confederate Armies.* Vol. II. Chapter 9. Government Printing Office. Washington, D.C.

Meide, Chuck, Olivia McDaniel, P. Brendan Burke and Samuel P. Turner
2016 450th Anniversary Shipwreck Survey: Report on Archaeological Investigations. Lighthouse Archaeological Maritime Program, St. Augustine Lighthouse & Maritime Museum, St. Augustine, FL.

Turner, Samuel P., Anthony Randolph, Kristen Meier, and Jean B. Pelletier
2005 Additional Phase I Cultural Resource Survey of One Survey Block and Archaeological Diver Investigation of Two Targets Adjacent to Poplar Island, MD. Technical Addendum to EA Engineering, Science, and Technology, Hunt Valley, MD from R. Christopher Goodwin & Associates, Inc. Frederick, MD.

Rush, Richard and Robert H. Woods
1896 Official Records of the Union and Confederate Navies of the War of the Rebellion. Ser. 1, Vol. IV. Naval War Records Office. Washington D.C.

Swain, Craig
2011 Dahlgren Guns Against Fort Sumter. https://markerhunter.wordpress.com/2011/04/10/ix-inch-dahlgren-fort-sumter Accessed 27 February 2016.

Thompson, Bruce F.
1998 "The Terrible Calamity on the Lower Potomac"; An Historical and Archaeological Assessment of the Shipwreck USS *Tulip* (18ST644), Potomac River, St. Marys County, Maryland. Revised (1995). Maryland Historic Trust. Crownsville, MD.

2004 Exploring a Wreck in 'A Land A-Part'. Naval History. 18(4)

Tilp, Frederick
1978 *This Was the Potomac River.* privately printed.

P. Brendan Burke
Lighthouse Archaeological Maritime Program (LAMP)
81 Lighthouse Avenue
St Augustine, FL 32080
904-829-0745
bburke@staugustinelighthouse.org

The 450th Anniversary Shipwreck Survey: Applying Updated Methodologies to the Search for Historic Shipwrecks in the Nation's Oldest Port

Olivia McDaniel, P. Brendan Burke, Chuck Meide

During the 2015 field season, the Lighthouse Archaeological Maritime Program (LAMP) completed remote sensing and target testing in the waters offshore St. Augustine, Florida with the objective of locating early colonial shipwrecks. The 450th Anniversary Shipwreck Survey, named in honor of and coinciding with the 450th anniversary of the founding of St. Augustine, focused on the re-investigation of a magnetic dataset collected in 2009 using updated remote sensing survey, data analysis, and target testing methodologies in order to better understand and better prioritize magnetic targets for further investigations, which ultimately led to the discovery of two new historic shipwrecks.

Introduction

In 2009, the Lighthouse Archaeological Maritime Program (LAMP), the research arm of the St .Augustine Lighthouse & Maritime Museum, carried out an extensive remote sensing survey as part of the initial phase of the First Coast Maritime Archaeology Project (FCMAP) (Turner and Kennedy 2010). This remote sensing program sought to resurvey 45 anomalies previously recorded during magnetometer surveys between 1995 and 2003, first by Southern Oceans Archaeological Research, Inc. (SOAR) and subsequently by an earlier team at LAMP (Franklin and Morris 1996; Morris et al. 1998; Franklin et al. 1999; Morris et al. 2002 and 2003). The anomalies were grouped into 23 survey areas, each of which was named after a different comic book character (Marvel for offshore targets, and DC Comics for inshore targets). For the resurvey, both side scan sonar and sub-bottom profiler were deployed along with a more advanced magnetometer and positioning system, and researchers refined their methodology in order to gain a more sophisticated understanding of the characteristics and positioning of targets. Target testing began at the most promising anomalies, and a single historic shipwreck (the 1782 Storm Wreck, 8SJ5459) was discovered during the 2009 field season (Meide et al. 2010:109-111, 184-183; Turner and Kennedy 2010). Many of the potential targets delineated during the survey remained untested, however. In 2015, with funding from a small matching grant from the State of Florida's Division of Historical Resources, LAMP researchers completed the 450th Anniversary Shipwreck Survey (hereafter referred to as the 450th Survey), which served as an extension of LAMP's FCMAP work and sought to re-investigate the 2009 dataset and the remaining untested targets in hopes of identifying early colonial shipwrecks offshore St. Augustine (Meide et al. 2016). Much like the initial 2009 survey, the 450th Survey employed updated survey and data analysis methodologies in order to better understand the magnetic anomalies in question and better prioritize them for further investigation. The following summary discusses the methodologies employed during the 450th Survey, and the results of subsequent target testing activities.

Survey Methodology and Instrumentation

The 2009 survey and the 450th Survey shared many similarities. Both surveys employed the same survey areas designated in 2009, assigned potential targets a name associated with each survey block's assigned comic book character name, and used the same two primary geophysical devices: a Marine Magnetics Explorer Mini Magnetometer and a Klein 3900 side scan sonar. The same Trimble DSM-232 WAAS-enabled DGPS was utilized for positioning, though the sub-bottom profiler was omitted in 2015. In both surveys Hypack software was used to create pre-plotted track lines in each survey block.

There were methodological differences between the two surveys. In 2009, data was collected at 5 m (16.4 ft.) intervals, while running the boat alternatively north to south and then south to north. The magnetometer was also floated on the surface during data collection. While the resurvey was limited in 2015, all survey lanes were spaced 7 m (23.3 ft.) apart and all were run only in one direction. Directional uniformity results in smoother, more consistent readings in any particular sea state, which was demonstrated during LAMP's 2014 survey operations off Canaveral (Meide et al 2015:43). All data was collected while traveling from south to north during the 450th Survey. The remote sensing instruments were also towed in the water column at a relatively consistent altitude above the sea floor, between 5 m (16.4 fsw) and 7 m (22.9 fsw).

Magnetic Data Analysis

The 2009 data analysis and the reanalysis of the 2009 dataset undertaken in 2015 employed the Hypack Single Beam Editor function to first scrutinize each line of raw magnetic data in cross section, allowing researchers to identify and record individual deflections, both positive and negative in nature, from the ambient magnetic field. Once identified, these anomalies were imported back into Hypack software as edited data files where they were contoured and prioritized for further investigation. In 2009, high priority designations were assigned to anomalies featuring spatial adjacency (signatures that were detected across multiple adjacent survey lanes), higher amplitudes (measured in gammas or nanoTeslas), and longer durations (measured in meters). Generally, this meant focus was placed on dipolar and multi-component signatures, although LAMP researchers also prioritized some anomalies that lacked spatial adjacency but otherwise featured substantial amplitude and duration, like some large monopoles (Meide et al. 2010:106-155 ; 2016: 42-62).

The 450th Survey data analysis took these characteristics into consideration, but differed from the 2009 analysis in that it relied most heavily on contouring magnetic data in order to assess polar orientation, or magnetic moment, described in detail below. This was done by normalizing the ambient magnetic field in Hypack Single Beam Editor, effectively bringing its value to zero gammas, and leaving the anomalous magnetic signatures more readily visible against a magnetically neutral background. Once imported back into Hypack as edited data files, an individual color palette was assigned to each survey area, using blue to indicate negative deflections from the ambient magnetic field and red to indicate positive deflections (Figure 1). Contoured in this fashion, the anomalies were analyzed and prioritized based on their magnetic moments, a technique that has been recently developed primarily by Jeffrey Enright (et al. 2006) and Robert Gearhart (2011).

Magnetic moment is a term used to describe the orientation of a magnetic field derived from a single ferrous object, or an assemblage of ferrous objects, and it is influenced by both permanent and induced magnetic

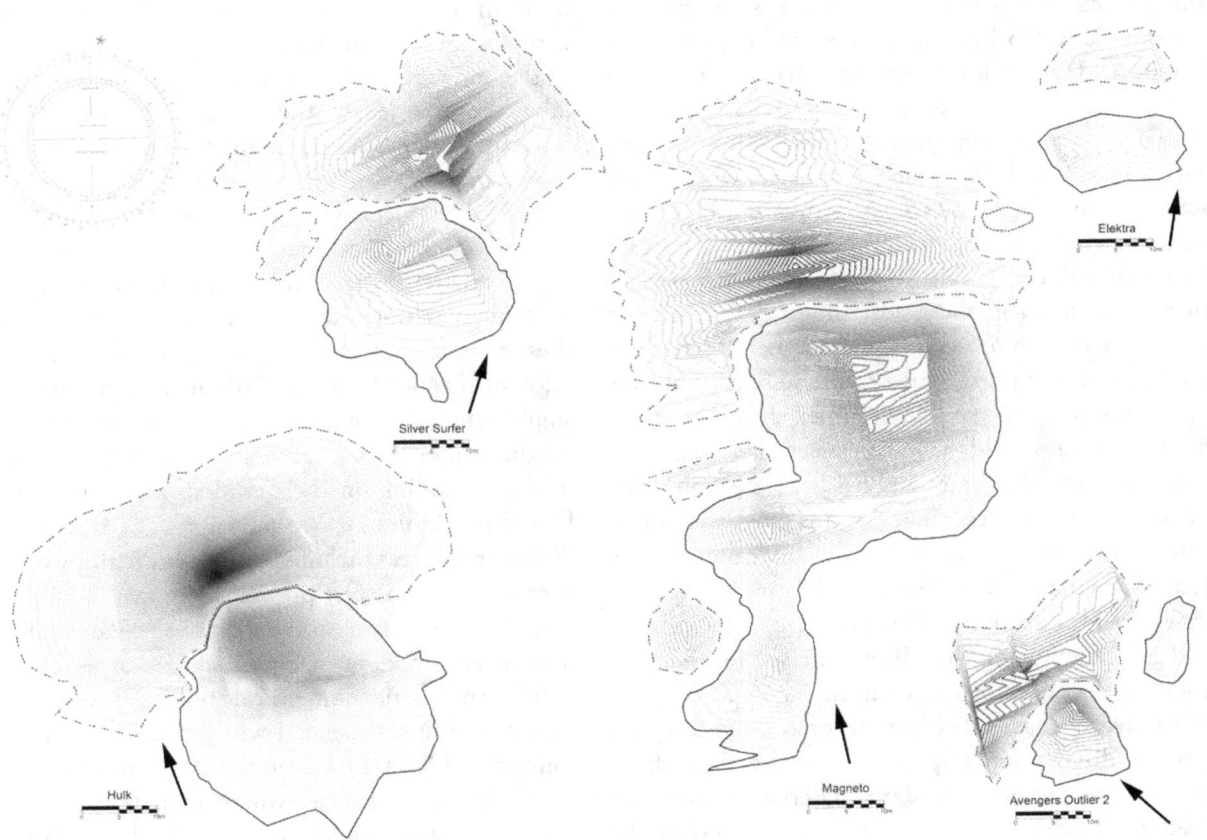

Figure 1. The magnetic contours for each of the anomalies chosen for further testing during the 450th Anniversary Shipwreck Survey are shown here to scale. The orientation of their magnetic moments, as assigned by LAMP analysts, is represented by the black arrows. Each contour is assigned an individual color palette to clearly illustrate each anomaly's amplitude. The dashed outlines indicate the negative lobes of each anomaly. The solid outlines indicate the positive lobes.

Anomaly Name	Magnetic Moment	Maximum Amplitude (gammas)	Duration (meters)	Associated Wreck or Debris
Hulk*	7°	704.3g	65m	Nine Foot Under Site (8SJ6460)
Silver Surfer	45°/21°	58.2g	54m	Anniversary Wreck (8SJ6461)
Elektra	-56°/10°	20.3 g	22m	Modern debris – concrete slab with reinforcing rebar
Magneto	-15	75.6g	53m	Iron Box Site (8SJ3526)
Avengers Outlier 2	-40°	35.5g	38m	Unidentified
Storm	0°	30.7g	36m	Storm Wreck (8SJ5459)
Juggernaut**	-6°	225.5g	47m	Unnamed shipwreck site (not yet assigned a site file number)
Avengers Outlier 3	-51°/-17°	369.5g	66m	*Industry (8SJ3478)*
Captain America	-12°	1959.7g	100m	Modern pipes and construction debris
Phoenix	-54°	69.8g	55m	Comptons' Wreck (8SJ3525)
Magneto (a)	-10°	135.5g	71m	Centerboard Schooner (8SJ3309)

Note: The characteristics included here were observed in the 2009 data set, except where otherwise noted. In the case where two magnetic moments are given, the first is determined by the objective method, whereas the second is determined by the whole anomaly approach.

*Observed in data set collected in 2015

**Observed in a data set collected in 2016

Table 1. Characteristics of Magnetic Anomalies Associated with Identified Wrecks or Debris Located Offshore St. Augustine, Florida.

fields. For example, the magnetic moment of a single ferrous object, such as a steel pipe or other single piece of ferrous modern debris, is determined by its permanent magnetic field, which is fixed and will change orientation if the ferrous object in question changes orientation. However, every ferromagnetic object also has an induced magnetic field, which is created when small amounts of atomic dipoles in a ferrous object realign towards magnetic north whenever the object is moved. In general, induced magnetic fields are much weaker than permanent magnetic fields, and are therefore not often detected when observing the magnetic signatures of single ferrous objects. When multiple ferrous objects lie in close proximity to each other, however, their various permanent fields tend to cancel each other out, leaving their induced magnetic fields as the dominant force, which more or less align towards magnetic north. Shipwrecks, which usually feature multiple ferrous objects, have magnetic moments indicative of induced magnetic fields (Gearhart 2011: 92-95; 102-103).

This phenomenon has been known for decades outside the archaeological community, but only in the last decade has it become a commonly accepted practice to differentiate shipwreck anomalies from those associated with isolated modern material through the concept of permanent and induced magnetism (Enright et al 2006:135-136; Gearhart 2011:102-109). When contoured, a complex source anomaly tends to display a dipolar pattern with its polar axis aligned with the earth's magnetic field, regardless of the orientation of the site itself. In the Northern Hemisphere, this means that for complex source anomalies, the negative lobes are situated in the northern portion of the anomaly, and the positive lobes are oriented to the south. Gearhart (2011:102) asserts that this polar orientation, or magnetic moment, has proven to be the single most effective discriminating factor when identifying simple-source anomalies and complex-source anomalies, including shipwrecks.

Gearhart (2011:97-102) demonstrated with a sample of 29 known shipwreck sites that the magnetic moment of these complex source anomalies is always oriented within ±26° of magnetic north. Gearhart also confirmed that single magnetic items of modern origin display varying magnetic moments based on their permanent magnetic fields, depending on their random position on the sea floor. In addition to unknown magnetic targets, the 2009 survey areas included both historic shipwrecks and sites of modern debris previously known to researchers, intended to create a comparative dataset for both historic and modern magnetic signatures. For the most part, the magnetic moment rule holds true when applied to the contours associated with these known magnetic sources (Table 1). However, the rule is not foolproof, as there are some instances where a single ferrous object, whose magnetic moment is influenced by its permanent magnetic field, happens to be randomly oriented within ±26° of magnetic north and therefore mimics a complex or shipwreck like anomaly. The probability of a single ferrous object falling so that its permanent magnetic field is oriented within this specific 52° span of the possible 360°, is approximately one out of seven occurrences, or around 14%. There are also instances where scatters of modern debris, such as a pile of modern pipes or braided steel cable in tangled loops, can exert magnetic fields indicative of complex source anomalies (Gearhart 2011:103). At the same time, a single historic object, such as an anchor with a magnetic moment determined by its permanent magnetic field, could look like modern debris and be overlooked. However, despite these exceptions to the rule, this method of analysis provides a reliable means of determining which targets are likely to represent complex historic shipwrecks, and allows researchers to more confidently devote limited resources to further investigations at these potential targets. Using this method, five anomalies were designated as high priority for further investigation during the 450th survey. They included Hulk, Elektra, Avengers Outlier 2, Silver Surfer, and Magneto (Figure 1).

It is worth discussing the method with which researchers estimated magnetic moments for each individual contours, as there does not seem to be a standard practice in place for determining the magnetic moments, and it is believed that it may be a somewhat subjective process with results varying depending on individual data analysts. In an attempt to objectively determine each anomaly's magnetic moment, the LAMP analyst initially recorded the angle between the maximum positive and minimum negative deflections for each anomaly. In most cases this seemed to work well, but it was occasionally problematic. The first time a problem was recognized was with the Avengers Outlier 3 target, which is associated with the 1764 *Industry* shipwreck (8SJ3478). Upon casual observation, the lobes of the Avengers Outlier 3 anomaly appear to be oriented in the north-south manner consistently associated with shipwreck signatures. Indeed, when measuring the angle from the approximate center of the positive lobe to the approximate center of the negative lobe, the resultant angle was -17°, well within the expected ±26° expected of a complex source anomaly. When the seemingly objective method was applied the resultant magnetic moment was measured at -51°, which would normally indicate a simple-source, non-shipwreck anomaly. This discrepancy occurred at two other anomalies as well, one of which was another 18th-century shipwreck (Anniversary Wreck, 8SJ6461).

After further investigation of the issue, researchers believe the discrepancy arises from the fact that this seemingly objective method rests in the ability to choose single points of magnetic data (the highest gamma reading and lowest gamma reading), and while it may provide an objective way to establish a line between those points, this method would not necessarily conform to the hypothesis that shipwrecks will exhibit a magnetic moment within 26° of magnetic north. This method relies on the probability that the survey vessel will collect a line of data directly over the highest and lowest points of magnetism, which is not guaranteed. Rather, researchers believe taking a more whole-anomaly approach that ignores exact data points and instead focuses on establishing a line that bisects the anomaly's positive and negative poles as equally as possible. A line drawn perpendicular to the bisecting line, from the approximate center of the positive pole to the approximate center of the negative pole, would then represent the magnetic moment. The magnetic moments indicated for the five magnetic contours in Figure 1 were derived using this method. LAMP researchers believe this represents a more consistently accurate method of determining magnetic moment from contours, and will rely on this method during future data analysis.

Table1 lists the characteristics associated with the high priority anomalies and those derived from known sources. In cases where magnetic moments determined by the objective method varied significantly from the whole anomaly method, both results are included.

Target Testing

A total of 161 dives were completed over the course of the project for a total cumulative bottom time of 140 hours and 43 minutes. Divers completed 353 probe tests, and three 1 × 2 m test excavations at five high probability targets. Three of the five targets (Hulk, Silver Surfer, and Magneto) appear to be shipwrecks. Of the two remaining targets, Elektra represents modern debris, and no magnetic material was encountered at Avengers Outlier 2.

Target Testing Methodology

Sonar imagery collected in previous seasons at each of the five targets indicated that the magnetic material associated with each anomaly was likely buried, which is typical for sites offshore St. Augustine. Therefore, divers employed a hydraulic probe to penetrate the substrate to confirm the presence of wreckage or other man-made material. As with the remote sensing, the target testing methodology was also modified and improved for this survey. The process began by deploying a buoy at the central point of the anomaly, ideally as close to the nexus of the negative and positive lobes as possible. In previous surveys this location had been refined using a handheld magnetometer, but a malfunctioning handheld magnetometer employed during the 2014 field season forced LAMP archaeologists to experiment with new ways of refining target locations (Meide et al. 2015). This new method, which relied on the computer generated contours of the anomalies and a survey-grade GPS, was found to be more reliable than employing the handheld magnetometer even after it had undergone repairs, and was therefore applied during the 450th Survey. By keeping the georeferenced contour open on a survey laptop equipped with Hypack, archaeologists were able to pick a specific point on the screen that was most likely to represent the magnetic source, or in other words, the nexus of the positive and negative lobes in the magnetic contour. Hypack was used to generate coordinates for this spot, which for each target was designated D1, or Drop 1, to represent the intended drop position for the first buoy.

After deploying the first buoy near these coordinates, the buoy weight was secured with a T-probe by a diver, and a swimmer equipped with the antennae of a highly accurate (sub-meter) survey GPS, swam to the drop buoy, and pulled the buoy line tight enough to eliminate slack in the line, but not so much as to move the buoy, while researchers on the boat recorded the position and plotted it directly on the target contour in Hypack. It should be noted that this method of collecting GPS coordinates is successful on sites in 30 ft. (9.1 m) of water or less, but has not been tested on sites at deeper depths at this time. The buoy location, designated D1A, or "Drop 1 Actual," allowed researchers to measure exactly how far the actual drop buoy was from its intended location (D1). A team of divers could then be instructed how far and in what direction to move the buoy in order to place it at the desired position. Once moved, the new buoy location was again recorded using a swimmer with the GPS antennae. The refined buoy location was designated D1B, and that became the primary datum for divers to begin hydraulic probing. If for any reason the buoy needed to be moved again, the new location was designated D1C (with consecutive letters for additional moves as needed). If researchers felt a new drop was required on the same target, but in a different area than that of D1, it was designated D2 (Drop 2), with letter extensions applied for each move as described above. This naming system was used consistently for each of the five targets tested during the 450th Survey.

With the datum established, hydraulic probing then took place at one meter intervals along a transect line centered at the datum. The pattern of probe tests and the orientation of the transect line was determined before divers entered the water and was customized to each anomaly, aiming to thoroughly cover the interface between the positive and negative lobes of the magnetic contours. This maximized the chances of encountering magnetic source material. The probe itself was a 10 ft. long, 1 in. diameter pipe attached to a water pump by lengths of garden and fire hose to create a water jet. Its entire length was forced into the sea floor, and if material was encountered, the depths and locations of each positive return were recorded by divers.

If the depth of burial allowed, a 1 × 2 m test unit was placed over the shallowest positive returns and excavated using two 4 in. diameter handheld dredges.

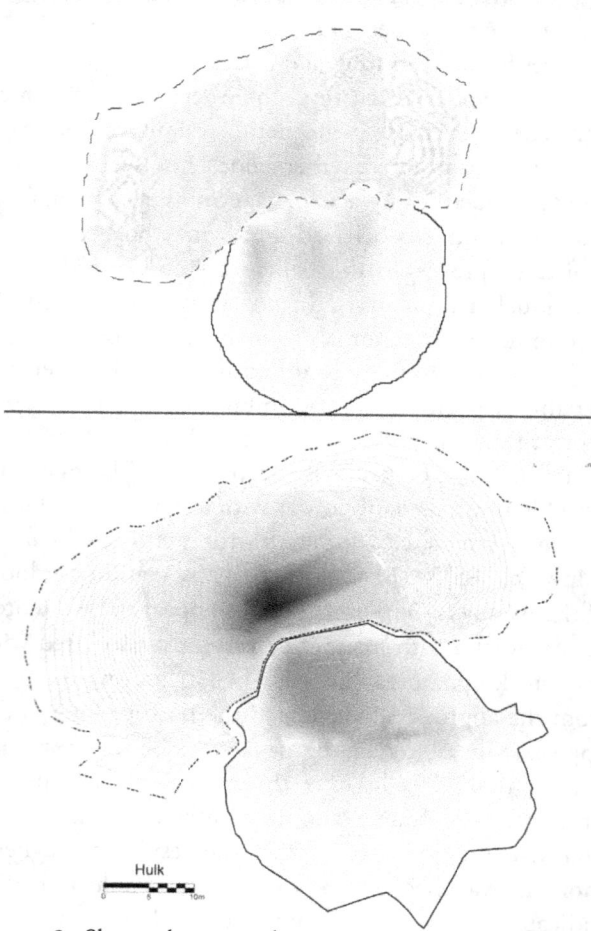

Figure 2. Shown here are the contours associated with the 214.5g Hulk anomaly as observed in 2009 (top) and the same anomaly after undergoing additional refinement survey in 2015 when its maximum amplitude was recorded at 704.3g (bottom). The same color palette is assigned to both contours to better illustrate the differences in gamma intensity between the two surveys.

While extensive excavation was not the goal of the project, exposing the buried material in this manner was the only definitive way to identify it as modern debris or historic material.

Target Testing Results

Hulk

Hulk was the first of the 2009 anomalies to be reanalyzed, and consisted of a large dipole with an ideal magnetic moment of 4°, and a maximum amplitude of 214.5 g. As the first target tested, before refining the methodology outlined above, divers placed 41 probes along two 20 m transects, laid out running north-south and east-west, intersecting at D1B. When no positive returns were detected, D1B was plotted on top of the georeferenced contour in Hypack, showing D1B was several meters north of the nexus of the anomaly's positive and negative lobes. The drop buoy was pulled and redeployed (D2A), but when hand-held magnetometer readings at the new drop indicated inconsistent readings, the decision was made to resurvey the entire area using the updated survey techniques discussed earlier.

The anomaly captured during the 2015 refinement survey was significantly larger than that of the 2009 data set (Figure 2). The 2015 contour indicated a dipole with a maximum amplitude of 704.3 g. Its magnetic moment at 7° was still within the ideal range. The 489.8 g discrepancy between two surveys of the same anomaly is due to different survey parameters, most importantly the depth of the sensor. Using the new contour as a guide, divers were instructed to move D2A 3.6 m closer to the dipole's center, designating that point D2B. Probing commenced from there. Divers immediately recorded three hard positive returns directly adjacent to D2B, validating the use of the magnetic contour to pinpoint the source of the anomaly. The returns were buried over two meters deep, meaning it would be extremely difficult to reach with handheld dredges. Therefore, a more extensive probing scheme was enacted on the Hulk target in order to thoroughly delineate the extent of the buried site. There were 51 positive returns out of 145 probes, all buried between 1.6 m (5.2 ft.) and 3 m (9.8 ft.) deep (Figure 3). Thirty of these returns were described by divers as hard returns, most likely indicative of metal or concretion. Divers described the other 21 positive returns as "soft" returns, saying they felt like pushing the probe into a mattress, or other softer material that was somewhat giving, and yet could not be penetrated. It is hypothesized that these soft returns may represent wood.

While the positive returns encountered at the Hulk

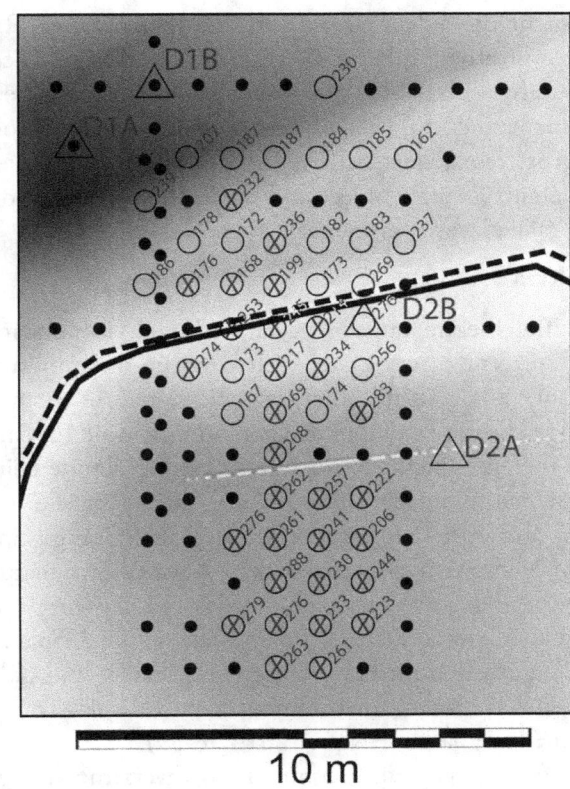

Figure 3. Due to the deeper burial of material at the Hulk target, more extensive target testing was performed in order to better delineate the nature of the site, the results of which are illustrated here.

target are too deep to effectively dredge for positive identification at this time, the combination of a contour featuring a magnetic moment indicative of shipwrecks, and the high number of positive probe hits indicating a deeply-buried large object or dense scatter of objects, seemingly made up of wood and metal, has convinced researchers that the Hulk target does indeed represent a historic shipwreck. The target was reported to the Florida Master Site File as the Nine Foot Under Site (8SJ6460).

Avengers Outlier 2

The Avengers Outlier 2 target is a dipolar anomaly featuring a maximum amplitude of 35.5 g. The target was initially assigned a favorable magnetic moment and chosen for further target testing. However, divers completed 55 test probes at the target, only one of which indicated a positive return, at a significant depth. After the mostly inconclusive hydraulic probing, the contour was revisited and it was found that the initial estimated magnetic moment was incorrect. After reanalyzing the contour a second time, researchers recorded a magnetic moment of -40°, well outside the desired range. The single positive probe was, at 2.3 m (7.5 ft.), too deep to easily access, but given the unfavorable magnetic moment and the lack of any adjacent positive probe returns, researchers believe the positive contact likely represents a single object and no further investigations will take place at this target.

Elektra

The Elektra target is a small dipole visible across five adjacent survey lanes, with a maximum amplitude of only 20.3g. While the magnetic signature is small, it did reflect a favorable magnetic moment of 10°, and was therefore included for further testing despite being considerably smaller in signature than other known 18th and 19th-century wrecks sites off St. Augustine. Archaeologists hypothesized that the smaller signature may be indicative of an older 16th-century wreck, or a smaller vessel such as those that supplied Spanish St. Augustine from Hanava, as these smaller and older wrecks have been shown to occasionally display weaker magnetic signatures (Krivor 2014:58-59).

When target testing commenced, divers immediately observed a human-made object on the sea floor adjacent to D1B. Initially believed to be a massive concretion, a 1 × 2 m test unit was established over the object to expose more of it in order to better understand its basic characteristics. Excavation revealed that it was in fact a massive slab of concrete that appeared to be damaged on two sides. It measured 1.23 m (4.0 ft.) long, 1.16 m (3.8 ft.) wide, and 0.55 m (1.8 ft.) thick. A manual probe one meter in length was used to penetrate extensively around the slab, but no further material was encountered. The hydraulic probe was then deployed to test the greater area around the slab. Five 10 m transects were laid out and a total of 53 probes were completed, of which only one was positive. This was approximately 80 cm (2.6 ft.) from the slab, but divers believe they may have placed the probe off the transect line in the low visibility and hit the slab itself. It therefore appears that the slab is an isolated object.

A hand-held metal detector deployed to scan the slab indicated the presence of metallic objects inside the concrete, most likely indicating reinforcing iron, steel, or rebar. This seemed to confirm that the slab was in fact the magnetic source of the Elektra target, and in this case illustrates one of the instances where a single ferrous object happens to be oriented to within 26° of magnetic north, mimicking the signature of a complex induced field anomaly.

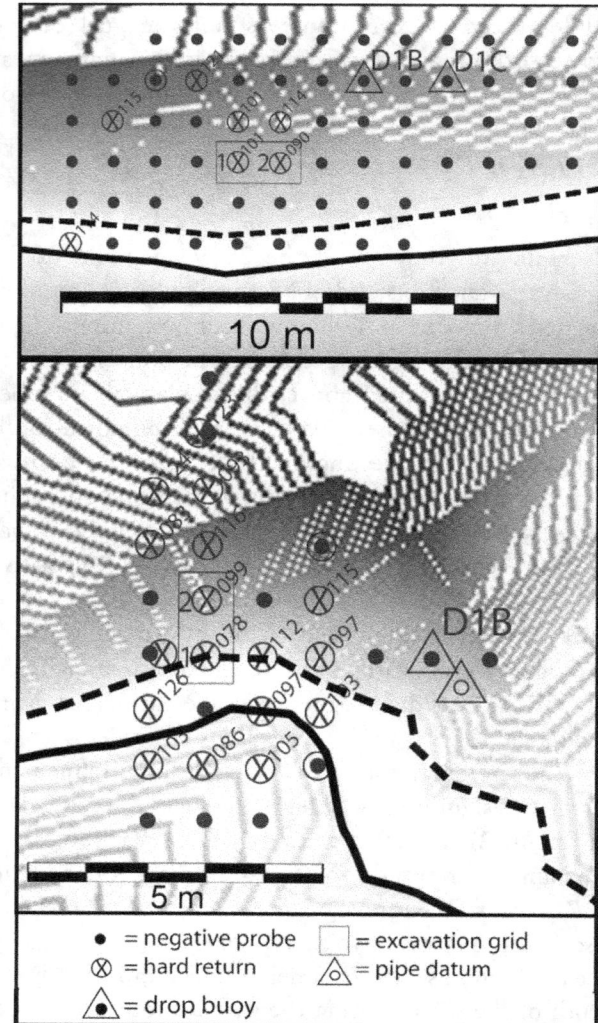

Figure 4. Shown here are the target testing maps for Magneto (top) and Silver Surfer (bottom). Note, the circle filled with a black dot on the Magneto map indicates a possible positive probe test, whereas the same mark on the Silver Surfer map indicates a shell layer.

Magneto

The anomaly designated as Magneto during the 450th Survey featured a favorable magnetic moment of -15° and a maximum amplitude of 75.6 g. While a likely candidate for shipwrecked material, it was also of interest due to its close proximity to the coordinates of the Iron Box Site (8SJ3526), a probable 19th-century shipwreck documented by SOAR divers in 1999 that included a pile of iron debris, including chain, and a large, partially exposed iron box-like structure with wooden timbers beneath it (Franklin et al. 1999: Appendix C5). The Magneto anomaly was chosen for further investigation to determine if it was a separate shipwreck or an outlying extension of the Iron Box Site, or if perhaps the reported location of the Iron Box Site was incorrect and the anomaly was actually the site itself.

A total of 68 probes were completed at this target, seven of which were positive returns, with a possible eighth positive return recorded as well. The returns were shallow enough to allow for dredge excavation, and a 1× 2 m test unit was established over the two shallowest positive returns (Figure 4, top). The subsequent excavation exposed a large concreted mass that appeared to be primarily composed of chain, and was consistent with the 1999 description of the Iron Box Site (Meide et al. 2016:78-84). While the iron box itself was not observed in 2015, researchers believe the Magneto target is the Iron Box Site, and the coordinates for the site have been updated accordingly.

Silver Surfer

The Silver Surfer Target was without question the most significant of those chosen for further investigation during the 450th Survey (Meide et al. 2016:90-110). The Silver Surfer anomaly was one of the targets that exhibited significantly different magnetic moments: an unfavorable 45° when determined with the "objective" method, but with the much more favorable estimate of 21° when applying the whole anomaly approach. It has a maximum amplitude of 58.2 g. Thirty-one probes were performed at the target, of which 17 resulted in positive returns (Figure 4, bottom). A 1 × 2 m test grid was established over the two shallowest returns and designated Units 1 and 2. Subsequent excavation in the units revealed a dense scatter of historic material, including cauldrons, barrels, pewter plates, and a stoneware sherd. Preliminary analysis suggested the site dated sometime between 1750 and the early 1800s. The site was reported as the Anniversary Wreck (8SJ6461), named in honor of the 450th anniversary of the founding of St. Augustine being celebrated that year. More extensive excavations began at this site the following year (Meide, this volume).

Future Research

In the coming field seasons, LAMP's main research focus will shift to excavation and research at the Anniversary Wreck, but the remote sensing and target testing activities initiated during the 450th Survey will continue. The use of magnetic moment as a tool to prioritize unknown magnetic anomalies for testing proved to be extremely successful over the course of the 450th Anniversary Shipwreck Survey, as it led to the discovery of two new shipwreck sites and the refined location of another last seen by archaeologists in 1999. LAMP archaeologists plan to continue applying this method to prioritize unidentified targets for further investigation. Additional remote sensing refinement surveys employing the updated survey and data analysis methods applied during this project will take place as well, in new areas and also at locations of other known sites. A continued focus on remote sensing in these waters will lead to not only a better understanding of the magnetic signatures of various types of shipwreck sites and other ferromagnetic debris, but also to the furtherance of our knowledge and understanding of the submerged cultural resources located in Florida's First Coast region.

References

Enright, Jeffrey M., Robert II Gearhart, Doug Jones and Jenna Enright
2006   Study to Conduct National Register of Historic Places Evaluations of Submerged Sites on the Gulf of Mexico Outer Shelf. LA OCS Study MMS 2006-036. U.S. Department of the Interior, Minerals Management Service, Gulf of Mexico OCS Region, New Orleans, Louisiana.

Franklin, Marianne, and John W. Morris III
1996   The St. Augustine Shipwreck Survey, Phase One. Southern Oceans Archaeological Research, Inc. Survey Report No. 1. Report 4451 on file at the Bureau of Archaeological Research, Division of Historical Resources, Tallahassee, FL.

Franklin, Marianne, John W. Morris III, Norine Carroll, Kelly Bumpass, and Andrea P. White
1999   The St. Augustine Shipwreck Survey 1998. Updated in May 1999 to include April Fieldwork. Southern Oceans Archaeological Research, Inc. Survey Report No. 3. Report submitted to the Bureau of Archaeological Research, Division of Historical Resources, Tallahassee, FL.

Gearhart, Robert
2011   Archaeological Interpretation of Marine Magnetic Data. In The Oxford Handbook of Maritime Archaeology, Alexis Catsambis, Ben Ford and Donny Leon Hamilton, editors, pp. 90-113. Oxford University Press, Oxford.

Krivor, Michael C.
2014   Submerged Cultural Resources Remote Sensing Survey and Diver Assessment of the Nassau County Shore Protection Project, Nassau County, Florida. Report prepared for the US Army Corps of Engineers, Jacksonville District, by Southeastern Archaeological Research, Inc., Jacksonville, FL.

Meide, Chuck, Olivia McDaniel, P. Brendan Burke and Samuel P. Turner
2016 450th Anniversary Shipwreck Survey: Report on Archaeological Investigations. Lighthouse Archaeological Maritime Program, St. Augustine Lighthouse & Maritime Museum, St. Augustine, Florida.

Meide, Chuck, Samuel P. Turner and P. Brendan Burke
2010 First Coast Maritime Archaeology Project 2007-2009: Report on Archaeological Investigations and Other Activities. Lighthouse Archaeological Maritime Program, St. Augustine Lighthouse & Museum, St. Augustine, FL.

Meide, Chuck, Samuel P. Turner, P. Brendan Burke and Olivia McDaniel
2015 The Search for the Lost French Fleet of 1565: Report on 2014 Archaeological Investigations. Lighthouse Archaeological Maritime Program, St. Augustine Lighthouse & Museum, St. Augustine, FL.

Morris, John W. III, Marianne Franklin, and Norine Carroll
1998 The St. Augustine Shipwreck Survey. Southern Oceans Archaeological Research, Inc. Survey Report No. 2. Report submitted to the Bureau of Archaeological Research, Division of Historical Resources, Tallahassee, FL.

Morris, John W. III, Jason M. Burns, Robin E. Moore and Jeff T. Moates
2002 The St. Johns County Submerged Cultural Resources Inventory and Management Plan 2001-2002. Lighthouse Archaeological Maritime Program, St. Augustine Lighthouse & Museum, St. Augustine, FL.

Morris, John W. III, Jason M. Burns, and Robin E. Moore
2003 The St. Johns County Submerged Cultural Resources Inventory and Management Plan 2002 – 2003 Phase II. Lighthouse Archaeological Maritime Program, St. Augustine Lighthouse & Museum, St. Augustine, FL.

Turner, Samuel P. and Kendra Kennedy
2010 LAMP 2009 Remote Sensing Survey. In ACUA Underwater Archaeology Proceedings 2010, Christopher Horrel and Melanie Damour, editors, pp. 11-16. Advisory Council on Underwater Archaeology, Amelia Island, FL.

Breiner, S.
1999 Applications Manual for Portable Magnetometers. Geometrics, Sunnyvale, CA.

Olivia McDaniel
Lighthouse Archaeological Maritime Program
St. Augustine Lighthouse & Maritime Museum
81 Lighthouse Ave.
St. Augustine, FL 32080

P. Brendan Burke
Lighthouse Archaeological Maritime Program
St. Augustine Lighthouse & Maritime Museum
81 Lighthouse Ave.
St. Augustine, FL 32080

Chuck Meide
Lighthouse Archaeological Maritime Program
St. Augustine Lighthouse & Maritime Museum
81 Lighthouse Ave.
St. Augustine, FL 32080

The Dish Ran Away with the Spoon: Revisiting Unprovenienced Foodways Artifacts from the Spanish Fleet Wrecks of Eighteenth Century Florida

Olivia Thomas

The Spanish empire was the first European power to establish permanent settlements on several Caribbean islands and coasts of North America, which facilitated prosperous trade between the New and Old Worlds. The distance between Spain and the colonies led to differences in the lifestyles and customs of these frontier spaces. Archaeological investigations have yielded numerous pieces of material culture reflecting Spanish life and trade in the territories of Florida and the Caribbean. This paper addresses lifestyles of frontier communities by examining artifacts associated with colonial Spanish foodways in two shipwreck assemblages from the early eighteenth century coast of Florida.

Introduction

The destruction of archaeological sites and their context is present in both terrestrial and maritime contexts. This is particularly true for shipwrecks, which can be less protected than terrestrial sites for several reasons including access, policing, and legislation. The 1715 and 1733 Spanish shipwreck fleets in Florida are prime examples of sites that have been destroyed by treasure hunters. State permits and illegal looting have led to the removal of countless artifacts from their original context and their placement within private collections or the hands of the state, per state-sanctioned contracts. The archaeological community has been hesitant to address these collections because of the lack of context for the artifacts. This paper will argue for the study of artifacts without archaeological context, or "unprovenienced" artifacts, by providing a case study of artifacts from collections of the 1715 and 1733 Spanish shipwreck fleets. This paper is a preliminary report reflecting ongoing research and analysis, and further conclusions are forthcoming. The primary research objectives of this project include creating usable typologies for the study of 18th century cutlery artifacts, creating a case study which utilizes unprovenienced artifacts in a meaningful way, and examining foodways artifacts using artifact biographies. This project seeks to answer the following research questions: What conclusions can be reached regarding Spanish colonial foodways of the 18th century through the examination of unprovenienced foodways artifacts recovered from shipwrecks in Florida waters? What are the biographies of cutlery from the 1715 and 1733 Spanish shipwrecks? What do these biographies relate about 18th century Spanish colonial foodways and trade?

Background

In late July 1715, the Tierra Firme Squadron and the Spanish *Flota*, comprised of a total of 11 ships, met in Cuba to begin the transatlantic journey to Spain (Peterson 1975:362-363). Though the voyage began with favorable weather, the fleet was sailing in the middle of hurricane season and was soon caught in a storm during which the ships were scattered along the Florida coast south of Cape Canaveral. (Peterson 1975:366). While waiting for supply and salvage ships, the remaining crew members set up a survivor's camp onshore which was soon raided by English-Bermudian pirate Henry Jennings, who made off with a sizeable quantity of the recovered specie (Peterson 1972:262).

Eighteen years later, in July 1733, the New Spain Fleet, made up of 8 galleons and 13 or 14 other vessels, departed Havana for Spain. Again, sailing during hurricane season, the fleet experienced several days of favorable weather before being caught in a storm off the Florida Keys. Several of the ships were lost or wrecked, and again salvaged by surviving crew members (Peterson 1972:263). Unlike the 1715 fleet, these survivors were not attacked by pirates and thus much of the recovered cargoes did ultimately arrive in Spain as intended (Peterson 1972:263).

The first of the 1715 shipwrecks were rediscovered in 1961 and have almost all been looted by illegal and state-sanctioned treasure hunters in the years since (Peterson 1972:263). Some of the 1733 *Flota* shipwrecks were rediscovered in the early to mid-20th century. Extensive treasure hunting and state-sanctioned salvage has taken place on all the known shipwrecks associated with this fleet as well (Peterson 1972:263-264).

In 1982, Dr. Russell K. Skowronek's master's thesis examined the artifact collection of the 1733 *flota* in comparison to terrestrial collections of colonial St. Augustine. Skowronek's study was the first and only artifact analysis of the 1733 *flota* and used Stanley South's (1977) frontier theory to examine the material recovered from those shipwrecks. This study will utilize Skowronek's initial artifact analysis as a basic framework for the study of the 1733 and 1715 artifact collections.

Theoretical Framework

There are four key concepts that form the theoretical framework of this study: material culture studies, artifact biographies, frontier economies, and foodways. Material culture studies can be defined as "a range of studies which looked at material objects, buildings and landscapes in both the prehistoric and recent past and present, in which the methods of archaeology, ethnography and related areas were combined" (Johnson 2010:66). Kathleen Deagan's (1987, 2002) two-part survey of artifacts from colonial Florida and the Caribbean serves as a model for the theory and methodology applied in this study. The intention of each of her studies was to synthesize existing information about Spanish colonial material culture. She states that "material culture is, after all, not only the most basic category of our archaeological database but also the one category that separates archaeologists from social historians, geographers, philosophers, and poets" (Deagan 2002:4). Barbara Mattick's (2010) study of bone toothbrushes was key to the development of typologies for artifacts in this study. The artifacts in the material culture study being undertaken in this project lack context because of the unscientific manner by which they were removed from their respective archaeological sites. This study will, therefore, include only morphological types as described by Mattick (2010:28), and will not attempt temporal typologies, save for the differentiation between fleets.

An aspect of material culture studies that serves as the second theoretical concept in this project is the model of artifact biographies. An artifact biography may be defined as "the concept of sequences of production and consumption" (Ashby 2011:1). This includes each stage of production, consumption, and deposition; it also accounts for the varying cultural values that would have had an impact on the raw materials, method of manufacture, design, method of transport, utility, and eventual discarding of an object (Kopytoff 2013). By looking at an artifact in terms of the stages or phases it underwent to result in its current state, scholars create a more comprehensive view of the entirety of cultural influences in the appearance of an artifact. Artifact biographies will be utilized, despite lack of archaeological context, to infer details of origin, manufacture, treatment, use, and deposition of the artifacts in this study.

Frontier theory and economics are the third theoretical concept in this study, and will be utilized as a basis of understanding the general temporal and physical context, rather than specific archaeological location, of the artifacts in this study. The term "frontier" is used with the understanding of the following statement by Kenneth Lewis:

> *Frontiers associated with European expansion are perhaps the most intensively studied examples of colonization ... intrusive societies were forced to adapt to conditions similar to those encountered by all migrating groups ... are also likely to disclose behavioral regularities common to colonization in general* (Lewis 1984:8).

Daniel Usner, Jr.'s study of frontier exchange economies focuses on the interactions between cultures "within a geographical area in a way that emphasizes the initiatives taken by the various participants" (1992:8). Frontier economics includes illicit trade which, in eighteenth century colonial Spanish territories, is well known to historians and archaeologists alike due to the numerous documents regarding the practice, or prevention, of the movement of contraband throughout colonies and trade ships (Harman 1969; Sanders 1977; Skowronek 1992; Deagan 2007; Thompson 2012). These alternative economies can be understood by referencing the following definition: "the informal economy is typically defined as consisting of all actions related to the illegal production, commerce, and/or transportation of goods that fell outside of formal (i.e., legal) economic systems" (Thompson 2012:56). The study of such systems has led to the development of diagnostic artifact typologies that suggest the presence of illicit trading activities including ceramics, precious gems and metals, textiles, and agricultural goods (Newquist 2011:93). The artifacts in this study will be examined for indication of frontier manufacture, use, and mercantilism in the context of maritime life and trade.

The fourth and final aspect to the theoretical framework of this project is the study of foodways, which can be defined as "the interaction of food and culture" (Thursby 2008:176). The study of foodways has been increasingly utilized by archaeologists and professionals in other disciplines to understand past and present cultures. Food, and its preparation, is universal in nature and provides an inherent link to past cultures. Foodways, for the purposes of this study, can include any item related to the procurement, storage, preparation, serving, consumption, and refuse of food by humans. Material culture examples include jars, baskets, kettles, pots, pans, platters, cutlery, and cups. This study will focus specifically on cutlery: forks, knives, spoons, and broken handles thereof. The specific nature of the artifacts in this collection will eventually be broadened, but will act, for the time being, as a baseline for analysis and interpretation of frontier maritime life.

Methodological Framework

The methodological framework for this project was twofold – the phases included historical research and archaeological artifact analysis. The first phase involved the consultation of several primary accounts of trans-Atlantic voyages to and from the Spanish colonies in the 18th century. Sources from the 16th and 17th centuries were also consulted to build a solid background for the analysis of trade, life, and foodways in that era. Primary source documents, including personal travel accounts, colonial records, official depositions, and archival records of the 18th century, were invaluable to the completion of this study. These sources were utilized both as a basis of knowledge and comparison to the artifacts that will be discussed later. Secondary sources by historians and specialists specific to the two fleets of shipwrecks in question, contemporary archaeological sites (both terrestrial and maritime), and general sources on the topics of Spanish colonialism and the history of foodways were consulted to establish a background for the major topics in this study.

The second methodological phase of this project focused on the consultation of material culture studies, which was instrumental in conducting an artifact analysis for this study. Examination of cutlery artifacts led to statistical analysis of distribution of artifacts between fleets, as well as the creation of artifact typologies. The artifacts in the archaeological collections of the 1715 and 1733 fleets were studied in the locations where they are held, at the Museum of Florida History as well as in the laboratory at Mission San Luis de Apalachee, both in Tallahassee, Florida. Types of artifacts associated with each set of shipwrecks were examined in relation to their physical characteristics, the frequency of said artifacts, and the commonality of those artifacts within other Spanish colonial sites, to allow for the interpretation of "common" vs. "uncommon" items, and the elaboration on value and subsequent meaning. The comparison between the artifacts of each fleet will help to shed light on the presence and extent of foodways items onboard the ships of the 1715 Tierra Firme Fleet and the 1733 New Spain flota.

Preliminary Typologies

The artifact collections of the 1715 and 1733 Spanish fleets' shipwrecks include a range of cooking and tablewares that were common in the 18th century, including metallic plates, trays, utensils, ceramic cups, metallic and ceramic pots, stone pestles, metates, glass bottles, ceramic jars, and metallic kettles. Of over 800 metal kitchen and table artifacts between the two fleets, 154 cutlery items were ultimately analyzed. Forty-two percent of the total cutlery items were broken handles (N=66), 26% were identified as forks (N=41), 26% spoons (N=41), and 4% of the artifacts in this study were knives (N=6). The 1715 fleet collection accounts for 88% of the items in this study (N=137), while the remaining 12% (N=17) are attributed to the 1733 fleet. Aside from basic identification and measurement, the artifact analysis in this project has been heavily centered on statistical analysis of variation in shape, size, form, and function between the two fleets (Table 1). Since the largest percentage of these artifacts are broken handles, it is no surprise that only 12% of the total artifacts in the study are complete, while the remaining 88% are fragmentary, either handles or working ends. Of the fragmentary artifacts, 57% are 50% complete or less. The most common material composition of these artifacts is silver (78%), the remaining identified metals (gilt gold, copper, and pewter) are each represented in 1% or less of the total artifacts. Nearly 18% of the artifacts in this collection are either unidentified in terms of material, or are still encrusted with marine growth and the material has yet to be revealed. Finally, nearly 30% of the artifacts in this study have linear breaks which are distinctive from breaks that occur at soldering points on the utensils.

Thus far, 12 unique handle design types have been identified; their general characteristics are shown in Figure 1. Of the recognized types, at least 10 designs are consistent with known cutlery designs of the time. The distribution of designs between the two fleets is shown in Table 2. The first handle design, demonstrated by 12 examples, is a fiddle-type end with a central ridge

Fleet	Total Artifacts	Fragmentary	Forks	Handles	Knives	Spoons	Silver	Stamped
1715	123	105	38	60	0	25	105	23
1733	17	14	3	4	6	4	3	1

Table 1. 1715 and 1733 artifact frequency distributions.

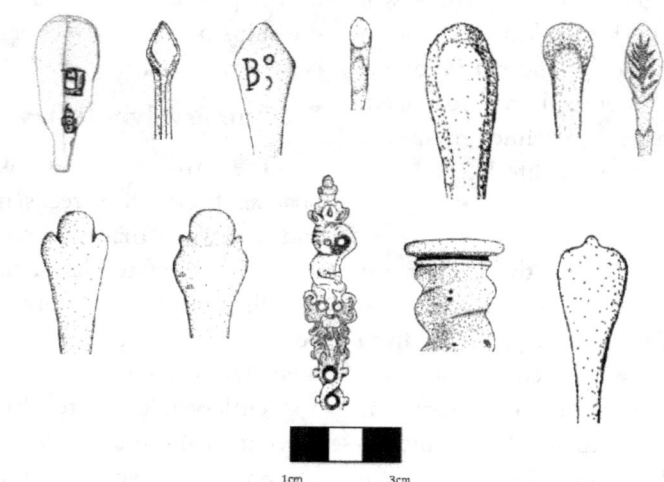

Figure 1. Variation of handle terminals. Top row (L to R): Fiddle, Spade 1, Spade 2, Oval 1, Oval 2, Oval 3, Floral. Bottom row (L to R): Trefoil 1, Trefoil 2, Figurine, Twisted, Dog-nose. (Illustrated by Kristina J. Fricker, 2017).

running lengthwise from working-end to terminal-end. Two types of spade-shaped terminal handle designs are included in the artifact collection. The spade-shaped handles are differentiated by cross-section shape: the first is diamond shaped and the second is flat, with 12 and 11 specimens, respectively. There are three similarly shaped terminal designs that share an oval theme; the first is a slanted oval with a spherical handle shape (17 examples), the second a flat handle with a rounded terminal (6 examples), and the third is flat on the underside of the handle, but has a raised, oval-ended section running the length of the middle of the topside (4 examples). There are three examples that show a floral (flower or leaf) motif. There are five examples of cutlery with a figurine shown on the terminal end of the handle. The twisted handle terminal shape has 12 examples in total. There are two variations of a trefoil designed handle terminal which are differentiated by the curvature or pointed nature of the outside tips, with seven and three examples, respectively. Finally, there are two pieces with a dog-nosed terminal end, both from the 1715 collection.

Potential Identification and Diagnostics

Approximately 20% of the artifacts in this collection have stamps of some kind. Stamp location varies between the working end, the medial section of the handle, and the handle terminal. Mint and assayer marks are visible on several pieces, giving a corroboration of time and place of origin for many of these pieces. The identification of place of origin adds to the interpretation of artifact biographies, adding a key piece to the puzzle of the story of these objects. Although preliminary, it is hoped that several things can be learned from this study. Information related to potential illicit trade within these fleets has already come to light. The common linear breaks of artifacts in this study could be explained as the intentional breaking of artifacts to be used as raw-silver currency for trade in lieu of specie (Craig 2000).

Conclusions

This is a preliminary report, as more research is being conducted, with more data collection and conclusions forthcoming. Recommendations related to the topics of this study include the following: the knowledgebase of the study of foodways in the archaeological record, particularly with respect to maritime contexts, should be expanded upon to incorporate a wider variety of items to complete the picture of colonial shipboard foodways. Frontier alternative economies have been studied in relation to terrestrial sites and sites with known contexts. It would be beneficial to create a framework for identifying subtle indications of alternative economies

Fleet	Fiddle	Spade (both variations)	Oval (all variations)	Floral	Figurine	Twisted	Trefoil (both variations)
1715	7	22	26	3	5	12	10
1733	5	1	1	0	0	0	0

Table 2. 1715 and 1733 handle terminal design distributions.

in the maritime world, beyond the typical "pirate booty" or smuggling. Finally, unprovenienced, looted artifacts have often been ignored for fear of unethical connotations on academic work. These artifacts are left tucked away in museum vaults or private collections where they are of no use to the academic or public communities. Although they would undoubtedly be more useful if their context had been preserved, these artifacts can, could, and should be studied and put on display -- not to condone the disreputable methods by which they were unearthed, but to be studied in terms of what information can be gleaned from them as they are, and what could have been if systematic archaeological methods had been employed.

Acknowledgments

The author would like to acknowledge those individuals who have been key to the development of and research related to this project: Dr. Jennifer McKinnon (East Carolina University), Dr. Dan Seinfeld (Florida State Archaeological Collections), Dr. Charlie Harper (Florida State Archaeological Collections), Kristina Fricker (East Carolina University), and Jessica Stika (Florida State Archaeological Collections).

References

Ashby, Steve
2011 Artefact Biographies: Implications for the Curation of Archaeological Ivories. <http://www.ebur.eu/userfiles/file/Artefact%20biographies%20final%20doc.doc>. Accessed 16 December 2016.

Craig, Alan K.
2000 Spanish Colonial Silver Coins in the Florida Collection. University of Florida Press, Gainesville, FL.

Deagan, Kathleen
1987 Artifacts of the Spanish Colonies of Florida and the Caribbean 1500-1800, Vol. 1, Ceramics, Glassware, and Beads. Smithsonian Institute Press, Washington, DC.

2002 Artifacts of the Spanish Colonies of Florida and the Caribbean 1500-1800, Vol. 2, Portable Personal Possessions. Smithsonian Institute Press, Washington, DC.

2007 Contraband through Archaeology: Illicit Trade in 18th Century St. Augustine. Historical Archaeology 40(3):98–116.

Harman, Joyce Elizabeth
1969 Trade and Privateering in Spanish Florida 1732-1763. The St. Augustine Historical Society, St. Augustine, FL.

Johnson, Matthew
2010 Archaeological Theory: An Introduction, 2nd edition. Wiley-Blackwell, Oxford.

Kopytoff, Igor
2013 The Cultural Biography of Things: Commoditization as Process. In The Social Life of Things: Commodities in Cultural Perspective, Arjun Appadurai, editor, pp. 64–91. Cambridge University Press, New York.

Lewis, Kenneth E.
1984 The American Frontier: An Archaeological Study of Settlement Pattern and Process. Studies in Historical Archaeology. Academic Press, Inc., New York.

Mattick, Barbara E.
2010 A Guide to Bone Toothbrushes of the 19th and Early 20th Centuries. Xlibris Corporation, United States of America.

Newquist, Ingrid Marion
2011 Contraband in the Convento? Material Implications of Trade Relations in the Spanish Colonies. In Islands at the Crossroads: Migration, Seafaring, and Interaction in the Caribbean, L. Antonio Curet and Mark W. Hauser, editors, pp. 87–103. University of Alabama Press, Tuscaloosa, AL.

Peterson, Mendel
1972 Traders and Privateers across the Atlantic: 1492-1733. In A History of Seafaring Based on Underwater Archaeology, George F. Bass, editor, pp. 253–280. Walker and Company, New York.

1975 The Funnel of Gold: The Trials of the Spanish Treasure Fleets as They Carried Home the Wealth of the New World in the Face of Privateers, Pirates and the Perils of the Sea. Little, Brown & Company Ltd., Boston, MA.

Sanders, G. Earl
1977 Counter-Contraband in Spanish America: Handicaps of the Governors in the Indies. The Americas 34(1):59.

Skowronek, Russell
1982 Trade Patterns of Eighteenth Century Frontier New Spain: The 1733 Flota and St. Augustine. Master's thesis, Department of Anthropology, Florida State University, Tallahassee, FL.

1992 Empire and Ceramics: The Changing Role of Illicit Trade in Spanish America. Historical Archaeology 26(1):109–118.

South, Stanley
1977 Method and Theory in Historical Archaeology. Academic Press, Inc., New York.

Thompson, Amanda
2012   Evaluating Spanish Colonial Alternative Economies in the Archaeological Record. Historical Archaeology 46(4):48-69.

Thursby, Jacqueline S.
2008   Foodways and Folklore: A Handbook. Greenwood Press, Westport, CT.

Usner, Jr., Daniel H.
1992   Indians, Settlers, and Slaves in a Frontier Exchange Economy: The Lower Mississippi Valley before 1783. The University of North Carolina Press, Chapel Hill, NC.

Olivia Thomas
East Carolina University
Program in Maritime Studies
302 East 9th St.
Greenville, NC 27858

A Preliminary Autopsy on Coffin's Beach, Gloucester, Massachusetts

Leland S. Crawford, Victor Mastone

In the spring of 2014, the partially uncovered skeletal remains of a wreck appeared in the sands of Coffin's Beach in Gloucester, MA. A team headed by State Underwater Archaeologist, Victor Mastone, under the auspices of the Massachusetts Board of Underwater Archaeological Resources, began an investigation of the site. Based on the data collected in this investigation, it is believed that wreck is a Chebacco Boat.

Introduction

In the spring of 2014, the skeleton of a wooden vessel started slowly emerging from the sands of a lightly visited private beach in Gloucester, MA. The body of this creature had nearly been lost to history, but due to the timely observation and reporting of local residents, the Massachusetts Board of Underwater Archaeological Resources (MBUAR) was able to put together a team to investigate the site before it was reburied later in 2014. The finding of this vessel is crucial for it represents the moment that a community went from a backwater village to an industry that launched over a thousand ships.

The Site

(Figure 1) The site lies (see Figure 1) about half way along the stretch of Coffin's Beach seaward of Wingaersheek Road, in Gloucester. The site is just south of the opening to Essex Bay within the estuary of the Essex river. The area at the mouth of Essex Bay is known for its shifting sandbars, which have been observed first-hand in a short timeframe during the archaeological visits to the site. Wingaersheek Point, with Coffin's Beach forming its Atlantic Ocean side, represents the southern half of the protective barrier for Essex Bay.

Site Description

The site lies in the high-energy zone of the beach, near the low water mark. The beach is entirely made up of a medium grain sand. The wreck is entirely submerged during all but the hour before and after the nadir of low tide. Thus, most of the wreck rests below the water table even at low tide. As a result, the majority of on-site field work has been planned around extreme low tides to get as much of the wreck above the water table as possible.

The measured dimensions of the wreck itself are 35ft. 4.2 in. in length and 11 ft. 7.5 in. in breadth. Through probing the northwestern section (which is believed to be the stern), it is hypothesized that the true overall length is between 38-40 ft. Due to the markings on the southern end (believed to be the bow) the draft is minimally 6 ft. The wreck is entirely made of wood and the preliminary assessments of the wood species is oak. Originally, there were thought to be metal fastenings which, upon closer investigations, turned out to be intrusions that had attached to the wreck post-deposition. The percentage of the wreck that is exposed at the site has varied greatly over the time that it has been monitored. During the first visits to the site, approximately 1-2 ft. of the frames were above the sand. The following year the wreck had been completely reburied, only to surface, with only about 1foot above the sand, a year later.

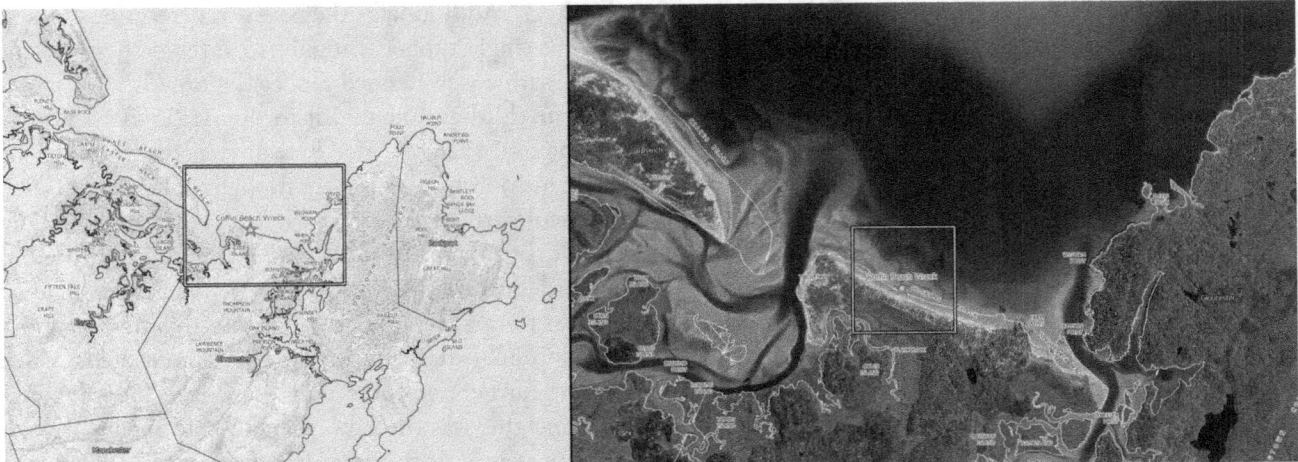

Figure 1. Location of the Coffin's Beach Site (Map by L. Crawford).

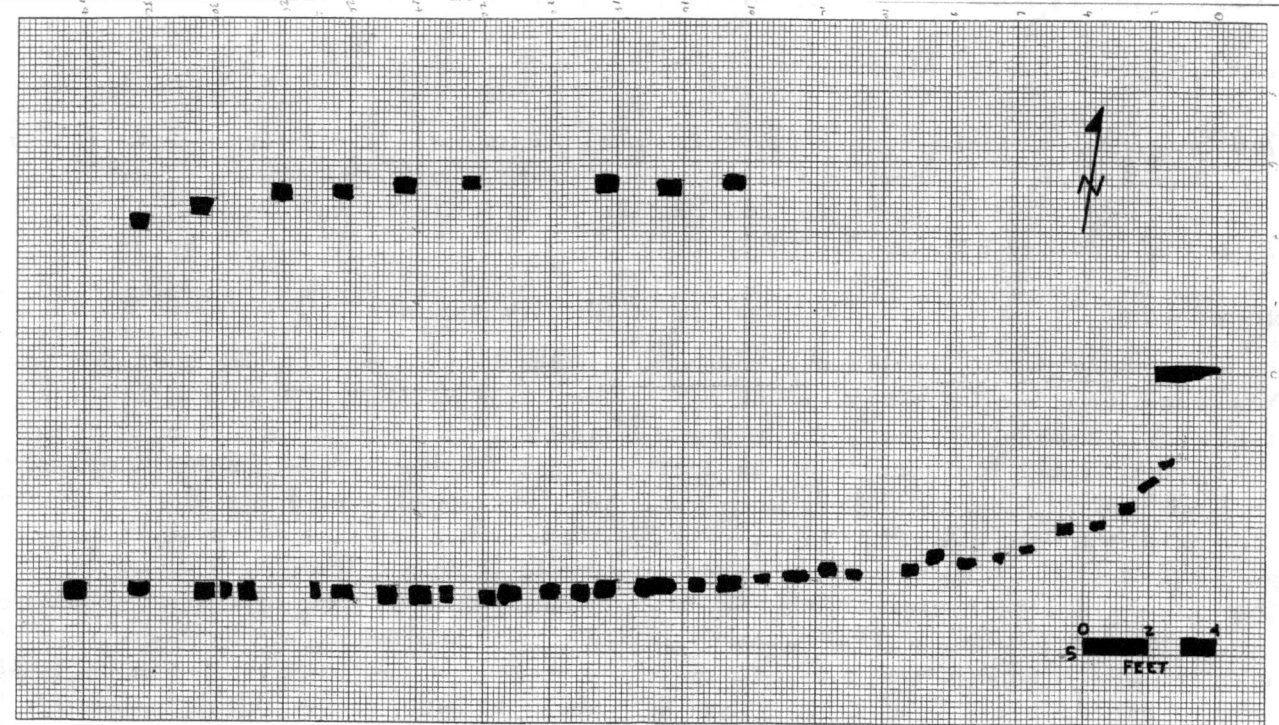

Figure 2. Site Map (Created by V. Mastone and L. Crawford).

Field Investigation

The MBUAR is the state government agency charged with the identification and protection of all archaeological finds that fall below the high tide line (The State of Massachusetts, West Group, and West Publishing Company 1958). Thus, in the spring of 2014, the MBUAR responded to contact from Jim Salem and Adam Ricciardiello, seasonal beach residents, about a previously unknown wreck that had been partially uncovered on Coffin's Beach, in Gloucester, MA. After correspondence with Victor Mastone, some preliminary photos were provided that clearly showed the framing timbers of a wooden vessel. Mastone reviewed MBUAR files and secondary sources to identify possible shipwrecking events in that area and then visited the site to determine if further research was warranted.

On 17 July 2014 the MBUAR team, consisting of Victor Mastone and Leland S. Crawford, visited the site in attempts to identify the vessel. Initially, the wreck was believed to be a small fishing or coastal vessel from the 1920s, possibly an early gillnetter lost in that area. However, after the first onsite visual inspection by the team, the apparent lack of any evidence of metal fittings or metal fastenings, or indications of an engine/engine mount led to a reassessment of the vessel dating to the 1880s. During this site visit, the team took preliminary measurements and created a basic site plan. The plan revealed that the vessel dimensions, form, and features strongly suggested it may be an early nineteenth/late eighteenth century shallop or early schooner, or even possibly a Chebacco Boat.

On 11 August of the same year, the MBUAR team with the additional help of Board member Graham McKay, and David S. Robinson & Associates, Inc. (consisting of David and his two sons Michael and Noah) made a small excavation of the wreck site. The primary focus of this work was the locating and documenting of the two ends of the wreck. During this work, the team found the first evidence of a clear draft mark (VI) (Figure 3) on what the team is identifying as the bow (Figure 3). Additionally, the bow was determined to be a massive single timber (roughly 15 in. wide by the same deep) with a well-defined rabbet (Figure 4).

The third and final visit to the site in 2014 was on 8 September. The MBUAR team was again joined by Graham McKay, but was additionally joined by NOAA Archaeologist Matthew Lawrence, local boat builder Harold Burnham (of the Essex Shipbuilding Museum) and local historian Jude Seminara (who has been of great help in researching the site). During this investigation, an additional draft mark, "V", was discovered, which helped further reinforce that these were depth marks and that this was the bow. A hand-held metal detector was utilized to confirm the lack of metal fittings (though wire fragments from lobster traps were encountered. While the team did not manage to excavate to the keel amidships, what was clearly a ballast pile was discovered. Amongst the ballast were found a number of pieces of brain coral (not indigenous to New England).

Additional archival research and observations of the extant remains has led to the belief that these vessel remains may be still older. Due to the difficulty of reaching the site (reburied naturally in Fall 2014), definitive conclusions could not be made. Thus, additional field investigation was the only means to determine vessel age and type.

In August 2016, an examination of the site was again undertaken with the MBUAR team, augmented by Captain Laurel Seaborn, Jude Seminara, Caitlin Gibbons and Catie Murpy. The objective over the three day period had been to uncover more diagnostic features. However, the beach profile was again significantly altered and the site was almost entirely covered by sand. A minor excavation of the stern end was undertaken to get a definitive length. Due to the sand and the fact that the wreck sits at the water table at low tide, a two-stage process was employed. The first stage involved divers in the water at high tide with a low volume suction dredge, capable of moving 5 square ft. per minute as per the permit. The second stage involved a shoreteam at low tide. It was believed that removing a good portion of the sand with the help of the water would allow the shore team to more easily access the wreck at low tide. However, the wave and tidal action proved to undo most of the dredging as the tide went out. Ultimately, little extra data was collected. Wood samples were collected and have been sent off to the University of Arizona's Laboratory of Tree-Ring Research; results are forthcoming.

Preliminary Findings

The current interpretation of the site as a Chebacco Boat is based on a number of diagnostic features. The sharp sweep of the bow is indicative of a number of specific vessels, such as the shallop, sloop, Chebacco Boat, etc., which were used in the area. The known breadth and hypothesized length (the measured dimensions of the wreck itself are 35 ft. 4.2 in. length and 11ft. 7.5 in. in breadth, but probing the northern section it is hypothesized that the true overall length is between 38-40 ft.) leads to a type of vessel that is longer than most of the known vessels with the steep bow (Chapelle 1960, 164) , which further eliminated potential alternative vessel types.

The bow post has a clearly engraved VI. This depth marker is of three-fold interest. Firstly, these depth markings indicate that there would have been six or more ft. of hull below this point. Second, it gives us a diagnostic indicator of what angle the bow sat at; it was at a slightly steeper angle than it currently lies. Third, and historically important, the depth indicators are in Roman numerals; their use fell out of favor at the beginning of the 1800s, which is based on anecdotal evidence by Harold Burnham. We have not been able to get a definitive reference that stated the switch. In addition, the lack of any clear bowsprit or any clear

Figure 3. Draft Marks (Photo by L. Crawford).

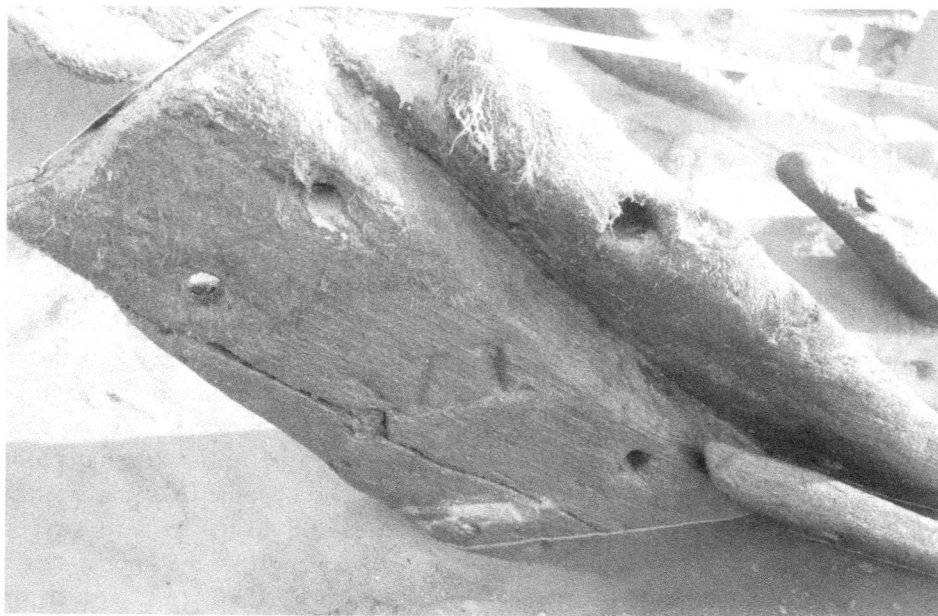

Figure 4. Rabbet in the Stem post (Photo by L. Crawford).

attachment point makes it similar to the "bow-spritless" Chebacco (Chapelle 1960, 164). All of these things taken together has led to the wreck being identified as a Chebacco Boat.

While the team did not find any mast-steps, our inability to access to the bilge of the vessel does not rule out the existence of two masts, which was typical of the Chebacco Boat. It is also not surprising that none of the cabins/standing-rooms of the traditional Chebacco Boat were found. This is due to the fact that the planks that sat on the beams as well as the wood for the cabins was usually made of white pine, which deteriorates quickly. In addition, if Henry Hall's research is correct, the masts would normally be made of either white oak, like the deck planking, or spruce (Hall 1884, 7). Both of these wood types would have rotted much sooner than the oak that makes up the sections that we found. To the extent that the stern of the vessel could be uncovered, it clearly shows evidence of the pined, "pink", stern. In a pink sterned vessel, the hull comes to a point making it essentially double-ended. This initially led to some confusion over stern and bow, but other features, especially the draft marks, have helped clarify this distinction.

Importance of the Chebacco style boat

While there is undisputed evidence of ships being built in Chebacco Parish by 1668 (Story 1995, 5), it is unclear when this vernacular tradition known commonly as a Chebacco Boat came into existence. The question still remains as to why the Chebacco Boat is important.

The Chebacco Boat would be important if for no other reason than the fact that it was the beginning of the rise of the Essex shipbuilding industry. While Essex is now known for its clipper ships, schooners, and other large fishing vessels, it was the Chebacco Boat that put Essex on the map, possibly quite literally.

"The period between 1775 and 1815, during which time occurred the war of the Revolution, the embargo act, and the war of 1812–1815, was a very unfavorable one for the American fisheries" (United States National Museum, Smithsonian Institution, and United States. Dept. of the Interior 1884, 653). The end of the American Revolution left New England in dire circumstances. The Revolution had affected the fishing industry in a number of ways. Firstly, "The Revolution, of course, put an embargo on Bank fishing, as well as an end to the exportation of fish, and the business soon dwindled to insignificant figures" (Procter Brothers 1882, 6). This had the effect of destroying some generations-old connections for trade, as well as losing a training ground for the next generation. Secondly, "The larger class of fishing vessels, those which had been employed on the Grand Bank and other distant fishing grounds, were compelled to lie idle, while, in most cases, the hardy men who had composed their crews were employed in the Army or Navy" (United States National Museum, Smithsonian Institution, and United States. Dept. of the Interior 1884, 653). While fishermen were not the first choice for any Navy Captains, as they were known to be poorly disciplined, they were nonetheless experienced seamen. The Revolution proved to be a huge drain on the work force of available fishermen, a drain that would never be returned due to the extensive loss of life. A great number of the fishing vessels, mostly the schooners that were capable of reaching and fishing the Banks areas, were turned into privateers during the war. While they were helpful in the process of gaining independence, an overwhelming number of these vessels were destroyed by British fleets. As the British fleets were leaving the New England area it did not hesitate to sink vessels it thought might or could have had any involvement in the war (Crawford 2017).

This created the need for a vessel that was big enough and safe enough to fish off-shore while requiring a minimum of crew. This is exactly what they re-designed the Chebacco Boat to be. The Chebacco Boat was the larger two masted evolution of common coastal fishing vessels such as the sloop or shallop. However, the Chebacco Boat was bigger in all dimensions and had what, at the time, seemed like an odd mast placement. For Chebacco Boat construction the average tonnage would have been between three and five tons (Maclay 1899, 314). This tonnage grew over time, and using drawings, models, and custom house records, Howard Chapelle believes that the model Lion in the Smithsonian collection exemplifies a Chebacco Boat with the dimensions of "37 ft. 9 in. between perpendiculars, 11 ft. 2 in. beam, 5 ft. 10 in. depth of hold, and 22.5 tons" (Chapelle 1960, 180). This is very consistent with our findings at Coffin's Beach. If we had found masts or mast-steps we would have expected to find the placement of the foremast just behind the bow and the second mast amidships. The two masts created enough sail area for the Chebacco Boat to be fast enough to get out to the banks while the gaff-rigged sail made the Chebacco Boat easy to maneuver by as few as two sailors, despite its larger size (Chapelle 1973, 26–34). The high sides and mostly enclosed hold ride the waves effortlessly even in storms. The deep standing-room hatches, which put the fisherman's feet just above the keel, put the fisherman's hands close to the water limiting the amount of bending over that was required for pulling in nets (Robinson and Dow 1922, 21). Due to all of these features the Chebacco Boat became wildly popular with New England fishermen. The Chebacco Boat led to the rebuilding of the New England fishing industry post-American Revolution with minimal building cost and minimal manpower per ton of fish.

Conclusion

The opportunity that the Coffin's Beach site provides as a window into the past cannot be undervalued. The community involvement, both archaeological and public, alone would be well worth the value of the archaeological investigation. However, due to the probable age of the vessel and the general design features, we have a chance to compare historical documents with archaeological findings. It is clear that there is an argument for the importance of the Chebacco Boat to be remembered for its own sake, however the Chebacco Boat stands as an important marker in history for the effect that it had on the place where it was being built. The Chebacco Boat gets its name from the area, the Chebacco Parish of the Town of Ipswich, MA, where it was "first built"(Procter Brothers 1882, 40). The building of the Chebacco early on was only truly understood by those in the Chebacco area, which created a huge influx of interest and capital. It was towards the end of the Chebacco Boat's hay-day that Chebacco Parish gained its independence and became the famous shipbuilding name that we know today: Essex. It is arguable that it was the ingenious creation and later demand for the Chebacco Boat that gave Essex the standing to become independent. However, it is clear that it was the Chebacco Boat that made the town of Essex the place for a fisherman to turn to find the best fishing vessels. In Dana A. Story's research, we see that Essex built and launched at least 1,364 ships between 1860–1980 (Story 1995, 3). When looking at the shipbuilding towns of the United States, "for sheer numbers, it's doubtful that any place exceeds Essex"(Story 1995, 3).

If, as is believed, the site represents a "lost" vessel type, then we have a priceless opportunity to rediscover the Chebacco Boat. So I ask, if Helen of Troy was so important that she launched a thousand ships, then where does that put the Chebacco Boat?

References

CHAPELLE, HOWARD IRVING
1973   *The American Fishing Schooners, 1825-1935*. Norton, New York, New York.

CRAWFORD, LELAND S.
2017   *Preliminary Title: The Chebacco Boat: The Creation of The Essex Shipbuilding Tradition (An Archaeological Investigation at Coffin's Beach)*. University of Southern Denmark, Esbjerg, Denmark.

HALL, HENRY
1884   *Report on the Ship-Building Industry of the United States*. Government Publishing Office, Washington, D.C.

Maclay, Edgar Stanton
1899   *A History of American Privateers.* Cambridge University Press, Cambridge.

Procter Brothers
1882   *The Fishermen's Own Book: comprising the list of men and vessels lost from the port of Gloucester, Mass., from 1874 to April 1, 1882, and a table of losses from 1830, together with valuable statistics of the fisheries, also notable fares, narrow escapes, startling adventures, fishermen's off-hand sketches, ballads, descriptions of fishing trips and other interesting facts and incidents connected with this branch of maritime industry.* Procter Brothers, Gloucester, Massachusetts.

Robinson, John and George Francis Dow
1922   *The Sailing Ships of New England, 1607-1907.* Marine Research Society, Salem, Massachusetts.

Story, Dana A.
1995   *The Shipbuilders of Essex: A Chronicle of Yankee Endeavor.* Ten Pound Island, Gloucester, Massachusetts.

The State of Massachusetts
1958   *Massachusetts General Laws Annotated, Under Arrangement of the Official General Laws of Massachusetts.* West Publishing Company, St. Paul, Minnesota

United States Department of the Interior and The Smithsonian Institution
1884   *Bulletin of the United States National Museum No. 27.* Government Printing Office, Washington, D.C.

Leland S. Crawford
Address: 1374 Main St Apt A2, Osterville, MA 02655
Phone: (Cell) 617-943-7712
Email: lelandscrawford@gmail.com

Victor Mastone
Address: MBUAR/MCZM, Suite 800,
251 Causeway Street, Boston, MA 02114
Phone: (Office) 617-626-1141

In Every Grain of Sand, there is a Story: The 19th-century schooner, *Ada K. Damon*, as a Case Study in Developing Maritime Archaeology Programs in Massachusetts

Calvin Mires

In 2015 and 2016, SEAMAHP and the Massachusetts Board of Underwater Archaeological Resources (MBUAR) part-nered with Salem State University, National Park Service (NPS), the Nautical Archaeology Society (NAS) and the PAST Foundation to offer a field schools that examined the life and death of Ada K. Damon - a 19th century schooner that has been a landmark on the shoreline for over 100 years. These field schools had immediate and long-term impacts for maritime archaeological programming in Massachusetts. This article examines the development and impacts of these field schools that were based on student-led, problem-based education, pivoted on the conceptual framework of a ship's life-cycle, and applied to Ada K. Damon.

Introduction

From 13-17 July 2015, the first maritime archaeological field school in Massachusetts was offered through Salem State University for college credit. This pilot program represented a collaboration between the Massachusetts Board of Underwater Archaeological Resources (MBUAR), the Nautical Archaeology Society (NAS), the Partnering Anthropology with Science and Technology Foundation (PAST), Salem State University (SSU), and the Seafaring Education and Maritime Archaeological Heritage Program (SEAMAHP). The results from this program were immediate and lasting. A second field school was immediately scheduled for 2016, there were NAS-certified volunteers for MBUAR projects, new maritime outreach opportunities developed throughout the state, another university south of Boston became interested in starting a maritime program, new partnerships were developed and existing ones strengthened, and a new program, *Telltales to Learning*, received funding from the National Park Service Maritime Heritage Grant Program. All of this was founded on the 2015 field school's problem-based, experiential learning, which pivoted on the concept of the "life-cycle" of a ship, and then applied these concepts to archaeological investigations of the 19th-century fishing schooner, *Ada K. Damon*.

Background

The 2015 field school started through an informal partnership between SEAMAHP's co-founders, Calvin Mires and Laurel Seaborn, and Chief Archaeologist at MBUAR, Victor Mastone. SEAMAHP is an educational and training program in maritime heritage and archaeology that focuses on human innovation, creativity, and endeavors in maritime industries throughout history. It believes in immersive, experiential learning to engage students and make connections between present and past cultures "by examining the 'life-cycle' of a vessel from its inception through ship design and construction, through its 'adult' life as a working vessel, and its 'after life' through training in maritime archaeology for both divers and non-divers alike" (SEAMAHP 2016). SEAMAHP's initial challenge was to find a suitable region where there were appropriate resources – active and historic shipyards, maritime museums, tall ships, and maritime archaeological resources. These resources needed to be close enough to each other to feasibly implement such a life-cycle concept. Massachusetts was immediately at the top of the list with 45 maritime museums, 17 museum ships, several sailing tall ships, and a vibrant historic and contemporary maritime heritage (Smith 2007).

Mastone was contacted and supported the concept. He facilitated efforts to develop a field course at Salem State University, and to find an appropriate site for study. Because there was to be no diving for safety and logistical reasons, Mires, Seaborn, and Mastone investigated several foreshore sites, gauging feasibility, workability, and environmental conditions. We selected the 19th century schooner, *Ada K. Damon*, located on Crane Beach, 5 miles northeast of Ipswich, Massachusetts (Figure 1).

The Fishing and Sand Schooner, *Ada K. Damon*

In 1875, Ebenezer Burnham built *Ada K. Damon*, a two-masted, 83 × 23 ft., 90 ton schooner in Essex (Figure 1). The vessel was one of an estimated 4,000 ships built in the small town of no more than 1,500 people through its history, and the Burnham name was one of the most prominent in the Essex shipbuilding industry since the

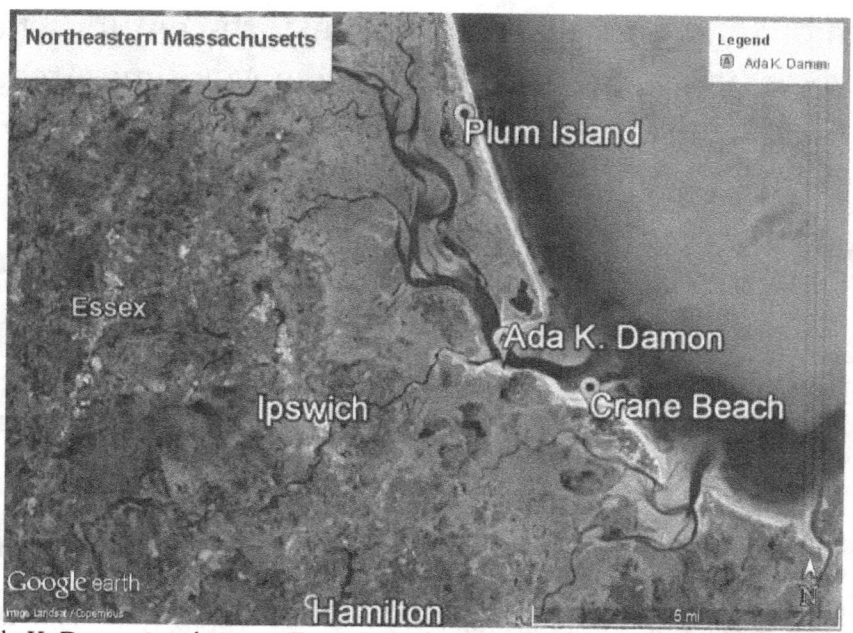

Figure 1. Location Ada K. Damon in relation to Essex, Ipswich, Crane Beach, and Plum Island (figure by author, map from Google Earth (10 May 2016, 42° 41.762' N 70° 46.778' W).

1630s (Story 1995; Peckham 2002). From 1876 to 1882, *Ada K. Damon* was a Gloucester fishing schooner, owned by Sylvanus Smith, a renowned Gloucester fisherman, captain, businessman, and a representative in both Massachusetts's House of Representatives and Senate (Proctor Brothers 1876; American Lloyds Registry 1877, 1880, 1882; Record of American and Foreign Shipping [RAFS] 1877, 1881, 1882; Cutter 1908). In 1882, it was sold to Philip A. Worf, who moved the ship from Gloucester to Provincetown, Massachusetts in 1885 where it continued as a fishing schooner for more than twenty years. It had a typical and unremarkable career, save for one incident in 1893 when a heavy snowstorm capsized one of its fishing dories, and the six crewmen aboard drowned (RAFS 1884, 1885, 1890, 1900; United States Life-Saving Service 1894). In 1909, it was sold to a farmer from Maine, Albert Knowlton "A.K." Brewster (Townsend 1913; Harris 2013).

A.K. Brewster was born in 1855 in York, Maine, to a Maine farmer and Scottish mother. The youngest of five children, Brewster spent some time as a Gloucester fisherman in his mid-twenties, lived in Boston around 1900, and soon thereafter moved back to York, presumably to run his family farm. In 1909, at the age of 54, he had a change of heart and decided to sell his farm and invest everything into purchasing and converting *Ada K. Damon* into a sand schooner (United States Census 1860, 1870, 1880, 1900a, 1900b, 1930; Townsend 1913). This decision was dramatic, but not without reason.

Sand was in demand by Boston construction companies that needed sand to make concrete. Further, sand from Plum Island (Figure 1), which was an easy day's sail from York, was prized for its "hardness and appearance" in floor surfaces used at the time in "fireproof buildings" (Thompson 1914:453). To load the sand, captains would sail their schooner broadside to a beach during high tide, and then anchor at the stem and stern. A long gangplank would be extended from the ship to the beach, and crew wheelbarrowed loads of sand onboard (Harris 2014). Brewster was apparently eager to start his new profession as a sand schooner skipper. He chose as *Ada K. Damon*'s maiden voyage to sail on 26 December, and learned the hard way that sailing with a new crew, on a new vessel, in the North Atlantic during the winter is a risky decision (Townsend 1913; Harris 2013).

On 23 December 2016, a weak cyclonic disturbance in southern Arizona turned eastward, and moved through Texas and the Midwest with increasing speed and precipitation. The storm that would become known as the "Christmas Storm of 1909," pummeled Pennsylvania with snow and winds through Christmas Day. It reached the New Jersey coast at midnight on December 26th, and turned northward towards New England. Along its way, the storm wrecked electric lighting; telegraph and telephone systems; and shut down streetcars, elevated trains, streets, and services, with reports of several horse drawn vehicles stalled in the drifts. In Philadelphia, it dropped 21 inches of snow in

23 hours. In New York, six people died due to exposure. Rhode Island experienced hurricane-strength wind gusts. In Massachusetts, two people drowned and 2,000 more were displaced in flooding when a dyke broke in Chelsea (Associated Press 1909a; Bigelow 1909; Mooke 1951). Those at sea did not escape either. Sixteen vessels were reported damaged or lost along Massachusetts's coast, the most tragic of which was the five-masted schooner, *Davis Palmer*. 12 of its crew perished (Associated Press 1909b; Coast Seamen's Journal 1910; Harris 2013).

Brewster did not escape the havoc caused by the Christmas Storm of 1909 either. He had decided to ride out the storm by anchoring in Ipswich Bay, 3.5 miles southwest of Plum Island. The winds, however, were too strong for his anchors, which dragged and eventually parted, sending *Ada K. Damon* onto Crane Beach, where the ship stuck fast. Crew from the Plum Island Life-Saving Station visited the wreck on 27-28 December, to find all of the ship's crew were safe, but the ship was full of water with the sea breaking heavily over it. The Life Saving Crew offered assistance, but Brewster declined because he believed he could still float the ship after the ballast was removed. When this proved impossible, he tried to sell the ship to wreckers, but found no one to buy it. On 2 January 1910, Brewster finally asked for assistance "to strip her on the following day. His request was complied with. The vessel was a total lost [sic]" (United States Life-Saving Service 1911:97). With his entire life's savings invested in *Ada K. Damon*, Brewster returned to Maine penniless, seeking farm work. He died in 1930 and records indicate that he had no family or heirs (United States Census 1930; Harris 2013).

Over the years, *Ada K. Damon* was continually exposed to natural and cultural site formation processes, such as wave-action, sediment deposition, and salvage activities, but it did not disappear. Instead, it became a local attraction and landmark for visitors to gather, hold picnics, and take pictures. Today, most of the vessel has deteriorated, but it still rests where it wrecked in 1909, with broken frames visible at low tide (Figure 2). While the site is open to the public, it has some protection because Crane Beach is part of Crane Estate, a 2,100 acre property owned by The Trustees of Reservations (TTOR), the oldest and largest statewide land conservation organization in the United States (The Crane Estate 2016; TTOR 2017).

The Life-Cycle of a Vessel as an Organizational, Structural, and Educational Framework

Ada K. Damon served as good case-study for the

Figure 2. Ada K. Damon circa 1910 (top) and in 2015 (bottom) (Top photo courtesy of Gordon Harris, originally taken by George Dexter (ca. 1910); bottom photo by author).

2015 pilot program. It was a workable site close to other cultural heritage resources, such as museums, shipyards, and tall ships, and has continued to play a visible role in maritime heritage as a landmark and recreation venue for people today. These factors fit well within and supported the concept of a ship's "life-cycle" (Figure 3) that the project directors (Mires, Seaborn, and Mastone) were leveraging as an organizational, structural, and educational framework. This conceptual framework was useful for several reasons.

First, it was a relatable metaphor to potential partner organizations and administrators as project directors discussed the program's vision and goals. Organizations immediately saw where they fit into the model, and how maritime archaeology augmented their educational goals as well. This created an ease of communication, which resulted in thought-sharing and interest in partnering. Second, it provided the project directors a road map to identify, contact, and partner with organizations that reinforced the model. For example, we partnered with the Essex Historical and shared a commitment towards education and maritime heritage preservation.

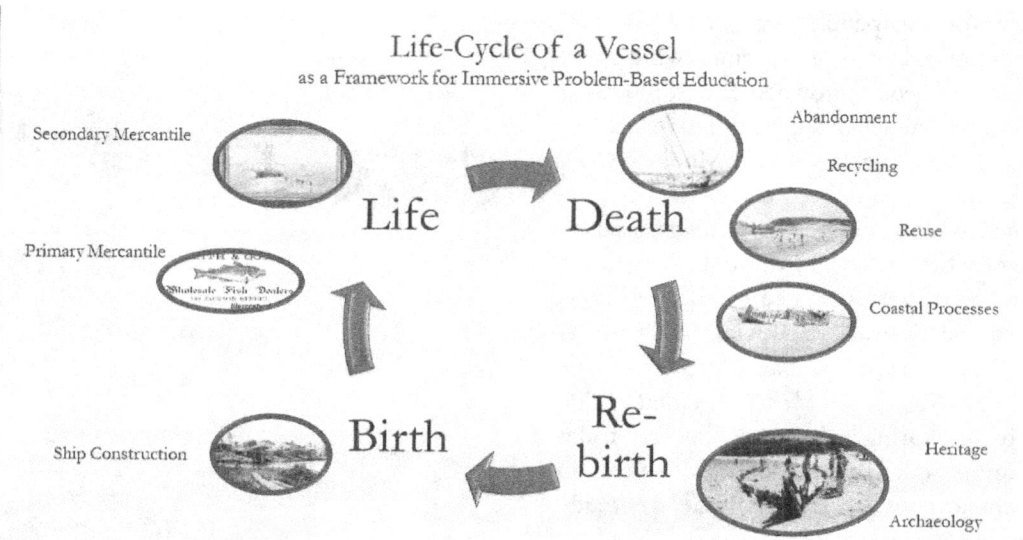

Figure 3. "Life-Cycle" of a Vessel as a Framework for Immersive Problem Based Learning (figure by author).

Society and Shipbuilding Building Museum (Essex Shipbuilding Museum), in Essex, Massachusetts, at a former shipyard near where *Ada K. Damon* was built. Established in 1976, the museum houses shipbuilding tools, exhibits, and two ships: *Lewis H. Story*, a replica of a 17th century vernacular watercraft, known as a Chebacco boat; and *Evelina M. Goulart*, an Essex-built fishing schooner (Essex Shipbuilding Museum 2016). The museum is also adjacent to a working shipyard run by Harold Burham, a master shipwright and possible descendant of Ebenezer Burnham. He has built several fishing schooners and watercraft using Essex shipbuilders' traditional methods. He is currently restoring *Ernestina-Morrissey*, a 19th century contemporary to *Ada K. Damon*, a National Historic Landmark Vessel, and the Official Vessel of the Commonwealth of Massachusetts (National Endowment for the Arts 2012; *Schooner Ernestina-Morrissey* Association 2017). The Essex Shipbuilding Museum allowed students to experience where and how a ship was born and nurtured.

To demonstrate a vessel during its working "adult life," we partnered with National Park Service Salem Maritime National Historic Site (Salem Maritime). Established in 1938, Salem Maritime is the first National Historic Site in the United States, and its mission is to preserve and interpret resources along the historic waterfront at Salem. It consists of nine acres of buildings, homes, stores, a lighthouse, three wharves, and the tall ship, *Friendship of Salem (Friendship)*, a replica of an 18th century East Indiamen merchant vessel (Salem Maritime 2016).

While Massachusetts has a rich and proud maritime heritage represented in almost 50 maritime museums, several tall ships still sailing, and all types of literature and culture, it did not have an academically sponsored field school in maritime archaeology. To change this surprising situation, the project directors contacted SSU, which is one of the largest state universities in Massachusetts (SSU 2016). We made presentations to SSU's administrators, faculty, and students because we knew accreditation was essential in developing a sustained program. Fortunately, all groups were receptive to the program and its leveraging of maritime archaeology to provide new perspectives and training. SSU's Department of History created a summer institute for the first maritime archaeological field school in Massachusetts (Victor Mastone, 2015 pers. comm.).

While the course was offered for undergraduate credit, we were aware that some people were not interested in the credits, but still wanted the training. For these students, we partnered with the NAS to offer certifications for its Introduction and Part I courses. NAS administration was extremely supportive in providing materials and curricula, and allowed us to work under a temporary license in 2015 and 2016.

While these partnerships were systematically pursued, others developed more organically. For instance, Mires was hired as the Director of Bridge Programs for the PAST Foundation in 2015. Since 2000, PAST earned a national recognized reputation as a leader and innovator in transdisciplinary, problem-based learning (TPBL) and science, technology, engineering, and math (STEM) related fields (PAST 2017). As Director of Bridge Programs, Mires was in charge of PAST's informal education (after-school and summer programming, and design challenges), and was able to leverage PAST's considerable experience and knowledge to the field school. Another example of this dynamic partnering occurred during the field schools as communication between project directors and TTOR increased. Management personnel from TTOR's cultural resources division saw the progress and interest in the field schools, and were willing to explore further opportunities and projects. Finally, the field schools benefitted immensely from the help of two doctoral candidates, Jennifer Jones and Leland Crawford from East Carolina University and University of Denmark, respectively, who shared their research experience in foreshore shipwrecks and volunteered their services.

With these organizational partnerships formed, a third benefit of using the life-cycle framework was structure of activities. For instance, at the start of each field school, students visited the Salem Maritime National Historic Site and the Essex Shipbuilding Museum to explore and reinforce lessons on ship construction and seafaring. At Salem Maritime, the 2015 crew learned ship construction and practiced archaeological documentation aboard *Friendship*. Unfortunately, *Friendship* was dry-docked for maintenance in 2016, so students learned ship construction and seafaring during a sail on a replica of an 1812 privateer, *Fame*, berthed at one of Salem Maritime's historic wharves (*Fame* of Salem 2016). At the Essex Shipbuilding Museum, students were able to understand better the scale, form, and functions of ship parts. Each year, they were able to speak with Burnham about his experiences in shipbuilding as well discuss with him what he hoped to learn from the *Ada K. Damon* that could help his restoration efforts. Combined with NAS's well-developed training curricula and PAST's problem-based, student-led approach that emphasized evidence of learning, the life-cycle framework provided a focused structure and consistent theme for students through the week.

Finally, the analogy of a vessel's life-cycle allowed students – who had no to limited experience in any maritime activity – to understand the specialized terminology, history, theory, and techniques involved with seafaring industry and maritime archaeology within a context that was simultaneously personal and universal. The educational impact was evidenced when students used the theme to facilitate discussion, inquiry, and idea-development between the instructors and themselves. This communication grew with their experiences at partner organizations through each week's curriculum. They stepped out of their comfortable, passive roles as students, and grew into a crew, working together to brainstorm and answer their questions. As they did, their learning curve and interest in the project increased as they grew invested through their own efforts. This was immensely rewarding to witness as an instructor, and offered immediate benefits in the field as we moved into the "after-life" phase of the cycle: that is, the maritime archaeological fieldwork on *Ada K. Damon*.

The Design Process in the 2015 and 2016 Field Schools

The 2015 field season represented the first half of a design process, the three components of which were planning, designing, and implementing. The conceptual framework of a ship's life-cycle, the NAS curricula, and PAST's TPBL all factored into the course's structure and design, which focused on educational goals as the priority. Before the students arrived at *Ada K. Damon*, they had grown as a crew and developed their own questions through the hands-on experiences at Salem Maritime and Essex Shipbuilding Museum. When they arrived at the site, they completed an assessment survey, creating site sketches, taking preliminary photographs, and observing environmental conditions. They discussed strategies for mapping, logistics, and safety for project management. Given the tides and travel distance to and from SSU, they had only eight hours over three days to document the site. Working in groups of two and four, they measured the exposed timbers using baseline offset and trilateration methodology. Under Mastone's supervision, they removed a limited amount of sediment at the stem and sternpost. They experienced the challenges of acquiring data from dynamic intertidal sites, and improved their techniques and communication through the week.

At the end of the week, their final project was to produce a scaled site map of *Ada K. Damon* in plan view, and profile views of the stem, sternpost, and selected frame sets. As they worked together to assimilate their individual raw data into a full site plan, students were encouraged to reflect on their experiences and growth over the week. This led to a student-led ad hoc symposium, in which they shared personal anecdotes and detailed analysis of fieldwork methods, the modifications they would make to increase efficiency, the importance of post-fieldwork activities, new appreciation for ethics and stewardship, and how they could further their training (Mires 2015).

Between 2015 and 2016, project leaders proceeded with the second half of the design process, which was to analyze, modify, and share. We looked at what worked and what did not during the 2015 season. We decided that the overall structure worked well, but we could increase the expectation, goals, and challenges for students. The second field school was offered from 25-29 July 2016, again for credit through SSU's Department of History. It followed a similar structure to the 2015 season with visits to Salem Maritime, the Essex Shipbuilding Museum and an interview with Harold Burnham, NAS training and certifications, and mapping the *Ada K. Damon*. Student expectations and goals, however, were increased to include everything from 2015, and the following: 1) to practice 3D techniques with Site Recorder 4; 2) to test open source 3D apps and imagery for use in public outreach; and 3) to design a website providing information about the site, its history, its environment, recording methodology, and results.

This final objective was a "Design Challenge." The Design Challenge is used as evidence of learning for many of PAST's Bridge Programs. It was brought to the 2016 field school to emphasize the importance of publishing and dissemination information, and to focus students' efforts around a real-world problem expressed by their research question: "How can the 2016 project help promote public stewardship of maritime heritage in Massachusetts?" Students were broken into teams of three and assigned one of the following pages to develop for the website: 1) *Build It* – page for ship construction; 2) *Sail It* – page for seafaring life and culture; 3) *Sink It* – page for causes and events of wrecking; 4) *Map It* – page for methodology description; and 5) *Manage It* – page for discussion about the research question. The point of the design was challenge was not necessarily to solve the problem, but to have students discuss it, brainstorm around it, and to put their learning, training, experiences, and activities within the context of solving it (Mires 2016).

The students met the challenge, and as in 2015, their experiences at the beginning of the week created independent and interdependent problem solving skills. Their results were impressive. They produced 2D site maps of *Ada K. Damon*, in plan and profile view. They created 3d images using photomosaics (courtesy of Leland Crawford) and open-source 3D apps on their smart phones. They had an opportunity to observe a drone operate and the imagery it captured (courtesy of Dr. Stefan Claesson). They practiced Site Recorder techniques of setting up a network and taking measurements. Finally, on Friday, they brought all of their experiences together to develop the Design Challenge website in four hours. They used the platform weebly.com to collaborate, design, and build their specific pages. Each team then had to present their page, the rationale for their choices, and how their choices fit within the question of promoting maritime heritage stewardship in Massachusetts. The presentations were given to their peers and were video recorded. Although the website was far from polished, it accomplished the goal of providing focus and meaning to all their education, activity, and training through the week. The Design Challenge engaged students because they knew they had the opportunity to share their knowledge in a meaningful way to the public – and that was an important lesson for them to learn about the purpose of maritime archaeology (Mires 2016).

Discussion

The 2015 and 2016 field schools have had immediate and long-term impacts for maritime archaeology in Massachusetts. Immediately, the 2015 pilot program brought renewed attention to the North Shore of Massachusetts for further maritime archaeological research. It was reported in various local, regional, and state media nearly every day. Students spoke with locals and visitors walking along the beach who stopped to ask questions. Salem State University promoted the project through university and social media outlets, and requested the 2016 field season. It provided a foundation for PAST's educational program, *Telltales to Learning*, a NPS Maritime Heritage Grant Education funded project. *Telltales to Learning* extends the principles of these field schools to middle and high school students and offering middle and high school teachers professional development. *Telltales to Learning* is scheduled for June 2017.

The 2015 and 2016 field schools would not have been as successful without the support of NAS. Students explicitly stated that they took the course for the NAS certifications and opportunities for further NAS education. Additionally, the Commonwealth of Massachusetts has received the benefit of a volunteer pool with 30 NAS trained students qualified to help Mastone on his projects. The NAS certifications also attracted a wider audience of students.

In 2015, there were 15 students, the maximum capacity for an SSU summer course. There ages ranged from 18 to 60s. In 2016, the course was again filled with 15 students, and the ages were from 17 to 50s. There were also five returning students from the 2015 course. Two were taking the class again because it satisfied another college requirement. One was returning as an independent study internship offered through SSU, and two volunteered simply because they enjoyed the previous so much. In 2016, students were given a pre - and posttest assessment to measure growth of knowledge, and to receive feedback. Some comments from students were:

> "Honestly, the best course I have taken."

> "Love the course, I wish I could take it for a 3rd year in a row."

> "Best on hands course that I have taken."

> "I learned how to properly set up a dig site and that's really cool." (Mires 2016)

As an instructor, these comments made the preparation and the effort extremely rewarding.

The field schools have also set up longer term impacts north and south of Boston, or as they say in Massachusetts, the North Shore and South Shore, respectively. On the North Shore, Salem Maritime has continued to partner with SEAMAHP for their various festivals, such as "Trails and Sails," and "Downrig or Die." Additionally, Salem Maritime is interested in developing outreach programming involving underwater robotics through Marine Advanced Technology Education, or MATE. On the South Shore, Bridgewater State University hired Mires to develop a program in maritime heritage and archaeology and teach maritime archaeological courses at their main campus in Bridgewater and their Cape Cod campus in Yarmouth. SEAMAHP is also looking to develop programs along the South Shore with possible partnerships with heritage agencies and museums, such as the New Bedford Fishing Heritage Center and Pilgrim Hall Museum in Plymouth.

Conclusion

Ada K. Damon, was a typical 19th century, Essex-built fishing schooner for most of its career, and it would have had a typical birth, life, and death if not for A.K. Brewster's dream of pursuing a new career and making money with a different gold: Plum Island sand. His ambitions and motivations caused him to take his new ship for its maiden voyage into the Atlantic and it cost him everything. *Ada K. Damon*, however, became part of the landscape and a venue where people gathered for recreation and photographs. In 2015 and 2016, it served as the site for maritime archaeological field schools, and as an illustrative case-study in the life-cycle of a ship. Structured on problem-based, student-led, hands-on learning, these field schools have had immediate and long term impacts for maritime archaeological outreach and programming in Massachusetts. Therefore, the direct and indirect contributions that *Ada K. Damon* has made in its "after-life," will likely outweigh its impact during its lifetime.

Acknowledgments

I would like to thank my colleagues, co-directors, and fellow instructors for all their efforts, Mr. Victor Mastone and Ms. Laurel Seaborn. I also would to thank the following: Jennifer Jones and Leland Crawford for their indispensable help; Beth Bower, Donna Seger, Tad Baker, Dane Morrison, and Cyndi Allison at Salem State University; Maryann Zujewski and the Park Rangers at NPS Salem Maritime National Historic Site; Lucinda Brockway and the staff at Trustees of the Reservations – Crane Estate; Mark Beattie-Edwards and Christopher Underwood at the Nautical Archaeology Society; Annalies Corbin, Sheli Smith, Ashley Bloom and the rest of the crew at the PAST Foundation; Nancy Dudley and Justin Demetri at the Essex Historical Society and Shipbuilding Museum; Our volunteers, Caitlin Gibbons, Annika Heinold, Greg Lott, and Catie Murphy; and all our students from 2015 and 2016.

References

AMERICAN LLOYDS REGISTER
1877 *American Lloyds' Registry of American and Foreign Shipping*. Digital Library: Ship Registers, Collections and Research, Mystic Seaport, Mystic, Connecticut https://research.mysticseaport.org/item/l0237571877. Accessed 11 February 2017.

1880 *American Lloyds' Registry of American and Foreign Shipping*. Digital Library: Ship Registers, Collections and Research, Mystic Seaport, Mystic, Connecticut https://research.mysticseaport.org/item/l0237571880. Accessed 11 February 2017.

1882 *American Lloyds' Registry of American and Foreign Shipping*. Digital Library: Ship Registers, Collections and Research, Mystic Seaport, Mystic, Connecticut https://research.mysticseaport.org/item/l0237571882. Accessed 11 February 2017.

ASSOCIATED PRESS
1909a Driven from Home by Water, *Evening News*, December 29. Roanoke, Virginia

1909b Storm Victims Added to List. *Los Angeles Herald*, December 29. Los Angeles, California.

BIGELOW, FRANK H. (EDITOR)
1909   *Monthly Weather Review.* United States Department of Agriculture, Washington Weather Bureau, Vol. XXXVII No. 12 (December). Washington D.C.

COAST SEAMEN'S JOURNAL
1910   Christmas on the Atlantic. *Coast Seamen's Journal*, Vol. XXIII, No. 16, January 5. San Francisco, California.

THE CRANE ESTATE
2016   About the Crane Estate. The Crane Estate a Property of the Trustees of Reservations Ipswich, Massachusetts http://www.thetrustees.org/crane-estate/about-the-crane-estate. Accessed 22 February 2017.

CUTTER, WILLIAM R. (EDITOR)
1908   *Genealogical and Personal Memoirs Relating to the Families of Boston and Eastern Massachusetts, Volume II.* Lewis Historical Publishing Company, New York, New York.

THE ESSEX HISTORICAL SOCIETY AND SHIPBUILDING MUSEUM (ESSEX SHIPBUILDING MUSEUM)
2016   About the Museum. The Essex Historical Society and Shipbuilding Museum, Essex, Massachusetts http://www.essexshipbuildingmuseum.org/about-the-museum-44.html>. Accessed 20 February 2017.

FAME OF SALEM
2016   About *Fame.* Fame of Salem, Salem, Massachusetts https://schoonerfame.com. Accessed 20 February 2017.

HARRIS, GORDON
2013   *Wreck of the* Ada K. Damon, *December 26, 1909.* Stories From Ipswich: An Antiquarian Almanac From Ipswich, Massachusetts, America's Best-Preserved Puritan Town https://storiesfromipswich.org/2013/10/31/shipwreck_ada-k-damon. Accessed 15 December 2016.

2014   *Wreck of the Sand Schooners.* An Antiquarian Almanac From Ipswich, Massachusetts, America's Best-Preserved Puritan Town < https://storiesfromipswich.org/2014/05/05/wrecks-of-the-sand-schooners/>. Accessed 15 December 2016.

MIRES, CALVIN
2015   SEAMAHP Maritime Archaeological Field School, Salem, MA, 2015 *PAST Bridge Program Annual Report*, PAST Foundation Publications, Columbus, OH.

2016   SEAMAHP Maritime Archaeological Field School, 2nd Season, 2016 *PAST Bridge Program Annual Report*, PAST Foundation Publications, Columbus, OH

MOOK, CONRAD P.
1951   Philadelphia's Greatest Snowstorm – December 25-26, 1909. *Weatherwise* 4(6):134-135.

PECKHAM, COURTNEY E.
2002   Essex Shipbuilding: Images of America. Arcadia Publishing, Charleston, South Carolina.

THE PAST FOUNDATION (PAST)
2017   Transforming Learning. The PAST Foundation, Columbus, Ohio https://pastfoundation.org/transforming-learning. Accessed 22 February 2017.

PROCTOR BROTHERS
1876   *The Fisheries of Gloucester from the First Catch by the English in 1623, to the Centennial Year, 1876.* Cape Ann Advertiser Office, Gloucester, Massachusetts.

NATIONAL ENDOWMENT FOR THE ARTS
2012   NEA National Heritage Fellowships: Harold A. Burnham. National Endowment for the Arts, Washington D.C. https://www.arts.gov/honors/heritage/fellows/harold-burnham. Accessed 20 February 2017.

RECORD OF AMERICAN AND FOREIGN SHIPPING
1877   *Record of American and Foreign Shipping.* Digital Library: Ship Registers, Collections and Research, Mystic Seaport, Mystic, Connecticut https://research.mysticseaport.org/item/l0179721877/2. Accessed 11 February 2017.

1881   *Record of American and Foreign Shipping.* Digital Library: Ship Registers, Collections and Research, Mystic Seaport, Mystic, Connecticut https://research.mysticseaport.org/item/l0179721881. Accessed 11 February 2017.

1882   *Record of American and Foreign Shipping.* Digital Library: Ship Registers, Collections and Research, Mystic Seaport, Mystic, Connecticut https://research.mysticseaport.org/item/l0179721882. Accessed 11 February 2017.

1884   *Record of American and Foreign Shipping.* Digital Library: Ship Registers, Collections and Research, Mystic Seaport, Mystic, Connecticut https://research.mysticseaport.org/item/l0179721884. Accessed 11 February 2017.

1885   *Record of American and Foreign Shipping.* Digital Library: Ship Registers, Collections and Research, Mystic Seaport, Mystic, Connecticut https://research.mysticseaport.org/item/l0179721885. Accessed 11 February 2017.

1890   *Record of American and Foreign Shipping.* Digital Library: Ship Registers, Collections and Research, Mystic Seaport, Mystic, Connecticut https://research.mysticseaport.org/item/l0179721890. Accessed 11 February 2017.

1900   *Record of American and Foreign Shipping.* Digital Library: Ship Registers, Collections and Research, Mystic Seaport, Mystic, Connecticut https://research.mysticseaport.org/item/l0179721900.

Accessed 11 February 2017.

SALEM MARITIME NATIONAL HISTORIC SITE – NATIONAL PARK SERVICE (SALEM MARITIME)
2016 Basic Information. Salem Maritime National Historic Site – National Park Service, Salem, Massachusetts https://www.nps.gov/sama/planyourvisit/basicinfo.htm. Accessed 20 February 2017.

SALEM STATE UNIVERSITY
2016 About. Salem State University, Salem, Massachusetts http://www.salemstate.edu/about/. Accessed 21 February 2017.

SCHOONER ERNESTINA-MORRISSEY ASSOCIATION
2017 Schooner *Ernestina*, ex. *Effie M. Morrissey*. Schooner Ernestina-Morrissey Association, New Bedford, Massachusetts http://www.ernestina.org. Accessed 20 February 2017.

SEAFARING EDUCATION AND MARITIME ARCHAEOLOGICAL HERITAGE PROGRAM (SEAMAHP)
2016 Welcome Aboard!. Seafaring Education and Maritime Archaeological Heritage Program https://seamahp.org/2016/10/16/welcome-aboard. Accessed 15 February 2017.

SMITH, ROBERT H.
2007 Massachusetts: Maritime Museums. Smith's Master Index to Maritime Museum Websites, Maritime Museums.net http://www.maritimemuseums.net/MA.html. Accessed 11 February 2017.

STORY, DANA A.
1995 *The Shipbuilders of Essex: A Chronicle of Yankee Endeavor*. Ten Pound Island, Gloucester, Massachusetts.

THOMPSON, SANFORD E.
1914 The Selection of Floor Surfaces in Fireproof Buildings. *Industrial Engineering and the Engineering Digest*, January 24(1):451-457. New York, New York.

TOWNSEND, CHARLES W.
1913 *Sand Dunes and Salt Marshes*. Dana Estes and Company, Boston, Massachusetts.

THE TRUSTEES OF RESERVATIONS (TTOR)
2017 Trustees History. The Trustees of Reservations, Boston, Massachusetts http://www.thetrustees.org/about-us/history. Accessed 22 February 2017.

UNITED STATES CENSUS BUREAU
1860 United States Census, 1860, Jane Brewster in entry for John Brewster, 1860, database with images, *FamilySearch* https://familysearch.org/ark:/61903/1:1:MDCM-P3P. Accessed 13 February 2017.

1870 United States Census, 1870, Albert Brewster in household of John Brewster, Maine, United States; citing p. 20, family 172, NARA microfilm publication M593 (Washington D.C.: National Archives and Records Administration, n.d.); FHL microfilm 552,064, database with images, *FamilySearch* https://familysearch.org/ark:/61903/1:1:M6DC-MG9. Accessed 13 February 2017.

1880 United States Census, 1880, Albert Brewster in household of Luke B Bassett, Gloucester, Essex, Massachusetts, United States; citing enumeration district ED 174, sheet 425C, NARA microfilm publication T9 (Washington D.C.: National Archives and Records Administration, n.d.), roll 0529; FHL microfilm 1,254,529, database with images, *FamilySearch* https://familysearch.org/ark:/61903/1:1:MH6Z-M2P. Accessed 13 February 2017.

1900a United States Census, 1900, Albert Brewster, Precinct 6 Boston city Ward 2, Suffolk, Massachusetts, United States; citing enumeration district (ED) 1180, sheet 11B, family 216, NARA microfilm publication T623 (Washington, D.C.: National Archives and Records Administration, 1972.); FHL microfilm 1,240,676, database with images, *FamilySearch* https://familysearch.org/ark:/61903/1:1:M9YS-J7C . Accessed 13 February 2017.

1900b United States Census, 1900, Albert Brewster, York township (part of), York, Maine, United States; citing enumeration district (ED) 260, sheet 10B, family 245, NARA microfilm publication T623 (Washington, D.C.: National Archives and Records Administration, 1972.); FHL microfilm 1,240,603, database with images, *FamilySearch* https://familysearch.org/ark:/61903/1:1:MMG4-ZDF. Accessed 13 February 2017.

1930 United States Census, 1930, Albert K Brewster, York, York, Maine, United States; citing enumeration district (ED) ED 61, sheet 21A, line 28, family 498, NARA microfilm publication T626 Washington D.C.: National Archives and Records Administration, 2002), roll 842; FHL microfilm 2,340,577, database with images *FamilySearch* https://familysearch.org/ark:/61903/1:1:XMDN-2T1. Accessed 13 February 2017.

UNITED STATES LIFE-SAVING SERVICE
1894 *Annual Report of the Operations of the United States Life-Saving Service for the Fiscal Year Ending June 1893*. Department of Treasury, Washington DC.

1911 *Annual Report of the Operations of the United States Life-Saving Service for the Fiscal Year Ending June 1910*. Department of Treasury, Washington DC.

Calvin Mires
257 ½ Sandwich Street
Plymouth, MA 02360
(252) 902-8351
calvinmires@gmail.com

A Lot Harder Than It Looks: Conservation of A Worst-Case Scenario

Christopher P. Morris, Andrew Fearon

Piecing together the scrambled skeletons of wooden shipwrecks during a planned archaeological excavation is a daunting undertaking under the best of circumstances. But, when the skeletal timbers are an unanticipated discovery, ripped from their resting place during a disaster recovery project, the circumstances are far from the best. Add to that scenario: jurisdictional complications resulting in the timbers being left exposed and unsecured for weeks, before being locked away untreated for over a year. The undertaking becomes a near impossible challenge. Conservators and maritime archaeologists employed modified conservation and recordation techniques in a race to prevent as much destruction as possible. These adaptations, coupled with robust communication between archaeologist, conservator, and consulting agencies, prevented a total loss of data and archaeological material

Introduction

Archaeological conservation ideally begins before excavation, often with years of preparation in place. Wooden artifacts found submerged or in wet environments pose complex conservation challenges, particularly when encountered or disturbed accidentally. Even with the best protocols and resources available, wet wood can present an assortment of conservation problems. These include mechanical damage, fungal/bacterial degradation, insect infestation, metal composites with related corrosion mechanisms, and most notably, permanent deformation or collapse due to stresses associated with drying.

In his seminal work on the conservation of maritime archaeological sites, Dr. Donny Hamilton laid the groundwork for the essentials of Maritime Archaeological Conservation, and clearly states the critical need for proper conservation on a maritime site:

> *Artifact preservation is one of the most important considerations when planning or implementing any action that will result in the recovery of material from a marine archaeological site. It is the responsibility of the excavator or salvor to see that material recovered is properly conserved. The conservation phase is time consuming and expensive, often costing more than the original excavation. Without conservation, however, most artifacts will perish, and important historic data will be lost. The loss is not just to the excavator but also to future archaeologists, who may wish to reexamine the material.*

Artifacts recovered from a salt water environment are often well preserved but of a very friable nature. In general, artifacts recovered from anaerobic marine environments (i.e., buried in sediment) are recovered in better condition than artifacts recovered from aerobic marine environments (i.e., the water column and surface sediment). Artifacts not properly conserved in a timely manner are apt to deteriorate at a very rapid rate and subsequently become useless as diagnostic or display specimens. Organic material, i.e., leather, wood, textile, rope, plant remains, etc., if allowed to dry without conservation treatment, can crumble and become little more than a pile of dust and debris in a matter of hours. Iron, on the other hand, can last for a few days to months according to the size and density of the artifact; however, it too will eventually deteriorate and become useless as a display or diagnostic specimen. Bone, glass, pottery, and similar material will, if not conserved, slowly devitrify and, in extreme cases, degenerate to a pile of worthless slivers. For these reasons, conservation must be of paramount concern when the excavation of a marine archaeological site is considered (Hamilton 1999:4).

Unfortunately in this case, no archaeology, hence no conservation, was planned. This project required planning and conservation preparation to be adapted months after the recovery of the material culture. Archaeological concerns arose during the installation of an 18,000-foot-long steel sheet pile wall in Ocean County, New Jersey, October 2014. In response to the ravages of Superstorm Sandy, state and federal agencies ordered the construction a bulwark to help protect the barrier island community, and obtained all required permits and reviews (including those related to Section 106 compliance). The undertaking was to avoid any known historic properties. However, as no historic concerns were noted, and the project proceeded without archaeological oversight.

The bulwark required immense vibratory pile drivers to install 45-foot-long marine sheet steel piles. When the progress of a pile-driving machine was halted by an unknown buried obstruction, a track hoe was used to remove the material and place it out of the way. The obstruction turned out to be several tons of primarily wooden material that had been buried 20 ft. (6.1 m) deep into a coastal dune, below the water table. The track hoe was able to wrench and excavate the cultural material from a 20 to 25 ft. (6.1 to 7.62m) diameter area extending the aforementioned depth, and pile it upon the dune face. Once the material was removed, the excavation was backfilled and compacted to facilitate the resumption of the driving activities. In an effort to keep the excavated material out of the way, it was redeposited several times until it was ultimately deposited upon a stack of sheet piling adjacent to the wall alignment. It was only after the removal and multiple re-depositions that monitors from state and federal agencies determined that the material could be historic. At this point, work was halted until a maritime archaeologist could be contacted to provide further analysis.

Initial Evaluation

The maritime archaeologist documented a scatter of approximately 200 to 300 artifacts consisting of medium to large timbers, shown in Figure 1; a mixture of disarticulated wooden timbers (possibly frames, or deck beams); hull planking with observable wooden treenails; copper alloy pieces; and ferrous metal components, which may have been related to a deck winch or windlass assembly. A full inventory was not conducted at that time for reasons to be explained later.

Within the assemblage, several timbers were at least partially articulated. The initial assessment found that most of the timber frames or beams and planks had sustained recent mechanical crush/scrape damage, indicative of handling via an excavating machine. The assemblage also contained parts of what appeared to be a winch or windlass, measuring more than 10 ft. (3.0 m) in length. The remains of the windlass assembly were timber-cored, and had corroded and concreted ferrous metal features. The windlass appeared to have been crushed or sheared-off on one end, and to have had something, perhaps a warping drum, pried off from the other. These features were found to be consistent with the construction and fastening of early- to mid-nineteenth century ocean-going vessels operating along the United States' Atlantic seaboard.

After interviewing onsite personnel and reviewing the recovered cultural material, it was concluded that neither the agencies in charge nor the contractor willfully disturbed the cultural deposit, it was truly inadvertent. They stated that prior to full excavation, the remains were thought to be buried modern storm debris. Site interviews revealed that the material had been removed from an at least partially intact structure, and that portions of the site most likely remained buried and *in situ*.

Exposure and Securing

Due to various state and federal agencies jurisdictional and contractual concerns, the maritime archaeologist was required to leave the site pending

Figure 1. Stockpile of shipwreck material initially observed on Mantoloking Beach in October, 2014 (Photo by author).

Figure 2. Stockpile of shipwreck material after suffering clear attrition, observed in November, 2014 (Photo by author).

further agency consultation. This unexpected and early departure preempted all but a brief, cursory examination of the stockpiled cultural material, and prevented full photo and inventory documentation. Before leaving, the maritime archaeologist strongly recommended that the recovered material be covered, and kept as secure as possible. They also recommended that all persons aware of the shipwreck material keep that information confidential as to prevent public interest and potential looting of the material. Unfortunately, within a week of the initial site assessment, the municipality held a press conference on site, and by Tuesday, November 4, 2014, the discovery had been picked up by local network affiliates and was further reported on national news networks.

By November 2014, consultations determined that the maritime archaeologist originally assigned to the response was contractually permitted continue their site investigation. They returned to the site, this time with an assistant. At least half, if not more, of the recovered shipwreck assemblage had disappeared, as evidenced in Figure 2. Missing material and vandalism suggested that significant looting of the site had occurred during the interim. Even during the first days the maritime archaeologists' return, significant portions of the assemblage were continuing to go missing. Pieces identified and recorded for analysis at the close of the day would be missing at the start of the next. Local law enforcement had to be called to remove individuals actively looting the site.

Consulting Agencies determined shipwreck assemblage the material should be secured offsite to minimize the threat of looting. Archaeological material was collected from the beach dune and loaded into an intermodal "Conex" box for transfer. After some delays, the Conex box was moved, and the material taken to a non-climate controlled building at a secure storage facility in a New Jersey State Park. Once the materials were offloaded, they were tightly packed and wrapped with plastic tarps secured with straps and bungee cords.

Starting Over

In April 2016, maritime archaeologists, along with representatives of the consulting state and federal agencies, met with conservator Andrew Fearon of Materials Conservation. The meeting took place at the New Jersey State Park storage facility where the remains were being temporarily housed. The shipwreck remains, recovered in late 2014 and sequestered in this facility since January of 2015, had been sitting untouched for over a year. There was concern that between the mechanical damage, exposure, material attrition, multiple transports, and time without treatment, the archaeological material, and hence all data, might be a total loss.

Under supervision of the conservator, the timbers were unwrapped and positioned for examination. This preliminary examination included visual inspections for stability, structural integrity, evidence of fungal damage, surface mold activity, mechanical damage, cracking, deformation, and evidence of insect activity. Corrosion products, concretions, and structural integrity of ferrous components were also recorded. It was found the general conditions of wooden materials had sustained a high level of structural integrity, with minor mold activity, no insect activity, and minor fungal related deterioration. Several wood fragments exhibited large cracks (2mm to 10mm wide), distortion, mechanical damage, and soft or degraded surface integrity, indicative of microbial and fungal degradation and associated with marine environments. Surface accumulations of soil and marine life from in situ context and some concretions including shell material were also observed. Advanced corrosion of ferrous metal components had occurred, including exfoliation on a 10 to 20cm portion of the lamellar structure of the windlass, which was found detached and easily fragmentable. Further, the windlass' wrought iron shaft was found bent at approximately 45 degrees from drum axis.

Moisture content readings were immediately recorded from approximately 20 locations over several artifacts using a Wagner 210 pin-less moisture meter. This model instrument was limited to 0.75" reading depth, a 32% moisture content range limit, and maximum specific gravity of .70. The meter was calibrated to .70 specific gravity, the maximum amount, which was an appropriate setting based on the timbers' cursory species identification as white oak (Quercus alba). Onsite moisture content readings ranged from 9.6% to 32%, with an average reading around 20%. This indicated that many of the wood materials had begun to dry out, and in some cases, were already fully dry. Changes in density across a given sample could potentially impact and distort readings. In some cases, moisture readings on single artifacts ranged over 10%, suggesting an uneven distribution of moisture content or an uneven drying process, likely related to differentiated exposure to heat and air inside the tarp enclosure.

The conservator concluded that despite the lack of preservation measures or climate control, the wooden artifacts had survived in a fair, but not ideal state of preservation. Their survival was likely due to the environmental conditions while the timbers were in situ, high levels of humidity post excavation, the tight packing and wrapping for storage, and a good bit of luck.

Four diagnostic artifacts (VSM-002, VSM-003, VSM-004, and VSM-005) were carefully transported to the Materials Conservation laboratory in Philadelphia for a more detailed analysis. The artifacts were photo-documented prior to their removal from the storage facility. Remaining artifacts were placed on ridged polystyrene foam insulation floor padding, and then covered with tarps to arrest further rapid drying.

Triage

The conservator directed the archaeology team to take immediate triage measures on the timbers to prevent the propagation of fungi/mold-fungi, cracking, and deformation related to rapid drying. It was emphasized that the wooden artifacts should be kept damp under plastic and sprayed with a 2% isopropanol in water solution every two days before full triage measures could be implemented.

Based on the conditions assessment, the triage program was designed to provide stable micro-climates for the artifacts using a double layer of permeable, high density woven polyethylene sheeting (Tyvek Homewrap) while applying disodium octaborate tetrahydrate (DOT) to deter higher order decay fungi propagation (i.e.; Basidiomycota) and insect activity (i.e.: Rhinotermitidae). To deter lower order mold-fungi species (i.e. fungi-imperfecti/Deuteromycota) iodopropynylbutyl carbamate (IPBC) was added to the treatment solution. While the triage used water as the primary solvent, the wood would eventually seek equilibrium with the relative humidity of the micro-climate, and the moisture content of the timbers would stabilize and slowly decrease over a period of months. Inert polystyrene blocks protected the surface of the artifacts from mechanical damage and allowed air to circulate around each object preventing uneven drying and resultant deformation. This technique was applied to wooden artifacts and wooden elements of metal artifact composites. Purely metal components did not require preservative applications.

The triage program was implemented by the archaeological staff beginning with an application of Tim-bor Professional® insecticide/fungicide (brand name for DOT) and Outlast Mold Buster® (brand name for IPBC). Eight gallons of a 10% solution of Tim-bor was mixed with 8 oz. of Outlast using two clean 5 gallon white buckets to mix the admixture back and forth. This solution applied twice to all sides of the artifacts, using a one-gallon Poly Lawn and Garden Sprayer. After the application, the artifacts were then double-wrapped in Tyvek and tied with cotton twill tape ribbon. After follow-up coordination calls between the archaeologists and Materials Conservation regarding the need for recordation, photography, and scanning of each specimen, it was determined that each artifact should only be wrapped upon completion of the analysis, as opposed to multiple episodes of wrapping and unwrapping a specimen.

Wood Identification and Analysis

Samples were extracted from detached or easily accessible portions of the artifacts, and transported to the lab. Extracted samples were split along their grain, then cut perpendicularly to the grain so that and exact transverse section could be surfaced with a hand microtome. Samples were moistened with water before plating and examination using a Leica M125 stereomicroscope at 10× to 50×. Based on macro anatomy, including ring porous configuration, large rays and abundant tyloses were found indicating that the three wooden artifacts (VSM-002, VSM-004, and VSM-005) were all white oak species (Quercus alba).

Maximum moisture tests were conducted to help quantify the degree of degradation of wood cell walls, which would have resulted from increased porosity and xylem saturation. Three samples measuring roughly 2cm³ were extracted from an accessible extremity of sample RT-35°C. The samples were saturated with boiling water for 15 minutes, submerged to cool for two hours, and then weighed at saturation point. These samples were then oven dried for 24 hours at 105°C, then weighed again. The following equation was used to calculate the maximum moisture content of the three samples.

% Maximum Moisture Content = (Weight, waterlogged - Weight, oven dried) × 100(Weight, oven dried)

Resulting weights of the three samples were recorded as shown in Table 1.

The condition or level of integrity of wet archaeological wood may be understood through a classification system based upon maximum moisture content (De Jong 1977).

CLASS I - Wood containing >400% water - Highly degraded wood predominates.

CLASS II - Wood containing 185 to 400% water - Comparatively small core present.

CLASS III - Wood containing <185% water - Sound core beneath a thin deteriorated layer.

All samples tested fell well below the 185% water content, suggesting the RT-35 materials retained a high level of integrity and could be considered well preserved.

Simultaneous dimensional change and maximum shrinkage calculations were conducted to determine maximum moisture content on the same samples. After the samples had been saturated, a 20mm long line was scribed across the sample's transverse face using a knife and a straight edge aligned parallel to the sample's tangential plane. Measurements of the line were taken before and after oven drying. The equation used to calculate the shrinkage of the samples is the as that used to calculate the moisture content, substituting dimensional data for weight.

% Maximum Shrinkage = (Length, waterlogged − Length, oven dry) X 100 (Length, waterlogged)

Results of the 3 samples were recorded as shown in Table 2.

Non- archaeological, green wood fibered white oak (Quercus alba) shows tangential shrinkage from fiber saturation point (FSP) to oven dry to be 8.8%. This value is consistent with our findings when testing the archaeological timbers, indicating that dimensional change recorded for the sample set is consistent with

Sample	Wet Mass (g)	Dry Mass (g)	Max Moisture %
RT-35C3.1	19.2	11.2	70%
RT-35C3.2	18.4	10.6	73%
RT-35C3.3	17.6	10.6	66%

Table 1. Percent Maximum Moisture Content for Sampled Material Table (Table by author).

Sample	Wet Length (mm)	Dry Length (mm)	Shrinkage %
RT-35C3.1	20	18.2	9%
RT-35C3.2	20	18.2	9%
RT-35C3.3	20	18.3	8.50%

Table 2. Percent Maximum Shrinkage Value for Sampled Material Table (Table by author).

the behavior of well-preserved wood. It should be noted that several cracks developed primarily on the material's radial plane, which resulted from being rapidly dried from FSP for 24 hours inside an 105 °C oven.

Metal and Composite Artifacts

Sample object VSM-003 was identified as cast iron with lead (Pb) sheet features. Sample object VSM-002 was identified as having a wrought iron band and shaft. Sample object VSM-005 was identified as having a copper alloy fastener. All ferrous material exhibit corrosion products, and the wrought iron features showed a delamination in lamellar structure. Lead and copper alloy material were found to be in stable condition with minor corrosion products. Desalination, mechanical cleaning, conversion treatment, or electrolytic reduction for ferrous metal components may be implemented locally. The copper alloy and lead components are stable – although some corrosion products exist, and may be reduced from the surface with a mild chelating cleaning solution. The degree of cleaning will depend upon display and related aesthetic requirements.

Further Treatment Options and Conclusions

The wood and metal composite objects in the lab have been treated with the same preservative materials applied in the field, and have each been monitored for eight months in a semi-closed system with data loggers measuring RH/T. Wooden material has been kept damp in a semi-closed system of polyethylene sheet with a 500ml container of water to keep the chamber sustained at 100% relative humidity and between 72° F and 75° F. The metal object RT-35C4 has been lightly flushed with water to reduce chlorides, and left at approximately 50 % RH. All preliminary field moisture content readings, FSP weight calculations, dry weight calculations, species identifications, microscopy examinations, treatment, and monitoring has indicated two things: first, the wood cell structures of the surveyed artifacts appear intact and exhibit high levels of integrity. Second, wooden archaeological materials had begun to dry out prior to triage, during their long period of exposure and storage.

In considering both of these findings, traditional bulking methods for wooden component stabilization will have limited effectiveness due to physical integrity of the xylem and species anatomy. However, slow controlled drying is critical to avoid further deformation, cracking, warping, and shrinkage. Freeze drying is a valid option for further conservation; however, it is questionable whether there is a sufficient water in the cell walls to justify such a measure. Propagation of lower and higher order fungi has been eliminated with the application of the DOT and IPBC preservative solution. The efficacy of fungi treatment has been confirmed in the lab over eight months of monitoring. Further treatment will

Figure 3. 3D Scanning set up of shipwreck timbers in May, 2016 (Photo by Author).

depend on the environments of future display and/or long term storage areas. If the majority of the materials are to be stored in the current environment or back-filled at the original site, or in similar conditions nearby, then treatment using a combination of Tyvek and DOT / IPBC will be sufficient. Any backfilled materials should be supplemented with additional geotextile landscape fabric providing a barrier from future excavation damage.

If any of the objects are to be displayed in a less or uncontrolled environment, then light aqueous cleaning is recommended, followed by a low-molecular weight surface consolidate/coating to ensure long term stability and facilitate future cleaning. The coating chemicals recommended for application may vary depending upon the stage of drying. A water-based consolidate may be applied while the wood is still drying to impart surface integrity to soft or friable material. Archaeological wood drying (without freezing) typically takes several months to several years to complete, due to the consolidates impedance to moisture loss.

Recordation and Data Capture for Study

Continued Triage

Once the timbers were cleaned, treated, and stabilized, archaeologists restarted the recording and inventorying the shipwreck assemblage in Spring 2016. During this analysis, materials were continuously treated with triage chemicals to prevent deterioration and degradation as they were being documented and measured. A total of 95 individual timbers and artifacts were analyzed. Despite the triage treatments and cleaning, there were several severely degraded and damaged wood fragments. The damaged wood fragments were essentially shredded timber, evidence of the substantial force during the non-archaeological excavation. Shredded timbers were stockpiled together for measurement. Cumulatively, the shredded timber mass measured approximately 9 ft.^{3} (2.29m^3). The shredded timber mass was photographed, but not inventoried, as part of the overall assemblage. Despite the significant damage, the shredded timbers were treated with triage chemicals to prevent further degradation and the spread of molds, spores, and fungi to the larger assemblage.

Hand Recordation / Digital Photography

Every artifact was inventoried and photographed. The inventory included metric measurements of each artifact's length, width, and depth; an identification and description of each artifact; an indication of the raw material; and an indication of what fastener types were present, if any. With limited time, and nearly a hundred timbers to record (some damaged beyond diagnostic potential), a recordation triage procedure was established. Samples from the most diagnostic timbers, and smaller samples of less diagnostic timbers, would have photographs taken of all faces and diagnostic features. They would then be hand measured and recorded in drawings, per standard maritime archaeological protocol. The data recovery methods called for hand-sketched recordations of approximately 30% of the sample. Of the hand-sketched recordations, 20% of consisted of timbers considered to be the most diagnostic; and approximately 10% were of the more damaged, less-diagnostic timbers. In total, hand sketch drawings were created for 29 of the recovered timbers.

All hand-sketched timbers were later three-dimensionally scanned to maximize data recovered from diagnostic and damaged timbers. Hand-drawn sketches of the timbers were analyzed against the 3D images for quality control. Graphic recordations of the timbers were produced for several reasons: to allow possible identification of timbers and further our understanding of the vessel structure; and to utilize traditional techniques for data recovery prior to further degradation.

For photographic documentation, each timber was placed on a photo stage backed with a blank Tyvek sheet and a photo scale. Each artifact face was photographed, measured, and recorded. Lighting in the storage facility was poor due to the building's the antiquated wiring; thus, each artifact was photographed both with and without flash to maximize potential of creating the best possible image. Data recordation, inventorying, and artifact photography was completed in May 2016. Upon completion, the assemblage was again treated and stored per the conservator's recommendations.

3D Laser Scanning

Per project method prescriptions, the 3D Laser scanning team and archaeologists scanned 69 artifacts. In addition to the 29 hand-drawn artifacts, an additional 40 artifacts. These artifacts were chosen for demonstrating diagnostic potential while having features that would have been inordinately time-consuming to hand-draw. Such features include amorphous concretions, multiple fasteners on multiple axes, slight angular shaping, and extensive structural damage. Scanning such objects tested the capability of the laser scanning tool, and the 3D scanning method in general.

The 3D laser scanning process required the installation of a tripod-mounted Leica Geosystems P40 laser scanner, which was positioned at various stations around the subject target(s). The scanner recorded thousands of points per minute from each station, and referenced the position of the target item in relation to other points in the scanning area (illustrated in Figure 3). Reference points remained static throughout the entire scanning process, and served as a basis for aligning data points collected from the various stations. The relational data is used to build a 3D point cloud of the target's surface. Each point in the point cloud represents a measurement between the instrument and a laser-thin spot on the artifact surface.

The scanner also records a series of digital images of the target(s). These images help orient the point cloud and assemble the points into a three-dimensional object. Digital images can also be applied to the points, adding color and texture to the target object's digital rendering. The target item is repeatedly rotated 90° or 180° to expose an un-scanned side; and the process of scanning and photographing is repeated. Overlapping of already scanned faces helps stitch the point clouds together and create the three-dimensional rendering. The 3D laser scanning of a artifact was completed once each of its faces had been scanned.

Each specimen required considerable handling during the scanning process; thus, triage chemicals were on-hand and applied as necessary. In some instances, treatment application or inclement weather (the scanning was done outside the storage facility) increased the amount of moisture on the surface of the target, which raised the potential for laser refraction and erroneous data. Puddling or even a droplet on an artifact surface can refract the beam. The laser scan would then measure the resulting surface targeted by the extent of that refraction. The scanning team and onsite archaeologists were mindful of moisture and potential refraction issues, and took precautions to prevent skewed data recordings.

Upon processing the 3D scanning data, it was found that over 70% of the timbers had potentially diagnostic features. Artifact shape; size; features including joinery and fastenings; and tool marks barely perceivable by eye; were discernable in the processed imagery. The windlass core's complex angles and damages are clearly visible in Figure 4. The windlass is extremely fragile and weighs several tons, making it difficult to study. After triage and scanning, the instrument can be virtually rotated to read, record, and measure any angle.

Summary and Conclusions

The RT-35 Maritime Archaeological Project suffered multiple false starts and setbacks. An initial concern was that no useful data could be reasonably and cost effectively recovered from the archaeological material. Had this been the case, it would have constituted an irreparable loss of data to the historic maritime cultural landscape of New Jersey. The treatment the excavated cultural material experienced prior to triage contravenes most tenets of maritime archaeological conservation. Significant loss was only prevented by the consulting agencies, maritime archaeologists, and conservators working in concert, communicating, and acting in good faith. Despite the significant damage and loss of material, proper archaeological conservation triage and

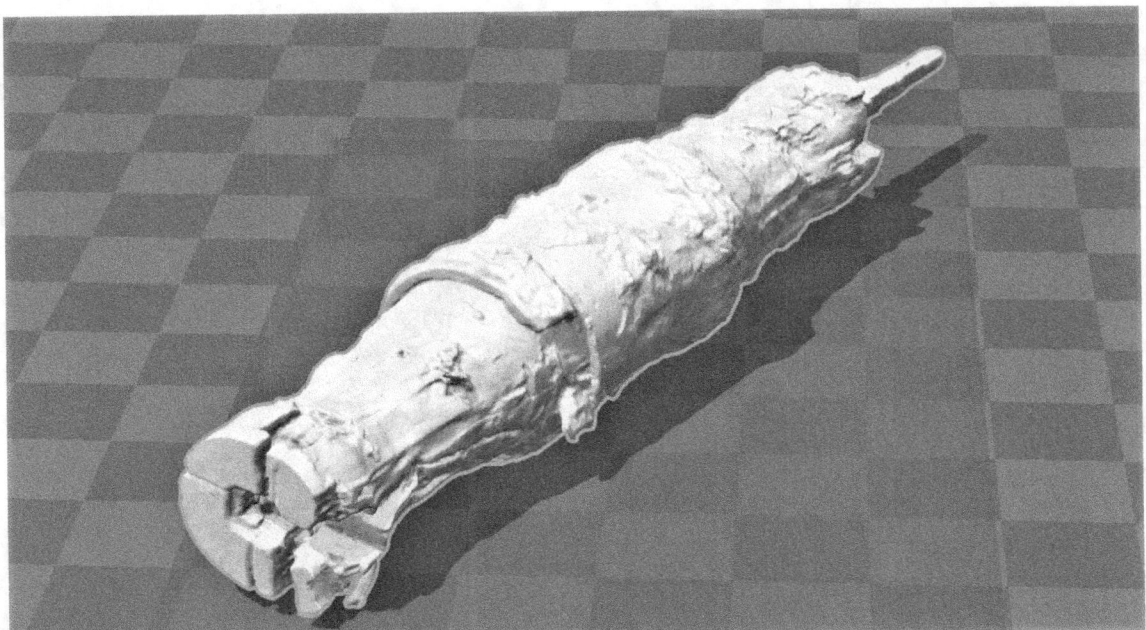

Figure 4. 3D dense point cloud model of windlass core (image by author).

creative recordation techniques rescued critical data, and allowed for a cultural resource management success.

It is difficult to say whether damage to the materials could have been prevented early on. The original multi-agency undertaking followed all standard procedures, yet still there was an unintended adverse effect on a potentially intact archaeological resource. There is nothing to indicate a specific failing on the part of any individual or part of the review process; this was not a case of agencies or contractors ignoring the rules. To the contrary, reports show immediate efforts to comply with 106 standards as soon as the discovery was recognized. Perhaps this case study highlights the fundamental need for a more critical look at how the regulatory and review process functions when addressing maritime cultural landscapes.

Acknowledgments

The authors would like to thank the management and staff at Dewberry, Materials Conservation, and the quiet diligence of Mr. Lauren Cook RPA. Also, the professionalism, and coordinated consultation of the representatives of the Consulting Agencies without whom this project would not have occurred: the Federal Highway Administration, State of New Jersey Department of Environmental Protection Division of Coastal Engineering, Historic Preservation Office, State of New Jersey Department of Transportation. Thanks also to Mr. Scott Bleeker II, who turned lost data into 3D history. Finally, we recognize the guidance and patience of Drs. Baugher, Switzer, and MD Morris PE.

References

DE JONG, J.
1977   *Conservation Techniques for old waterlogged wood from Shipwrecks found in the Netherlands.* London: Applied Science Publishers.

HAMILTON, DONNY L.
1999   *Methods of Conserving Archaeological Material from Underwater Sites.* College Station, TX: Nautical Archaeology Program, Texas A&M University.

Christopher Morris
1311 E. State Street
Ithaca, NY 14850

Andrew Fearon
1625 North Howard Street
Philadelphia PA, 19122

Luray Victory and the SS Ira: Identification and Deterioration of Wrecks on the Goodwin Sands

Elizabeth Krueger, Justin Dix

The Goodwin Sands has long been a major navigation hazard. Several previous projects have been undertaken to document the many shipwrecks in the area, and this study furthered this effort by utilizing recent bathymetric surveys to update the wreck database created during the English Heritage AMAP2 project. The bathymetric data was analyzed to independently confirm the presence of known wrecks and locate previously undocumented ones. Two wrecks listed in the AMAP2 database, the SS Ira and the Luray Victory, were flagged as potentially misidentified, and alternate identifications of the related wrecks were discussed. The rapidly changing geomorphology of the Goodwin Sands was also investigated to determine the extent of its effects on wreck sites in the area.

Introduction

The Goodwin Sands has long been an important maritime location, and its capacity for preserving shipwrecks has made it a major resource for archaeologists. Understanding the bank's patterns of sediment transport is crucial in predicting threats to sites due to exposure. This project used recent bathymetric and hydrodynamic data combined with previous known wreck databases to assess the vulnerability and archaeological potential of visible wrecks in the area.

Background

The Goodwin Sands consists of a pair of sandbanks, which combined measure 14 km long and 8 km wide (Figure 1). The formation lies between 4 and 8 km off the coast of Kent (Larn and Larn 1995b) and acts as a breakwater for The Downs, a channel that runs between the Goodwins and the mainland. The Goodwin Sands' bank structure is simpler than most sandbanks in the region, which allowed geologists to begin modeling and predicting its movements as early as the 1950s, when R. L. Cloet (1954) determined that the banks follow a general pattern of counterclockwise rotation, with the northwest arm of the bank moving shoreward and the southern tip of the bank moving eastward. This rotation happens irregularly over centennial timescales, with occasional periods of reversal.

The area has a long history of significance to maritime activity, both good and bad. On the one hand, it acts as a barrier between the North Sea and the Downs, creating a sheltered harbor that has allowed the Thames Estuary and the Deal coast to become thriving regions for international trade (Redknap and Fleming 1985). On the other hand, its ever-changing shape presents a constant navigational challenge, leading to numerous wrecks over the years (Larn and Larn 1995b). Of particular note is the area along the bend in the eastern margin of the South Goodwin bank, which acquired the nickname "Calamity Corner" in the early 1950s due to the large number of wrecks that occurred there within the span of a few years (Larn and Larn 1995b). Two of these wrecks were analyzed during this project.

The area's 16 ft. average tidal range is one of the

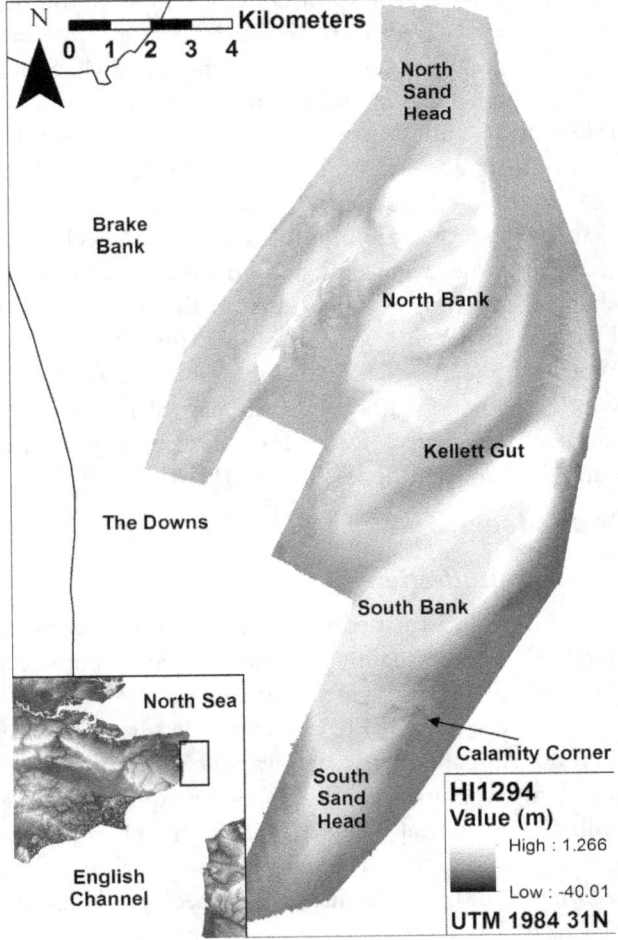

Figure 1. Overview map of the Goodwin Sands, HI1294 (Map by author, 2017; data from UKHO 2017).

largest in the world, and much of the bank uncovers at low spring tide (Larn and Larn 1995b). The large tidal range and strong currents around the Goodwin Sands create an extremely dynamic burial environment, which can be destructive to exposed shipwrecks (Bates et al. 2007). Studying the active site dynamics in the region is useful for prioritizing wreck sites in imminent danger of degradation for additional documentation and study. In addition, areas of erosion can be monitored for the emergence of previously undocumented wrecks.

Aims and Objectives

The main aim of this project was to examine the site dynamics, both locally and regionally, affecting the wrecks on the Goodwin Sands and combine this with prior knowledge of the wreck record to create a comprehensive catalog of the wrecks in the area. In addition, this project aimed to determine whether any wrecks of archaeological significance in the area were in urgent need of archaeological investigation due to natural deterioration or other potential threats.

The goals of this project were achieved through examination of recent bathymetric datasets to assess the condition of visible wrecks on the Goodwin Sands, and through comparison of this data with historical information and shipwreck records to determine the historical significance of the located wrecks. Time-lapse analyses of the bathymetric datasets were also used to examine how the condition of the located wrecks have changed in the recent past, and how it may continue to change. This project followed from the recent English Heritage 'AMAP2 - Characterizing the Potential for Wrecks' project (AMAP2), which created a composite wreck database for the southeast coast of England, the most complete wreck record for the region compiled to date (SeaZone Solutions 2011a, 2011b).

Methodology

Data Collection

This project focused on the use of available digital datasets, relying mainly on the AMAP2 shipwreck database; UKHO bathymetric surveys HI1294, HI1399, and HI1484; and DEFRA bathymetric survey number 235800. All bathymetric surveys were accessed through the United Kingdom Hydrography Office's public online data portal (United Kingdom Hydrography Office 2017). Hydrodynamic modeling analysis of the region output by the Managing Archaeological Cultural Heritage Underwater (MACHU) project was also analyzed. Additional historical information was acquired from Richard and Bridget Larn's (1995a, 1995b) work cataloging the shipwrecks of the British Isles, as well as the online shipwreck database Wrecksite (2017).

All bathymetric surveys used in this project were collected with multi-beam sonar equipment, and all were originally projected in the WGS 1984 UTM Zone 31 coordinate system, except HI1484, which was originally projected in GCS EPSG 4326 (NATO Military Geodetic Surveying). All surveys used Admiralty Chart Datum for vertical reference. The data for survey HI1294 was collected in 2009, for HI1399 in 2012, and for HI 1484 in 2015. Prior to download, the HI1294 dataset had been binned at 2 m, while HI1399 and HI1484 had been binned with 1 m spacing. The data for the DEFRA survey was collected in 2014 and the dataset accessed for this project had been binned at 2 m.

The hydrodynamic modeling data consulted during this project included several GIS layers detailing bed level change and residual sediment transport vectors for the Goodwin Sands area under various wave and tidal conditions. This model was originally created to better understand of the dynamics affecting underwater archaeological site formation processes (MACHU Project Team 2008a, 2008b; Dix et al. 2008; Carrizales 2010).

Data Processing

The geographic information systems software ArcMap 10.4.1 was used for all interpretation of environmental datasets. Microsoft Excel for Mac 2011, v14.6.7 was used for accessing and analyzing the data in the AMAP2 shipwreck database.

Before analyzing the various bathymetric datasets, the HI1484 survey was reprojected from GCS EPSG 4326 into the WGS1984 coordinate system using the ArcMap Project Raster tool. Copies of the HI1399 and HI1484 surveys were resampled at a bin size of 2 m for more direct comparison to the other two surveys, but both 1 m- and 2 m-binned versions were considered during visual interpretation of the datasets. Where relevant, the finer-grained versions were used for locating and analyzing shipwrecks, as the increased level of detail allowed for more accurate assessment of the size, shape, and condition of the observed wrecks. The versions with a larger bin size were used for time-lapse comparison with the earlier surveys in order to avoid any bias that may have resulted from differing bin sizes.

Bathymetric Interpretation

Slope, curvature, and hillshade maps were created for each of the bathymetric datasets. These, along with the initial bathymetry maps, were visually examined to locate possible wreck sites. Basic information about each of the located wrecks was recorded, including the water depth, the length, beam, height, and orientation of the wreck, and also the length, depth, and orientation of any scour trails present. This information was combined into a visible wrecks database, which is included in full in the original project report (Krueger 2016).

The individual values of the various bathymetry datasets were subtracted from one another to create difference maps showing the change in the seabed level between time-steps in order to analyze the changing shape of both the bank as a whole and individual wreck sites. Due to limited overlap between the surveys, not all areas of the sandbank could be analyzed this way, however several key areas of change were identified from the available data.

Wreck Analysis

The shipwreck database output by the AMAP2 project was the first point of reference for historical data about the shipwrecks visible on the bathymetry datasets. The location data provided in the AMAP2 database was used to match records from the database with anomalies located during the bathymetry analysis stage of the project. The HOID designation for the AMAP2 record matched to each located wreck was included in the visible wreck database created for this project in order to allow cross-examination of the two databases for future research.

Eleven wrecks were chosen for in-depth individual analysis based on quality of bathymetric signature and availability of historical information about the corresponding vessel in the AMAP2 database. Additional visual examination was performed on the bathymetric data available for each of these wrecks, and detailed descriptions of the bathymetric signatures were created. The aforementioned historical sources were consulted for each identified vessel to gain a more complete understanding of the vessel, the circumstances of its loss, and its potential archaeological significance. The historical information was then compared to the bathymetry to assess the validity of the identification, and future plans for documentation and monitoring were recommended. The full results of this analysis were detailed in the original project report (dissertation). Three of the located bathymetric anomalies, corresponding to two entries in the AMAP2 database, were discussed here due to the potential significance of the findings.

Results

Bathymetric Analysis

Figure 1 shows a bathymetric map of the Goodwin Sands with relevant features labeled. The HI1294 survey was used for the overview map, as it was the most extensive of the surveys used in this study. Both banks showed significant motion over the period between the surveys.

South Bank

Overall, the south bank (Figure 2) narrowed during the time between surveys, but the exact change could not be accurately measured due to the differing extents of the surveys. The central ridge running longitudinally along the bank shifted an average of 200 m west between the 2009 and 2015 surveys, with approximately three quarters of that shift occurring between 2009 and 2012. The movement of individual areas varied, with the largest change of around 400-500 m occurring near the

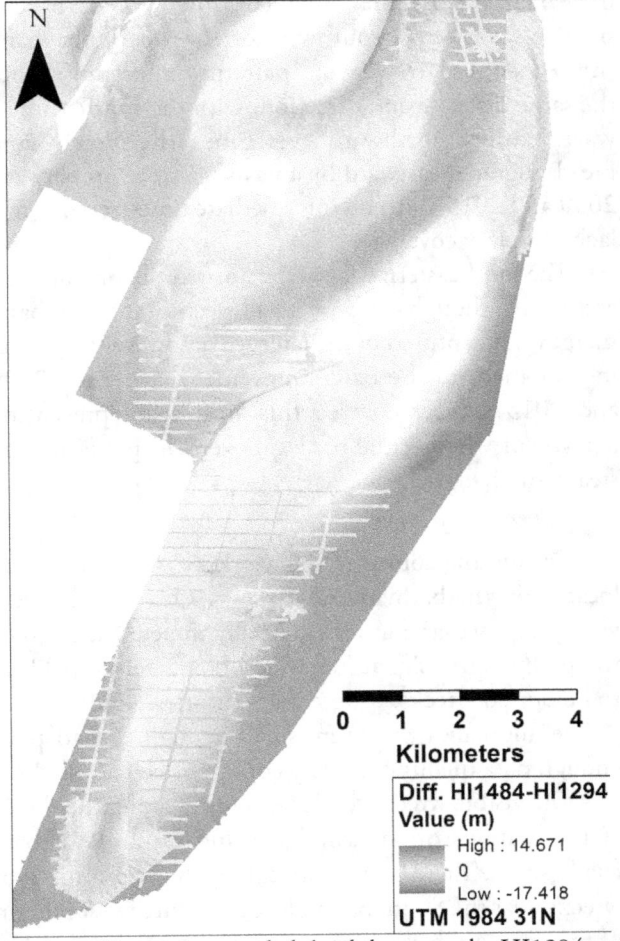

Figure 2. Change in recorded depth between the HI1294 and HI1484, South Goodwin sandbank, overlaid on the HI1294 bathymetry for reference (Map by author, 2017; data from UKHO 2017).

South Sand Head. On the northeast side of the southern bank, the sand migrated on average 50-100 m west between the 2009 and 2012 surveys, but has since begun to reverse direction, showing a small amount of eastward movement between 2012 and 2015.

The average water depth in some areas changed by as much as 10 m between 2009 and 2015, with around two thirds of this change occurring between 2009 and 2012. Over the surveyed period, the central ridge became less pronounced, and the line of the ridge changed from having a noticeable reverse S-curve to being approximately linear, though due to the wide spacing of the survey lines on the later surveys, the exact extent of the straightening was difficult to determine.

North Bank

The western arm of the North Goodwin bank (Figure 3) was one of the few areas completely surveyed at all three time-steps. It migrated westward by 100-200 m over the span of the surveys, with fairly steady movement across the observed time period. Several smaller sand waves southwest of the tip of the bank showed similar movement patterns, migrating about the same distance and direction, with the southernmost waves curling northward over time. The North Sand Head migrated eastward by an average of 60 m between 2009 and 2015, with no intermediate time-step due to a lack of survey coverage.

The southeastern edge of the northern bank migrated eastwards, though only a small section of the bank margin was captured in the later survey, preventing exact measurement of the bank's movement. Only the 2009 and 2015 surveys covered this area, again preventing analysis of whether the bank's movement patterns were steady or changing.

Wreck Analysis

During the course of this work, 68 anomalies were located on the bathymetric datasets. Of these, 29 were visibly exposed and at least partially intact. Nineteen of the bathymetric signatures were oblong mounds likely to be buried wrecks, 8 were debris scatters, and 12 were visible anomalies that were small enough or had poor enough data quality that they could not be classified.

The visible wrecks tended to cluster along the slopes at the margins of the sandbank and on areas of bare chalk shelf. There were particularly high numbers of wrecks near the South Sand Head, the northwest margin of the northern bank's western arm, the northern end of Kellett Gut, and the area of the eastern margin of the southern bank known as 'Calamity Corner'. Of these areas, the most visibly intact wrecks were found near

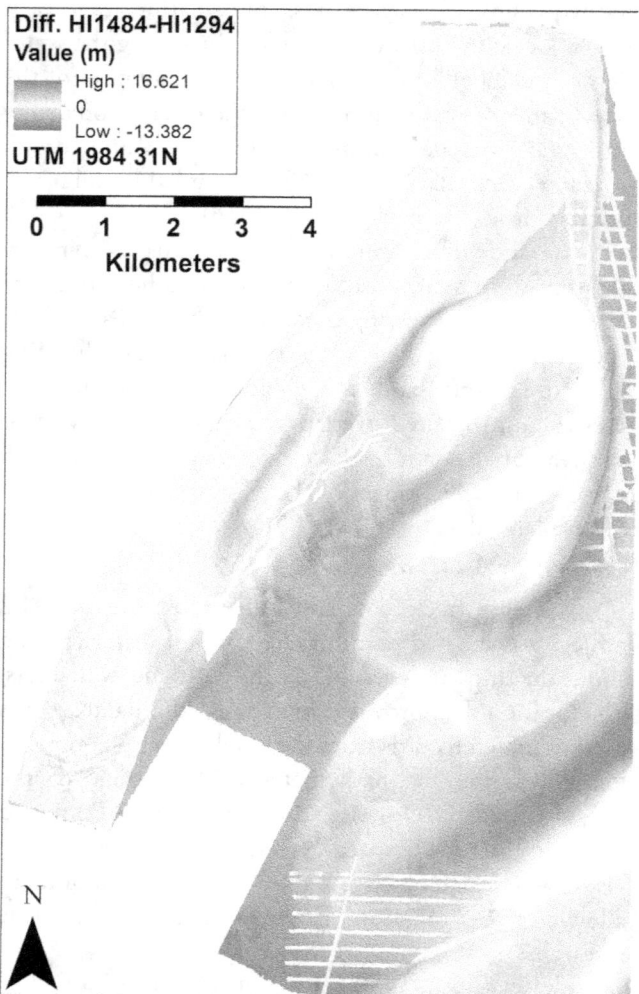

Figure 3. Change in recorded depth between the HI1294 and HI1484, North Goodwin sandbank, overlaid on the HI1294 bathymetry for reference (Map by author, 2017; data from UKHO 2017).

Calamity Corner.

Three of the anomalies located near Calamity Corner were discussed here (Figure 4). Two of these wrecks – labeled here as Wreck 46 and Wreck 48 – matched the locations of two wrecks listed in the AMAP2 database, named Luray Victory and the SS Ira, respectively. The last of these anomalies, Wreck 45, did not have a clearly associated AMAP2 entry.

Wreck 45

Wreck 45 was located on the eastern margin of the South Goodwin sandbank and appeared on both the HI1294 and HI11484 surveys. The wreck rested at the base of the eastern margin of the South Goodwin sandbank, near the bottom of the slope. The water depth as of the 2009 survey varied across the length of the wreck between 20 and 23 m, sloping downwards to the southeast. By the 2015 survey, the margin of

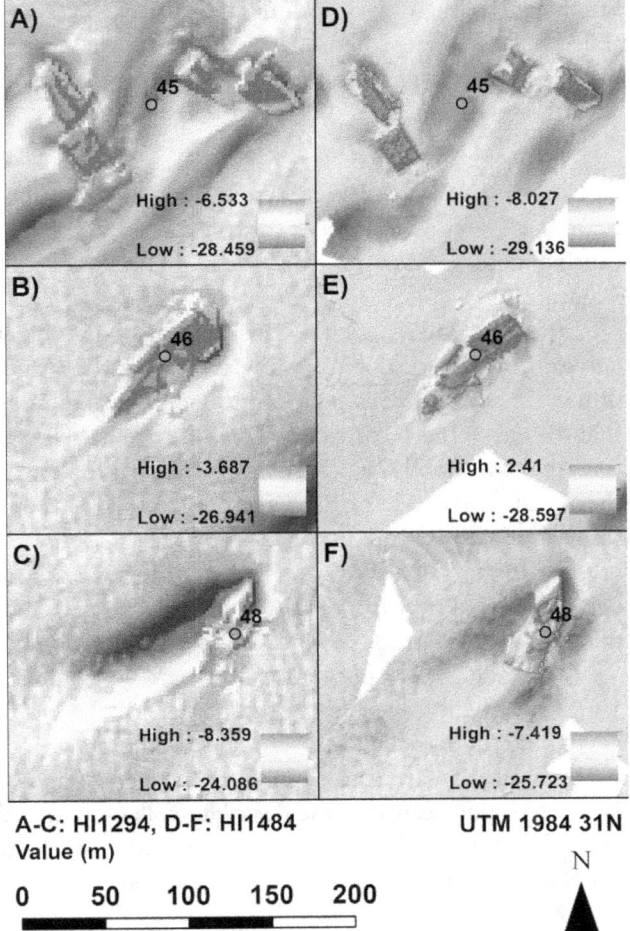

Figure 4. Bathymetric images of wrecks 45, 46, and 48, shown at two time-steps. A), B), and C) show HI1294, while D), E), and F) show HI1484 (Map by author, 2017; data from UKHO 2017).

the sandbank had migrated 600 m westward, leaving the wreck slightly deeper at 25 m with a flat seabed surrounding it.

The wreck was found in 4 pieces with lengths of 40 m, 30 m, 30 m, and 35 m, ordered from west to east, giving a total length of 135 m. The maximum width of the wreck was 17 m. The eastern half of the wreck rested 60 m northeast of the western half. Piecewise, the wreck appeared structurally intact. Both end pieces had tilted over to the northeast, the western one having settled at a diagonal, while the deck of the eastern one was close to vertical. The central pieces were approximately upright. The western end of the vessel narrowed significantly towards the lower half of the hull, while the eastern end narrowed gradually towards the keel.

The wreck had a maximum height of 16m above the seabed, which was achieved at the uppermost points of the diagonally tilted end pieces. Most of the wreck averaged 10 m high. There was a thin protrusion to the northeast of the westernmost piece of the wreck that was visible at all time-steps. It extended 14 m out from the wreck and was less than 4m wide. A similar protrusion was seen in the 2009 bathymetry extending 15 m out to the northeast from the wreck on the easternmost piece of the wreck, but it was not visible as of the most recent survey. As of the 2015 survey, a gap had appeared in the western end of the eastern midsection fragment, apparently having collapsed in on itself.

Wreck 46

Wreck 46 was found partway down the slope of the South Goodwin sandbank's eastern margin. It was located 135 m away from Wreck 45 at an azimuth of 294. The bathymetric signature was 87 m long and 21 m wide at its widest. The wreck had a pointed end to the southwest and a flat end to the northeast, and was mostly intact, though visibly degraded between the two surveys.

The wreck was covered by the HI1294 and HI1484 surveys. The water depth increased by 5 m between surveys as the sandbank retreated westward. In 2009, the water level ranged from 19 to 20 m across the wreck, sloping down to the southeast. In 2015, the water level was 24-25 m, but with the wreck lying at the base of the slope, the area to the southeast of the wreck flattened out rather than continuing to slope downwards as in the earlier survey.

As of the 2009 survey, the maximum height of the wreck was 14m above the seabed, increasing to 18 m by the 2015 survey. The north end of the wreck had two distinct levels, with the northwest side raised by 2 m in comparison with the southeast side, which averaged 11 m high as of 2009. The south end of the wreck measured 8-10 m off the seabed at that time-step. As of 2015, the northern end of the wreck measured 12 and 8 m high for the upper and lower portions respectively, while the southern end measured 8-9 m high with a maximum height of 12 m. There was a thin protrusion extending 16 m to the southeast of the vessel, which was visible on both the 2009 and 2015 surveys.

The southern end of the wreck was fairly intact in the 2009 survey, but appeared to be in the process of breaking apart, as there was visible deterioration of the wreck's structural integrity between the two surveys. A small section of the northern end's lower portion was no longer visible on the 2015 survey, and a section of the northwest side of the vessel appeared to be separating from the rest of the wreck. In addition, the southern tip of the vessel was blunter in the 2015 survey, appearing to have collapsed between the two time-steps.

Wreck 48

Wreck 48 was found on the upper slope of the eastern margin of the South Goodwin sandbank and lay exposed on the surface of the bank. The wreck had dimensions of 62 × 24 m and had one pointed end and one blunt end, with the pointed end oriented at an azimuth of 20°. At the time of the 2009 survey, the wreck rested on top of the sandbank, with the water depth a flat 16 m across the site. By 2015, the sandbank had migrated far enough west that the wreck was on the eastern slope of the bank margin, and the water depth varied across the site from 20 to 22 m, sloping down to the southeast.

In 2009, the maximum height of the wreck was 8 m above the seabed, which occurred on a raised section at the northern end of the wreck. As of the 2015 survey, maximum height had increased to 13 m due to the sandbank's retreat. Another raised section at the southern end of the wreck rose to a maximum of 11 m above the seabed, with the remainder of the wreck averaging 4-5 m high. These measurements did not change between surveys. There was a deep scour pit seen along the west side and northern end of the wreck in the 2009 survey, which migrated to surround the entire wreck in the 2015 survey. A section of the hull near the western corner of the vessel fell outward between 2009 and 2015.

Discussion

Sandbank Geomorphology

The South Goodwin sandbank showed a pattern of clockwise rotation across the time period studied here, suggesting that the Goodwin Sands was in a period of reversal, as described in Cloet's work (1954). The bank's movement was significantly slower between 2012 and 2015 than during the earlier time-step, suggesting that this reversal period may have been nearing its end, and some areas of the southern bank were already beginning to reverse their movement.

Most of the North Goodwin sandbank was not covered by the 2012 survey, so it was not possible to directly confirm whether it was undergoing similar rotational slowing to that seen on the South Goodwin bank. However, given the results of previous study of the geomorphology of the Goodwin Sands, it seems unlikely that the northern bank would move independently of the southern bank, since the two are part of the same hydrodynamic system.

The conclusions laid out in Cloet's work (1961) suggest that the western arm of the North Goodwin sandbank is likely to continue its current westward trajectory and eventually separate from the main bank to migrate shoreward, replacing Brake Bank as it merges with the shoreline.

Wreck Deterioration

The three wrecks considered here provide clear examples of the movement of the Goodwin Sands causing deterioration of shipwrecks due to increased exposure.

Wreck 45 maintained a consistent absolute height between the surveyed years while increasing the height difference between the wreck and the seabed, suggesting that the wreck was resting directly on the chalk shelf that underlies the Goodwin Sands. Several protrusions from the northeastern side of the wreck visible on the 2009 survey were absent or degraded as of the 2015 survey, suggesting that the less structural parts of the wreck were being degraded over time as the sandbank retreated and the wreck settled onto the chalk shelf.

The multi-level appearance of wreck 46 could be indicative of the two sides of the hull, with the wreck having tilted partially onto its side to the southeast. If this was the case, the sharp split between the two sections could mean that the deck had collapsed or was otherwise missing. In addition, the pointed bow of the vessel seen in the 2009 bathymetry appeared noticeably blunted in the 2015 survey, likely due to the collapse of the structure. A small scour pit appeared around the bow of the vessel in the later survey, which was not present in the earlier one, though it was unclear whether the increased scour caused the bow to collapse or if the collapse of the bow initiated the hydrodynamic change that created the scour pit.

Wreck 48 appeared to be collapsing in on itself as the sandbank shifted westward, though the structure of the northern end appeared to still be fairly intact as of the 2015 survey. Over the surveyed period, a section of the hull on the southern side of the vessel near the stern fell outwards, potentially exposing the interior of the ship to future deterioration. As a whole, the wreck appeared to be uncovering and deteriorating as the sediment around it receded.

Identification of the SS Ira

Historical Documentation

The AMAP2 database identified Wreck 46 as the Luray Victory, an American Victory VC2-S-AP3 class steamship with dimensions of 138.7 × 18.9 × 11.6 m, weighing 7618 gross tons. The vessel was equipped with a 127 mm stern gun, a bow-mounted 76 mm anti-aircraft gun, and eight 20 mm anti-aircraft cannons when it was stranded on the Goodwin Sands and broke in two on January 30, 1946. The wreck was noted as almost entirely buried as of a survey in 1997 (SeaZone Solutions 2011b; Wrecksite 2016).

Wreck 48 was identified as the SS Ira by the AMAP2 project. The SS Ira was a steel, Greek cargo ship with dimensions of 134.7 × 17.4 × 8.2 m and weighing 7176 tons. The AMAP2 database lists the vessel as an American ship, likely due to her origin as the Harry Percy, a Liberty EC2-S-C1 class steamship owned by the US Maritime Commission War Shipping Administration. Notable features of the vessel class included a pilothouse amidships and cargo winches midway between the pilothouse and the bow and stern of the ship. The SS Ira was additionally outfitted with a stern-mounted 102mm deck gun (SeaZone Solutions 2011b; Wrecksite 2016).

The SS Ira was reported to have run aground on the Goodwin Sands and broken in two on 7 March, 1947. The coxswain of the Walmer lifeboat, which was launched to rescue the vessel and its crew, reported witnessing an explosion that split the ship down the middle. Accounts of the sinking noted that the ship sunk midway between two sections of the Luray Victory, which had sunk just over a year prior (Larn and Larn 1995b). The wreck was listed as "dead (not found)" by the Wrecksite (2016) database, and the AMAP2 database labeled the data entry as "Ira (possibly)", suggesting that previous attempts at identification had not provided a definitive identification.

Data Comparison

The wreck labeled by the AMAP project as the Luray Victory was about 80 m in length, which falls significantly short of the historically documented vessel length 138.7 m. However, assuming the wreck identified as the Ira by the AMAP2 project was actually the other half of the Luray Victory wreck, the combined length of the two pieces would add to 140 m, which is within reasonable error of the Luray Victory's historically recorded vessel length, and the beam measurement was similarly accurate. The shape of the two anomalies also supported this idea, as both had abrupt blunt ends, which do not match historical descriptions of either ship but would make sense if the two wrecks were originally one vessel. Historical accounts of the SS Ira's sinking also corroborated this theory, describing the location of the Ira's sinking to be between the two halves of the Luray Victory, implying that the latter was in two distinct pieces far enough apart from each other that such a description would be reasonable.

The dimension measurements for Wreck 45 matched closely to those of the SS Ira, and the shape of the wreck bore several similarities to schematics of the Liberty EC2-S-C1 class, namely the location and size of the pilothouse and the existence of the two northeastern protrusions, which could be the remains of cargo winches. The pieces of the wreck had a combined length of 135 m, which fit closely with the 134.7 m length listed in the AMAP2 database for the SS Ira. Between the accurate length measurement and descriptions of the wrecking suggesting that the ship was violently split in half by a boiler explosion, it seemed reasonably likely that Wreck 45 was in fact the SS Ira.

Significance and Recommendations

Both the Luray Victory and the SS Ira were lost to mundane causes during routine non-wartime shipping activities, and neither vessel was unique, as both were from classes of ships that were mass-produced during WWII. However, both vessel classes have very few surviving examples, which makes any remaining ones more important than they might be otherwise. In addition, both vessels were lost in the Calamity Corner area during the period when it earned the moniker, and both wrecks were significant events in the history of the Deal coast lifeboats.

Both wrecks showed deterioration between 2009 and 2015, and given that the current movement of the sandbank will uncover them further, it is likely that their states of preservation will continue to worsen. Given the imminent danger to the wrecks, further monitoring to check for deterioration is highly recommended, and if any site work is to be done to record the wrecks, it should be done sooner rather than later. It would also likely prove useful to analyze the original Generic Sensor Format (GSF) data from the relevant surveys in order to assess finer details of the wrecks not visible on the binned data, both for the purpose of verifying the identifications proposed here and for more accurate analysis of the wrecks' deterioration.

Conclusion

This project was undertaken with the goal of better understanding the site dynamics affecting the wrecks on the Goodwin Sands in the hopes of using this knowledge to better monitor and protect them. Understanding how the sandbanks interact with shipwrecks, both on a local and regional scale, will allow archaeologists to make better predictions as to which wrecks might soon be buried or destroyed and suggest appropriate recommendations for future archaeological study. Wrecks that are buried will likely be preserved, but will be lost to study unless they resurface, while wrecks that become exposed are susceptible to increased degradation as they are subjected to the strong tidal forces that affect the Goodwin Sands.

Of the wrecks both listed in the AMAP2 database and visible on the analyzed bathymetric surveys, few had sufficient historical detail to attempt to confirm the identity of the wreck. Of the identifiable wrecks, the majority appeared to be correctly labeled in the AMAP2 database. However, the cluster of wrecks consisting of The SS Ira and the two halves of the Luray Victory were likely misidentified, and an alternate interpretation was presented here that alleviated several discrepancies between previous identifications and evidence from recent bathymetry data.

One potential direction for future work would be to acquire and examine the raw GSF data files for the surveys analyzed here. With GSF point cloud data rather than meter-scale binned rasters, a much more detailed examination of the wrecks would be possible. This could allow for more confident identification of the located wrecks, and would also provide more detailed data for analyzing and monitoring changes to both the sandbank and the wrecks themselves. Further research into the geomorphology of the Goodwin Sands via computer modeling and analysis of bathymetric surveys of the area would also be useful to provide a better understanding of sandbank's movement patterns. Such analysis could assist in predicting where and when known, buried wrecks might become unburied, which would be of immense use for monitoring known wrecks in the area.

This project has advanced the effort to document and protect the wrecks of the Goodwin Sands by synthesizing recent bathymetric surveys with previously compiled wreck databases to assess the continually changing state of the sandbank and the wrecks buried there. It has laid the groundwork for future research into both geomorphological and wreck record patterns as well as furthered the state of knowledge about specific known wrecks in the area.

The Goodwin Sands has great potential for future archaeological investigation. The constant shifting of the sandbank presents both an opportunity and a challenge by both protecting the wrecks buried within the bank and making archaeological documentation and monitoring difficult. This project was but one small part of the continuing effort to protect and preserve the wrecks buried beneath the Goodwin Sands.

Acknowledgments

I would first like to thank my dissertation advisor, Fraser Sturt, for all of his support and guidance throughout this project. I am grateful to the Santander Universities scholarships program for their financial support of this research. I appreciate the encouragement my friends and family have provided throughout this project and my degree program as a whole. Lastly, I am immensely grateful to my late grandfather, Harold W. Krueger, for providing me with the personal funding that allowed me to complete this work. You are dearly missed.

References

Bates, Richard, Martin Dean, Mark Lawrence, Philip Robertson, Fernando Tempera and Sarah Laird
2007 Innovative approaches to Rapid Archaeological Site Surveying and Evaluation (RASSE). Final report, Project no. 3837.

Carrizales, Adam
2010 Development and refinement of regional sediment mobility models: Implications for coastal evolution, preservation of archaeological potential, and commercial development. AMAP2 Project Report, Project no. 5653. English Heritage.

Cloet, R. L.
1954 Hydrographic Analysis of the Goodwin Sands and the Brake Bank. The Geographical Journal 120(2):203-215.

Cloet, R. L.
1961 Development of the Brake Bank. The Geographical Journal 127(3):335-339.

Dix, Justin, Pierre Cazenave, David Lambkin, Tim Rangecroft, Chris Pater and Ian Oxley
2008 Sedimentation-Erosion Modelling as a tool for Underwater Cultural Heritage Management. In: MACHU Final Report Nr. 3. European Union Culture 2000 Programme, Amersfoort, Netherlands, pp.48-53.

Krueger, Elizabeth
2016 The Goodwin Sands: Patterns of Burial and Updating the Wreck Record. Master's thesis, Archaeology Department, University of Southampton, Southampton, UK.

Larn, Richard, and Bridget Larn
1995a Shipwreck index of the British Isles: Vol. 2. Lloyd's Register of Shipping, London.

Larn, Richard, and Bridget Larn
1995b Shipwrecks of the Goodwin Sands. Meresborough, Rainham.

REDKNAP, MARK, AND MIKE FLEMING
1985   The Goodwins archaeological survey: Towards a regional marine site register in Britain. World Archaeology, 16(3):312-328.

MACHU PROJECT TEAM
2008a   MACHU Report Nr. 1. European Union Culture 2000 Programme, Amersfoort, Netherlands.

MACHU PROJECT TEAM
2008b   MACHU Final Report Nr. 3. European Union Culture 2000 Programme, Amersfoort, Netherlands.

SEAZONE SOLUTIONS
2011   AMAP2 – Characterising the potential for Wrecks: Year 1 Update. Project 5653, English Heritage.

SEAZONE SOLUTIONS
2011   AMAP2 – Characterising the potential for Wrecks: Final Report. Project 5653, English Heritage.

UNITED KINGDOM HYDROGRAPHIC OFFICE
2016   UKHO INSPIRE Portal & Bathymetry DAC, United Kingdom Hydrographic Office. http://aws2.caris.com/ukho/mapViewer/map.action. Accessed 7 March 2017.

WRECKSITE
2017   Wrecksite. http://www.Wrecksite. Accessed 7 March 2017.

Elizabeth Krueger
251 Webster Street, East Boston,
    Massachusetts, 02128
+1-857-928-4986
ekrueger@alum.mit.edu

Justin Dix
+44-023-8059-3057
j.k.dix@soton.ac.uk

The Pirates of the Pamlico: A Maritime Cultural Landscape Investigation of the Pirates of Colonial North Carolina and Their Place in the State's Cultural Memory

Allyson Ropp

During the colonial period, North Carolina was a backwater of the British Empire. The landscape provided ample opportunities for pirates to establish operational bases. This study shows that the colony was used as a pirate haven, due to geographical, socio-economic, and political influences. Through the lens of the maritime cultural landscape, various remains are identified for the pirate bases. Overlaid maps of pirate locations and colonial settlements suggest varying degrees of pirate-colonial interactions. Further, investigations of the contemporary urban landscapes reflect the collective memory of piracy manifested in place and street names. Between 1694 and 1724, pirates frequented Colonial North Carolina for different reasons. Many sought the colony as a place for a base of operations for their actions as pirates, others viewed it as a quick hideaway to avoid capture by the Royal Navy, and still others saw it as a place to begin a new life away from piracy. While in the colony, many of the pirates interacted with the colonists they encountered in North Carolina, and these interactions were essential to the success or failure of their operations. Pirates, or those who commit criminal violence upon another ship from their own vessel, often required interaction with others to exchange goods or acquire protection and human company. These men traded with the colonists, took lovers amongst them, attempted to hide amongst them, and integrated into their society. These various interactions manifested into physical and cognitive archaeological remains as well as the cultural memory of today's North Carolinians. There are a limited number of tangible remains reflecting pirate presence in the state, yet the vast array of intangible remains elucidates their place in the colony. The state's memory of piracy results from the combination of historical and archaeological records. Although piracy in North Carolina often refers to one man, Edward "Blackbeard" Teach, this paper explores other pirates that came, including Henry Avery and Charles Vane. Through examining these other well-known pirates, this study links the historical and archaeological evidence of the legacy of piracy with the memory of current North Carolinians.

Project Overview

This project aimed to explore the pirate-colonist relationship in Colonial North Carolina and its manifestation in the archaeological record as well as its role in creating the current state of pirate memory among today's North Carolinians. The research questions were:

(1) how and to what extent did pirates interact and engage with the colonists in Colonial North Carolina?

(2) what factors made certain colonial towns and geographic areas attractive as pirate havens?

(3) what are the types and volume of landscape signatures that reveal the cultural memory of piracy in North Carolina today?

Although pirates could be colonists and colonists could be pirates, for the purposes of the study they are separate entities. This project offers tangible and intangible evidence to illuminate North Carolina attachments to the pirate as a symbol of their history using maritime cultural landscape and cultural memory theory.

The maritime cultural landscape concept was developed by Christer Westerdahl in the early 1990s. The maritime cultural landscape is defined as "[signifying] human utilization (economy) of maritime space by boat: settlement, fishing, hunting, shipping, and its attendant subcultures, such as pilotage, lighthouse and seamark maintenance" (Westerdahl 1992:5). The idea combined "physical aspects of landscape and seascape to analyze the culture of maritime peoples within a spatial context while retaining the recursive culture-nature relationship of landscape study" (Ford 2012:4). A large portion of the maritime cultural landscape approach relies on the study of place names or toponyms. Researchers attempt to identify the origins and meanings of place names, which have "some specific reference either to a feature of the place, or to an event that occurred thereabout, or to a person or thing associated with the place" (Ehret 1976:15). Cultural memory, first developed by Jan Assman in the 1980s, signifies a comprehension of cultural reflections of certain events and people and the institutionalization of the memory. It focuses on a fixed point or moment in time, known as "figures of memory." The memory of these figures requires institutionalization through items such as monuments or texts to cement their place in people's memory. These connections to the figures bond the memory of individuals and the social and cultural context that surrounds them (Assmann and Czaplicka 1995:129; Erll 2008:4).

To conduct this investigation, a search area was established for the area east of NC-17. A database was compiled of all the pirate-related places in this area which include their exact locational information. The points from this database were imported into ArcMap to project on digital maps. Maps were created focusing on typological, geographical, and pirate connectivity divisions. These maps were analyzed independently for their distribution patterns and overlaid with historical maps to see their relation to historical pirate locations.

Historical Background

Colonial North Carolina had its beginnings in the sixteenth century with the arrival of Spanish, French and English explorers (Lawson 1709:68; McCrady 1901:41, 43, 47-48). After the Roanoke expeditions failed, colonists did not arrive on North Carolinian shores until 1663 when King Charles II signed a charter to eight men, the Lords Proprietors. This charter gave them all the land between the 30th and 36th degree parallel (Charles II King of England 1663:20-33; 1665:112). By 1700, this large expanse of land had been divided into a northern section and a southern section, each ruled by separate governors appointed by the Lords Proprietors (Lords Proprietors 1698:852-858; Lords Proprietors 1710:749-750; Doyle 1882:443).

The colonial split reflected the rise of the rice economy in the southern portion, which took the interest of the Lords Proprietors. The northern half did not prosper as well for many reasons. Environmentally, the lack of deep accessible ports and the presence of shoals both in the sounds and ocean kept colonists and merchants from traversing to and around the colony. These features limited the economic potential of the colony forcing the colonists to engage in illegal and illicit activities to survive thus creating a welcoming environment for pirates. The Lords Proprietors took no interest in a colony that could not prosper economically, which allowed the officials in the northern segment of the colony to do as they chose. The colonists were a geographically widespread community and a rough sort of people that were uncontrollable and accepting of an illegal system for survival. This socio-economic dynamic created the atmosphere perfect for pirates to come and establish a pirate haven as many officials throughout the British Empire feared was happening. (Lawson 1709:68-69, 86-95; Camp 1963:1-3, 6-11; Butler 2007:6-11; McIlvenna 2009:13-14, 20; Molter 2014:9, 77)

Pirates and Colonists

In this environment, pirates arrived and thrived in the backwater colony. Through historical resources, eight well-known pirates have been identified—Henry Avery, John Redfield, Edward "Blackbeard" Teach, Stede Bonnet, Charles Vane, Richard Worley, George Lowther, and William Fly. Five of the eight pirates—Avery, Redfield, Bonnet, Worley and Lowther—focused their activity on the Cape Fear region. There, these pirates set up camp and attempted to avoid capture. One, William Fly, never landed in the colony but used the shoals off Cape Hatteras to take a prize, *John & Hannah*. The remaining three—Teach, Bonnet, and Vane—focused their efforts on the middle section of the colony. Like the Cape Fear pirates, these men created encampments for their themselves and their crew and sought to avoid capture (Bridgewater et al. 1696:475; Dann 1696; Cowse 1718:2-3; Rogers 1718; Governor and Council of South Carolina 1781a, 1718b; Spotswood 1719b; 1719c; Virginia Council 1719; North Carolina Council 1719; Johnson 1724: 51, 54, 74-78, 93, 96-97, 145, 343-344, 347-349, 361-362; Edwards 1726:7, 13; Midwinter 1732:8, 12, 24, 29-32, 43, 86-87).

While these activities were taking place, colonists already resided in the colony. Before 1705, there were no incorporated settlements. Colonists tried to establish settlements along the Cape Fear River and lower coastlines, but these were abandoned in 1667 as disaster kept striking those settlements (Modyford and Colleton 1663:39-42; Lee 1965:36-40). The presence of the natives and the ill-fated initial settlers tainted the image of the area. No further settlement was attempted at Cape Fear until the 1720s. A few settlers remained in the area, but they had to engage with the pirates and other smugglers that passed through. At the same time, the area around the Albemarle Sound was developing. Freed indentured servants and run-away slaves inhabited the area. They attempted to conduct business with Bermuda and New England traders, yet many of these traders were unable to enter the colony due to the dangerously shallow inlets of the barrier islands. This led to many of the colonists, even those that resided in Edenton to trade with pirates and smugglers (Lawson 1709:70; McIlvenna 2009:22-23, 43; Barth 2010:8). The first incorporated town in the northern colony was Bath in 1705. Throughout the area, colonists had to contend with a large native population that inhabited the area (Lawson 1709:173-175; Paul 1965:12-19;

McIlvenna 2009:17). The colonists, whether they lived in these towns or elsewhere, were a poor people. They did not have access to the same goods and services as others throughout the colony. Further, the Tuscarora Wars ravaged the entire colony during the 1710s and left the colonists even poorer than when they first settled in the area (Pollock 1712:873; la Vere 2013:17). These circumstances led many of the colonists to willingly accept pirates into their lives.

Discussion of Results

Pirates and colonists inhabited similar areas in the colony. Pirates sought out areas with easy access to the trade routes, fresh water, food sources, and seclusion. Similarly, colonists wanted access to the same trade routes, fresh water sources, and food. Although colonists did not need places to hide from naval forces, many wished to live in solitude. These reasons clearly show that these two desperate people sought similar places to make a life.

When examining the data seen in Table 1, the areas of interaction between pirates and colonists can be assessed. There is some overlap where pirates and colonists would have interacted. These interactions include recreation, such as engaging with colonists in town through drinking and merriment; labor, such as careening vessels, pillaging, and establishing a new life; criminal penalties, like incarceration and hanging; family and marriage; including marrying women in the area and starting a family; business transactions, including trading goods; and burial in the North Carolina area. Many of the pirates used the Cape Fear River, yet the settlements there were pretty much abandoned by the 1690s (Lee 1965:52). The interactions that occurred with the limited colonists in the area were only trading (business transactions) and pillaging (labor). Many the interactions occurred in the middle region of the colony. These interactions ranged from business transactions with local officials, labor through pillaging, recreation and drinking, family and marriage, and burial. Teach

	Henry Every	**John Redfield**	**Edward Teach**	**Stede Bonnet**	**Charles Vane**	**Richard Worley**	**George Lowther**	**William Fly**
Recreation	None	None	Spent leisure time in Bath and on Ocracoke Island in 1718	None	Spent time with Teach on Ocracoke Island for a few days in Oct 1718	None	Likely had leisure time while living in the Cape Fear region during his winter there in 1722	None
Religion	None	None	None	None	None	None	None	None
Labor	His crew that traveled to the Carolinas became part of the Cape Fear workforce in 1696	Started a life in the Cape Fear region while protecting Kidd's treasure in 1701	Pillaged and raided along the intercoastal waterways in 1718	Careened his vessel in the Cape Fear region in September 1718 and raided along the coastline	None	Careened his vessel in the Cape Fear region in late 1718	Hunt and fished for subsistence during the winter of 1722 in the Cape Fear region	Pillaged and raided along the Cape Hatteras coastline in 1724
Family & Marriage	None	Lived with his wife near Money Island near present-day Wilmington in 1701	Married Mary Ormond in Bath and relationships with other women throughout the area	None	None	None	None	None
Business Transactions	None	None	Traded with NC officials in Bath after taking ships and their items	None	None	None	None	None
Criminal Penalties	None	None	Attempted capture by Virgina officals in November 1718 at Ocracoke Island. Teach was killed in battle	Captured in the Cape Fear region by South Carolina officals, under the command of William Rhett in September 1718	None	Escaped capture by South Carolina officals in the Cape Fear region in 1718	None	Convicted of his crimes off Cape Hatteras
Burial	None	None	Body was thrown over board near Ocracoke Island after battle in November 1718	None	None	None	None	None

Table 1. Pirates of North Carolina and their interactions with colonists based on seven different types of interaction. From this table, trends of interaction are seen by the frequency pirates interacted with colonists and where these locations were taking place (Author 2017; Dann 1696, Cowse 1718, Johnson 1724, Edwards 1726, Midwinter 1732, Camp 1963; Paul 1965, Butler 2007).

and Bonnet both visited Bath to receive the King's Pardon, traded with these various colonists, and Teach even lived among them for a time marrying Mary Ormond (Spotswood 1719a; 1719c; North Carolina Council 1719; Johnson 1724:75, 77, 85-86, 93).

Maritime Cultural Landscape and Cultural Memory

There is much evidence both tangible and intangible for the pirate landscape in Colonial North Carolina. Of the two, the tangible evidence is the more difficult to find. The most prominent feature is the Beaufort Inlet Wreck, believed to be the wreck of Teach's flagship, *Queen Anne's Revenge*. Although there are still those who do not believe the ship is Teach's (Rodgers et al 2005), the consensus reflects that it is not only his flagship but also evidence of piracy in the colony (Miller et al. 2005; Moore 2005; Lusardi 2006:217-218; Wilde-Ramsing 2006:191-195; Wilde-Ramsing and Ewen 2012). Further evidence may have been found in Bath with a tar kettle located near where Teach supposedly lived in Bath (McLaughlin 2013:11-12). The rest of the tangible evidence lies in the potential for artifacts in areas of high pirate activity, such as the Cape Fear and Ocracoke, and the remains of another ship, named *Adventure*, in Beaufort Inlet (Overfield 2002).

The intangible or cognitive remains are much more prominent. First, the presence of high traffic trade routes off the North Carolina coastline provides ample opportunities for pirates to take prizes and make their living. Second, the natural topography aided in this quest to capture prizes, as well as to easily hide from the encroaching threats to their survival. Finally, the presence of pirates in certain areas inspired immediate adoption of pirate place names. The most immediate was Teaches Hole near the southern end of Ocracoke Island marking the location of his death in November 1718. This place was first noted by this name on the 1733 Moseley Map. Others include references to Stede Bonnet along the Cape Fear River, like Bonnet's Creek (Moseley 1733; Weslager 1954:47; Galvin 1991:114; Ulanski 2008:181; Hornsby 2012:29-30; Hanna 2016:4).

As mentioned earlier, the landscape evidence and cultural memory evidence is very similar. The evidence included for pirate cultural memory in North Carolina came from place names (i.e. businesses, restaurants, beach houses, and road names), festivals, mascots, archaeological sites, museums, historical markers, and geographical features. Overall, 229 different places of institutionalized pirate memory were identified (Figure

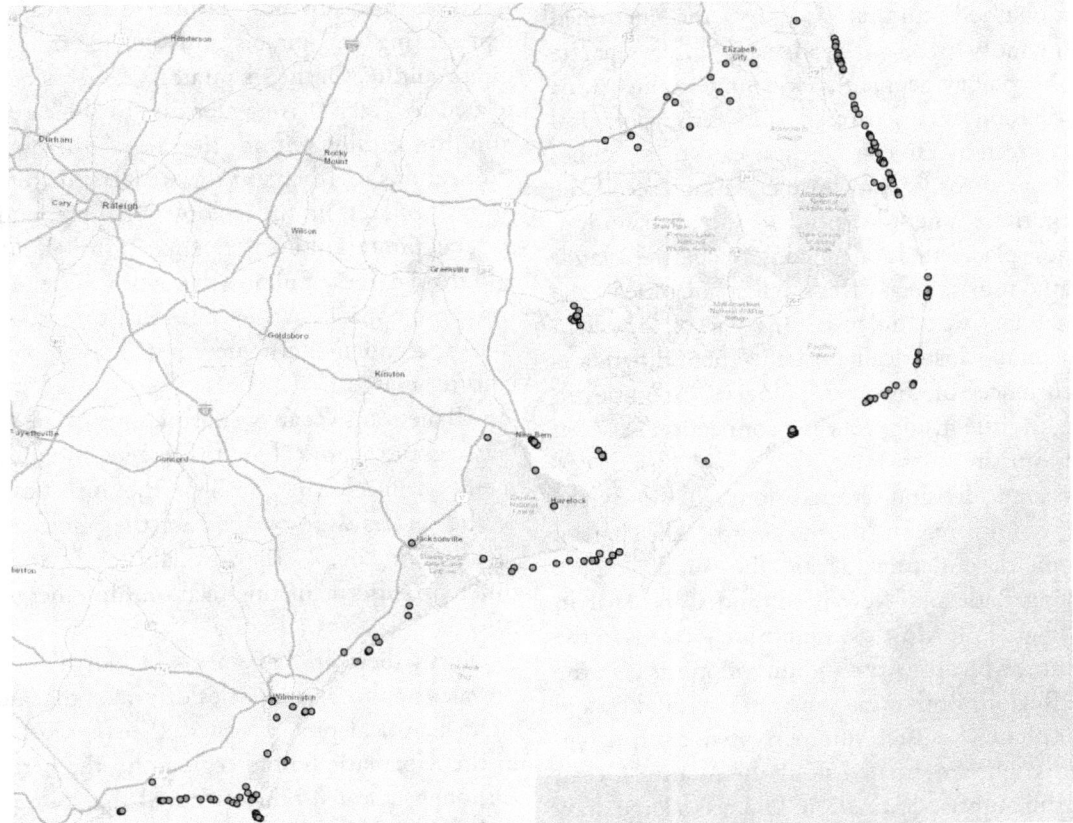

Figure 1. Map showing all the locations of pirate cultural memory throughout the search area (Author 2016).

	Albemarle	Barrier Islands	Middle Region	Cape Fear
Archaeological Sites	0	0	1	0
Business Names	1	20	8	9
Festivals	1	2	3	3
Historic Sites/Markers	3	1	5	3
House Names	13	45	4	17
Museums	0	1	2	2
Physical Feature	1	3	4	4
Restaurant Name	4	5	4	0
Road Name	7	8	16	25
School Mascot	1	0	2	3

Table 2. The frequency of the types of cultural memory and their location in the four geographic areas (Author 2016).

1). Almost all the points are situated on the coastline. These are places of both pirate history and high beach tourist traffic. Those that are found further inland are in areas with a strong connection to noted pirate history.

Discussion of Results

To understand the importance of the different pieces of institutionalized cultural memory, the identified pieces of memory were analyzed using three separate categories—typology, geography, and pirate connectivity. The first division was separated into ten typological categories, as seen in Table 2. Of these categories, names of beach houses, roads, and businesses far exceed the other categories. When looking at the distribution, many of these places are located along the barrier islands in high traffic tourist areas. The smaller categories—the historical markers, sites, and museums—are all located in places that pirates historically visited. These differences in the occurrences of various typological categories in locations with little history reflect a connection between piracy and tourism.

The second division created four divisions: the Albemarle Sound region in the north; the barrier islands along the Atlantic Ocean; the middle region encompassing Bath and New Bern; and Cape Fear in the south (Figure 2). Most the points are located on the barrier islands, while the least amount of points is in the Albemarle Region. Both areas were rarely visited by any of the eight pirates, yet their numbers are not surprising. The barrier islands are situated along the Atlantic Ocean and are a prime tourist destination. Piracy is a large draw for tourists, especially beach tourism in such places as the Outer Banks. The Albemarle region, on the other hand, does not have the same tourist appeal and therefore there is a smaller presence of pirate connected localities. The distribution frequencies in the Albemarle and barrier islands reflect a further connection between piracy and tourism regardless of the historical connections to piracy.

The third division created seven categories—six representing real pirates and one referring to general pirate culture. Of the six pirates, the frequency of locales related to Teach was greater due to the ease in placing him historically within the area. The multitude of connections to Teach's history reflects the remembrance of real pirates in the colony. The preponderance of general pirate culture references throughout the state and three names of pirates that never came to the colony show the opposite, an overall tourist draw of pirates in the state and modern predominance of piracy in our culture at large.

To help answer an overall question of the relationship between the historical pirate presence and pirate cultural memory in North Carolina, the historical locations of the pirates were overlaid on the pirate connectivity distribution map. The overlaid map shows several different patterns of this relationship emerging (Figure 3).

First, there are large areas in North Carolina with prevalent cultural memories of piracy that none of the eight historical pirates visited. This is most prominent in the Albemarle Sound region and the barrier islands. Although colonial officials noted that pirates sailed in and out of these inlets and interacted with the colonists

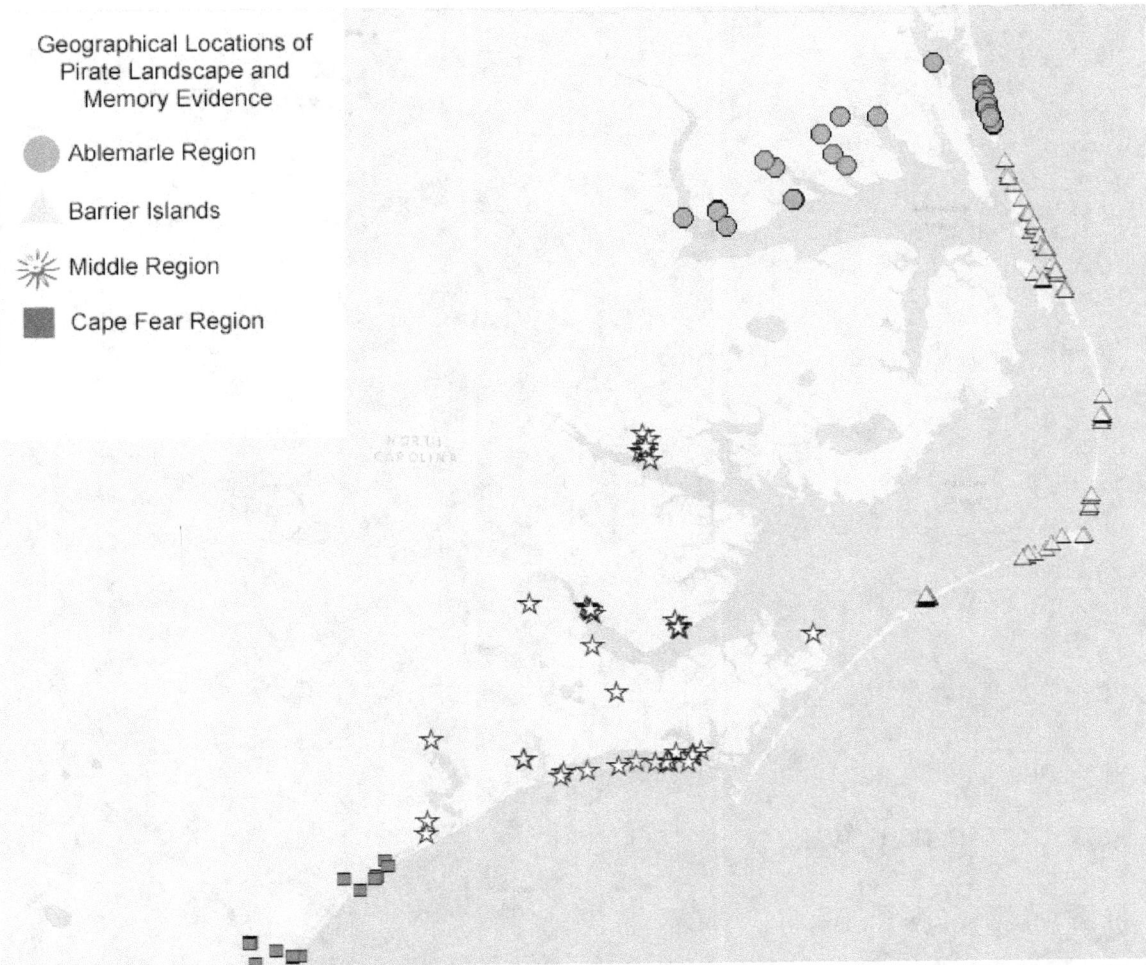

Figure 2. Map showing the memory locations divided by geographical regions. The lines drawn on the map separate the different regions: Albemarle at the top; barrier islands to the right; middle in the middle; and Cape Fear at the bottom (Author 2017).

in that region, these pirates were not named in the records (Randolph 1696:467). Second, not all the eight pirates had memory evidence. Further, a clear majority of the evidence referred to general pirate culture, such as The Buccaneer Motel and Mutiny Bay Mini Golf in Nags Head. This ties in with the third trend showing much of the public memory was created or named within the last century, well after the pirates inhabited the shores. These first three trends show the effectiveness of using pirate naming for touristic purposes and the influence of popular cultural romanticizing the Golden Age of Piracy.

The fourth and final trend is clearer with the removal of the general pirate connections. Once removed, the data show there are clear connections between pirate histories and institutionalized memory. The two pirates that provide the most prominent connections between history and memory are Edward Teach and Stede Bonnet. Figure 4 shows numerous elements of cultural memory that refer to Teach fall within the historical Teach's sphere of influence. These patterns in the data display the use of history and the landscape pirates used in colonial times to create an institutionalized memory. It also demonstrates that pirate histories outside of the areas they visited are to attract tourists.

Conclusion

The first research question explored the interaction between the pirates and the colonists in Colonial North Carolina. When looking at these seven types of interactions, the most frequent interactions focused on political engagements and business transactions, as pirates sought protection from the colonial officials and chances to trade the stolen goods for necessary supplies. Another large point of interaction was the incarceration of pirates, which occurred at the hands of colonists outside of Colonial North Carolina. Some pirates interacted more than others. Teach was the most involved pirate in pirate-colonial interactions, while others like Fly, who stayed out on the islands likely never

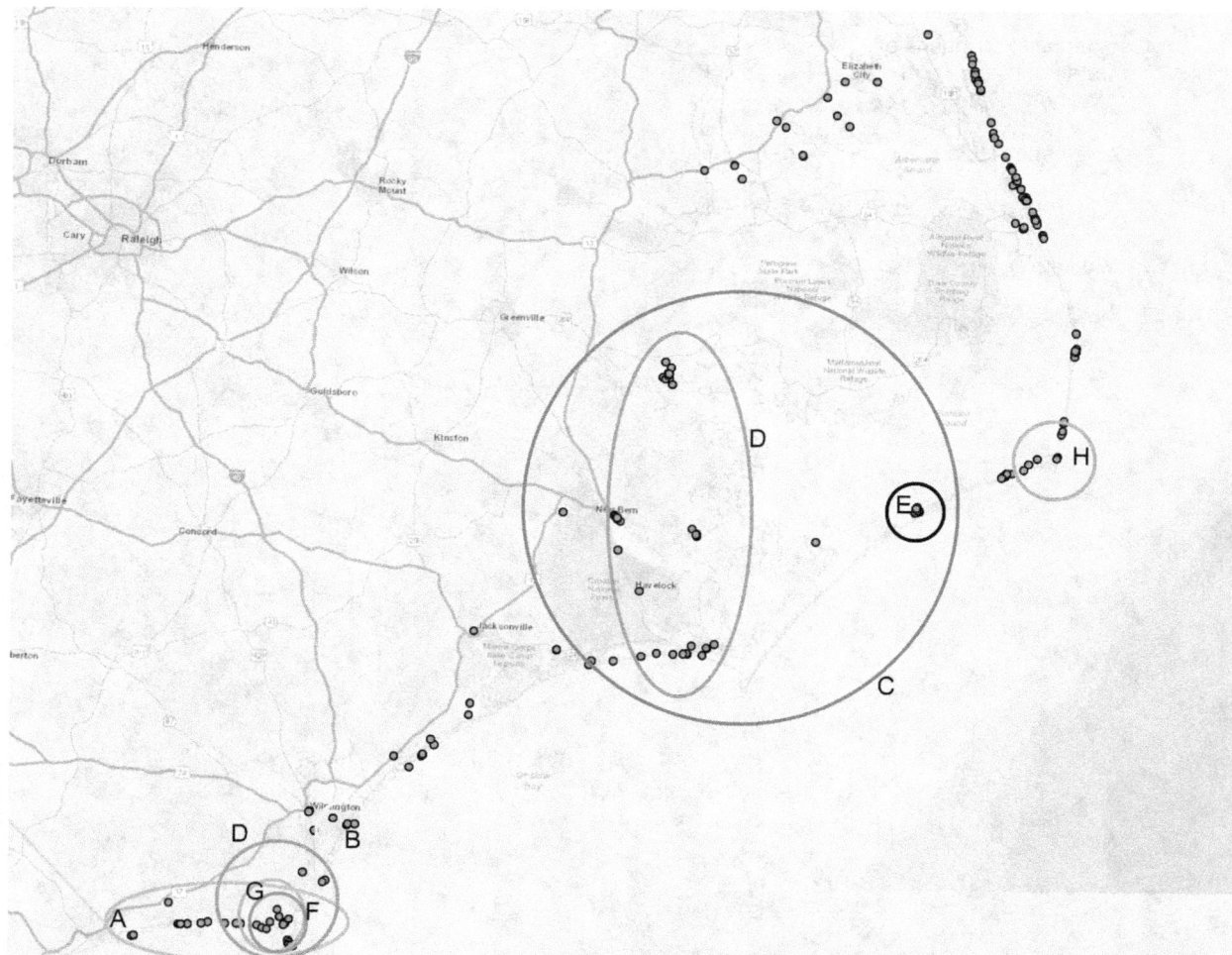

Figure 3. Map showing the overlaid locations of the pirate cultural memory with the historic pirate locations. The pirate cultural memory is defined by the legend in the map. The circles representing the spheres of pirate influence based on historical records are as follows: A-Henry Avery; B-John Redfield; C-Edward Teach; D-Stede Bonnet; E-Charles Vane; F-Richard Worley; G-George Lowther; H-William Fly (Author 2016; data from Dann 1696, Cowse 1718, Johnson 1724, Edwards 1726, Midwinter 1732, Camp 1963; Paul 1965, Butler 2007).

saw a colonist.

The second research question examined the creation of a pirate haven in Colonial North Carolina. Officials throughout the British Empire realized it was happening over a thirty-year period, as the pirate presence slowly increased in the colony peaking with the arrival of Teach in 1718. Colonial North Carolina had the natural, economic, political, and social features necessary for piracy to survive. The dangerous environment kept most people out. The economy suffered because colonists were unable to trade on the prominent Atlantic seaboard trade routes. The Lords Proprietors were indifferent to what their officials were doing in North Carolina allowing a rebellious population to rise. Demographically, the people were spread out and open to illegal activities. These features created a welcoming environment for pirates.

In answering the final question concerning maritime cultural landscape, cultural memory evidence, and their relationship with one another, maritime cultural landscape and cultural memory evidence are linked and can be the same. Many features of the colonial pirate landscape are ingrained in public memory. There are physical remains of their presence, along with the potential to find further remains. These remains still captivate today's North Carolinians and can help explain the predominance of pirate related institutionalized memory throughout the state. Much of that memory is for touristic purposes, but some are also tied to the deep pirate history from Colonial North Carolina.

Through this project, the pirate haven that existed during the Proprietary era of North Carolina's history and the various types of interactions that took place are shown. Further understanding of the pirate history of

North Carolina is provided by the historical sources, the limited physical remains, and the numerous intangible remains present. We can participate in remembering and recognizing pirate memory that exists across the coastline, as both a memorial to the pirate heyday and the rise of piracy in popular culture to further tourism.

Acknowledgments

I would like to express my deepest gratitude to East Carolina University's Program in Maritime Studies; my thesis advisor, Lynn Harris, for her endless support and direction; my committee, Nathan Richards, Christopher Oakley, and Paul Fontenoy, for all their continuous guidance; and the East Carolina University's Coastal Maritime Council for their funding to complete this project.

References

ASSMANN, JAN AND JOHN CZAPLICKA
1995 Collective Memory and Cultural Identity. New German Critique 65:125-133.

BARTH, JONATHAN EDWARD
2010 "The Sinke of America:" Society in the Albemarle Borderlands of North Carolina, 1663-1729. The North Carolina Historical Review 87(1):1-27.

BRIDGEWATER, JOHN, PHILIP MEADOWS, WILLIAM BLATHWAYTE, JONATHAN POLLEXFEN, AND ABRAHAM HILL
1696 Letter of the Council of Trade to the Lords Proprietors of Carolina. In The Colonial Records of North Carolina, Vol. I, 1662-1712, William L. Saunders, editor, pp 475-476. P.M. Hale, Raleigh, North Carolina.

BUTLER, LINDLEY S.
2007 Proprietary North Carolina: Politics, Shipping, and Pirates. Queen Anne's Revenge Shipwreck Project, Research Report and Bulletin Series QAR-R-07-03, Underwater Archaeology Branch, Office of State Archaeology, Department of Cultural Resources, Raleigh, North Carolina.

CAMP, CORDELIA
1963 The Influence of Geography upon Early North Carolina. The Carolina Charter Tercentenary Commission, Raleigh, North Carolina.

CHARLES II KING OF ENGLAND
1663 Charter granted by Charles II King of England to the Lords Proprietors of Carolina, 1663. In The Colonial Records of North Carolina, Vol. I, 1662-1712, William L. Saunders, editor, pp. 20-33. P.M. Hale, Raleigh, North Carolina.

1665 Charter granted by Charles II, King of England to the Lords Proprietors of Carolina, 1665. In The Colonial Records of North Carolina, Vol. I, 1662-1712, William L. Saunders, editor, pp.102-114. P.M. Hale, Raleigh, North Carolina.

COWSE, BENJAMIN
1718 The Tryals of Major Stede Bonne, and Other Pirates, who were all condemn'd for Piracy. As also the Tryals of Thomas Nichols, Rowland Sharp, Jonathan Clark, and Thomas Gerret, for Piracy, who were acquitted. At the admiralty Sessions held at Charles-Town, in the Province of South Carolina, on Tuesday the 28th of October, 1718, and by several adjournments continued to Wednesday the 12th of November, following. To which is prefix'd, an account of the taking of the said Major Bonnet, and the rest of the Pirates. Rose and Crown in St. Paul's Church-yard, London, England.

DANN, JOHN
1696 Examination of John Dann, mariner, of Rochester. In Calendar of State Papers Colonial, America and West Indies, Vol. 15, 1696-1697, J.W. Fortescue, editor. British History Online < http://www.british-history.ac.uk/cal-state-papers/colonial/america-west-indies/vol15/pp248-267>. Accessed 19 March 2015.

DOYLE, J.A.
1882 The English in America: Virginia, Maryland, and the Carolinas. Longmans, Green, and Co., London.

EDWARDS, JOSEPH
1726 The Tryals of Sixteen Persons for Piracy, Four of which were Found Guilty, and the Rest Acquitted. At a Special Court of Admiralty for the Tryal of Pirates, held at Boston within the Province of the Massachusetts-Bay in New-England, on Monday the Fourth day of July, Anno Dom. 1726. Pursuant to his Majesty's Commission, founded on an Act of Parliament, made in the Eleventh and Twelfth Years of the Reign of King William the Third, Intitled; An Act for the More Effectual Suppression of Piracy. And made perpetual by an Act of the Sixth of King George. Corner Shop on the North-side of the Town-House, Boston, Massachusetts. In British Piracy in the Golden Age: History and Interpretation, 1660-1730, Vol. 3, Joel Baer, editor, pp. 231–259. Pickering & Chatto, London, England.

EHRET, CHRISTOPHER
1976 Linguistic Evidence and its Correlation with Archaeology. World Archaeology 8(1):5-18.

ERLL, ASTRID
2008 Cultural Memory Studies: An Introduction. In Media and Cultural Memory: Cultural Memory Studies: An International and Interdisciplinary Handbook, Astrid Erll and Ansgar Nünning, editors, pp. 1-15. Walter de. Gruyter, Berlin, Germany.

Ford, Benjamin (editor)
2012 The Archaeology Maritime Landscapes. Springer, New York.

Galvin, Peter
1999 Patterns of pillage: a geography of Caribbean-based piracy in Spanish America, 1536-1718. Peter Lang, New York.

Governor and Council of South Carolina
1718a Letter to the Council of Trade and Plantations from the Governor and Council of South Carolina. In Calendar of State Papers Colonial, America and West Indies, Vol. 30, 1717-1718, Cecil Headlam, editor. British History Online < http://www.british-history.ac.uk/cal-state-papers/colonial/america-west-indies/vol30/pp404-424>. Accessed 20 March 2015.

1718b Letter to the Council of Trade and Plantations from the Governor and Council of South Carolina. In Calendar of State Papers Colonial, America and West Indies, Vol. 30, 1717-1718, Cecil Headlam, editor. British History Online <http://www.british-history.ac.uk/cal-state-papers/colonial/america-west-indies/vol30/pp359-381>. Accessed 19 March 2015.

Hanna, Mark G.
2016 Pirate Nests and the Rise of the British Empire 1570-1740. University of North Carolina Press, Chapel Hill.

Hornsby, Stephen J.
2012 Geographies of the British Atlantic world. In Britain's Oceanic Empire: Atlantic and Indian Ocean World, c. 1550-1850, H.V. Bowen, Elizabeth Mancke and John G. Reid, editors, pp. 15-44, Cambridge University Press, Cambridge.

Johnson, Charles
1724 A general history of the robberies and murders of the most notorious pyrates, and also their policies, discipline and government, from their first rise and settlement in the island of Providence, 1717, to the present year 1724. With the remarkable actions and adventures of two female pyrates, May Read and Anne Bonny. To which is prefix'd an account of the famous Captain Avery and his companions. To which is added, a short abstract of the statute and civil law, in relation to piracy. C. Rivington, London, England.

la Vere, David
2013 The Tuscarora War: Indians, Settlers, and the Fight for the Carolina Colonies. University of North Carolina Press, Chapel Hill.

Lawson, John
1709 A New Voyage to Carolina. Hugh Talmage Lefler, editor. University of North Carolina Press, Chapel Hill.

Lee, Lawrence
1965 The Lower Cape Fear in Colonial Days. The University of North Carolina Press, Chapel Hill.

Lords Proprietors
1698 Fundamental Constitutions of Carolina. In The Colonial Records of North Carolina, Vol. II, 1713-1728, William L. Saunders, editor, pp. 852-858. P.M. Hale, Raleigh, North Carolina.

1710 Minutes of a Meeting of the Lords Proprietors of Carolina. In The Colonial Records of North Carolina, Vol. I, 1662-1712, William L. Saunders, editor, pp. 749-750. P.M. Hale, Raleigh, North Carolina.

Lusardi, Wayne
2006 The Beaufort Inlet Shipwreck Artifact Assemblage. In X Marks the Spot: The Archaeology of Piracy, Charles Ewen and Russell Skowronek, editors, pp. 196-218, University of Florida Press, Gainesville.

McCrady, Edward
1901 The History of South Carolina under the Proprietary Government 1670-1719. MacMillan & Co., London.

McIlvenna, Noeleen
2009 A Very Mutinous People: The Struggle for North Carolina, 1660-1713. University of North Carolina Press, Chapel Hill.

McLaughlin, Erin
2013 Beyond Historic Bath: Archaeological Investigation of Handy's Point, Bath, North Carolina. Master's Thesis, Department of Anthropology, East Carolina University, Greenville, North Carolina.

Midwinter, Edward
1732 The History and Lives of all the most Notorious Pirates and their Crews, from Capt. Avery, who first settled at Madagascar, to Capt. John Gow, and James Williams, his Lieutenant, and who were hanged at Execution Dock, June 11 1725, for Piracy and Murther; and afterwards hanged in chains between Blackwall and Deptford. And in this edition continued down to the present year 1732. Giving a more full and true account than any yet published, of all their murthers, piracies, maroonings, places of refuge, and ways of living. Looking Glass on London-Bridge, London, England.

Miller, J. William, John E. Callahan, James R. Craig, and Katherine M. Whatley
2005 'Ruling Theories Linger:' Questioning the Identity of the Beaufort Inlet Shipwreck: A Discussion. The International Journal of Nautical Archaeology 34(2):339-341.

MODYFORD, THOMAS AND PETER COLLETON
1663 Proposealls of Severall Gentlemen of Barbadoes August this 12th 1663. In The Colonial Records of North Carolina, Vol. I, 1662-1712, William L. Saunders, editor, pp. 39-42. P.M. Hale, Raleigh, North Carolina.

MOLTER, CHERI D.
2014 Colonial North Carolina: A Safe Harbor for Pirates. Thesis. Methodist University, Fayetteville, North Carolina.

MOORE, DAVID D.
2005 Technical Comments Relating to 'Ruling Theory' and the Identification of the Beaufort Inlet Wreck. The International Journal of Nautical Archaeology 34(2):335-339.

MOSELEY, EDWARD
1733 A New and Correct Map of the Province of North Carolina. Three Crowns, London.

NORTH CAROLINA COUNCIL
1719 Council Minutes from 27 May 1719. In The Colonial Records of North Carolina, Vol. II, William L. Saunders, editor, pp. 341-349. P.M. Hale, Raleigh, North Carolina.

OVERFIELD, MICHAEL
2002 Search for Adventure. Master's Thesis, Program in Maritime Studies, Department of History, East Carolina University, Greenville, North Carolina.

PAUL, CHARLES LIVINGSTON
1965 Colonial Beaufort: The History of a North Carolina Town. Master's Thesis, Department of History, East Carolina College, Greenville, North Carolina.

POLLOCK
1712 A True Copy of a Letter to the Lords Proprietors Dated September 20, 1712. In The Colonial Records of North Carolina, Vol. I, 1662-1712, William L. Saunders, editor, pp. 873-876. P.M. Hale, Raleigh, North Carolina.

RANDOLPH, EDWARD
1696 Paper submitted to the Commissioners of Customs, 17 Aug. 1696. In Calendar of State Papers Colonial, America and West Indies, Vol. 15, 1696-1697, J.W. Fortescue, editor. British History Online <http://www.british-history.ac.uk/cal-state-papers/colonial/america-west-indies/vol15/pp71-91>. Accessed 29 Mar 2015.

RODGERS, BRADLEY A., NATHAN RICHARDS AND WAYNE R. LUSARDI
2005 'Ruling Theories Linger:' Questioning the Identity of the Beaufort Inlet Shipwreck. The International Journal of Nautical Archaeology 34(1):24-37.

ROGERS, WOODES
1718 Letter to the Council of Trade and Plantations, from Governor Woodes Rogers. In Calendar of State Papers Colonial, America and West Indies, Vol. 30, 1717-1718, Cecil Headlam, editor. British History Online <http://www.british-history.ac.uk/cal-state-papers/colonial/america-west-indies/vol30/pp359-381>. Accessed 19 March 2015.

SPOTSWOOD, ALEXANDER
1719a Letter to Lord Cartwright. In The Colonial Records of North Carolina, Vol. II, 1713-1728, William L. Saunders, editor, pp. 324-327. P.M. Hale, Raleigh, North Carolina.

1719b Letter to Secretary Craggs. In The Colonial and State Records of North Carolina, Vol. II, 1713-1728, William L. Saunders, editor, pp.333-336. P. M. Hale, Raleigh, North Carolina.

1719c Letter to the Council of Trade and Plantations from Governor Spotswood. In Calendar of State Papers Colonial, America and West Indies, Vol. 31, 1719-1720, Cecil Headlam, editor. British History Online <http://www.british-history.ac.uk/cal-state-papers/colonial/america-west-indies/vol31/pp85-101>. Accessed 20 March 2015.

ULANSKI, STAN
2008 Gulf Stream: Tiny Plankton, Giant Bluefin, and the Amazing Story of the Powerful River in the Atlantic. University of North Carolina Press, Chapel Hill.

VIRGINIA COUNCIL
1719 Minutes of the Virginia Governor's Council [Extract]. In The Colonial and State Records of North Carolina, Vol. II, 1713-1728, William L. Saunders, editor, pp.327. P. M. Hale, Raleigh, North Carolina.

WESLAGER, C.A.
1954 Place Names on Ocracoke Island. The North Carolina Historical Review 31(1):41-49.

WESTERDAHL, CHRISTER
1992 The maritime cultural landscape. The International Journal of Nautical Archaeology 21(1):5-14.

WILDE-RAMSING, MARK
2006 The Pirate Ship Queen Anne's Revenge. In X Marks the Spot: The Archaeology of Piracy, Charles Ewen and Russell Skowronek, editors, pp. 160-195, University of Florida Press, Gainesville.

WILDE-RAMSING, MARK AND CHARLES R. EWEN
2012 Beyond Reasonable Doubt: A Case for Queen Anne's Revenge. Historical Archaeology 46(2):110-133.

Allyson Ropp
209 Happy Valley Rd.
Middleburg, VT 05753

Loss of British Tanker *Mirlo* Revisited: New Considerations Regarding the Vessel's Loss off the North Carolina Coast during the First World War

John C. Bright

On 16 August 1918, British tanker Mirlo *sank off the North Carolina coast following an encounter with a German U-boat. Over the last century, specific details of the tanker's sinking were largely overshadowed by the legendary US Coast Guard rescue operation that ensued. Ambiguity remained as to whether a U-boat torpedoed* Mirlo, *or it struck a mine laid previously by the same U-boat. Similarly, review of primary source materials revealed that* Mirlo *was also equipped with a highly secretive minesweeping device developed by the British in 1917. These additional details shed new light on the circumstances of* Mirlo*'s loss.*

Introduction

During the First and Second World Wars, German U-boats waged aggressive naval campaigns against allied merchant shipping in the Atlantic. This was a strategic initiative during both wars intended to deprive the allies of personnel and material necessary to sustain military operations within the European theater of war. To this end, German U-boats sought to engage and destroy concentrations of allied merchant vessels along main shipping routes and at strategic locations throughout the Atlantic Ocean and, in some cases, beyond. One such location was Cape Hatteras, on the American eastern seaboard. Converging oceanic currents, geomorphology, and proximity to shipping lanes and major trade ports made this area ideal for German U-boat operations. Already notoriously hazardous to mariners, North Carolina's Outer Banks became the final resting place for nearly 100 allied military and merchant vessels during belligerent activities in the Second World War (Stick 1952:254-257; Hickam 1989:296-305).

North Carolina's Outer Banks, however, factored much less prominently into the First World War's Battle of the Atlantic naval activity. In the short period between May and October of 1918 when German U-boats operated in American waters, over 100 vessels were attacked and sunk along the Eastern Seaboard, but of these only 10 were adjacent to the North Carolina coast; an order of magnitude fewer than what would follow in the Second World War. Most of these vessels, however, were far offshore at the time of their sinking. Only five, in fact, were lost near the coast: *Harpathian, Nordhav, Merak, Diamond Shoals Lightship LV-71*, and British tanker *Mirlo*. Having been lost along Diamond Shoals proper, the remains of *LV-71* were since discovered and are presently listed on the National Register of Historic Places. The presumed remains of *Merak*, in the form of vessel remains currently under investigation at the edge of Diamond Shoals, have likewise been found. Thus, *Mirlo* stands as one of the last undiscovered vessels from the First World War along coastal Carolina waters (Marsh 1919; McMaster 1920:1-31; Stick 1952:193-208; Tarrant 1989:70-71; Blake 2006:138).

In the century since *Mirlo*'s loss, details of the vessel itself and inquiry regarding ambiguities of its loss were largely eclipsed by the legendary US Coast Guard rescue effort prompted by the tanker's destruction. In a narrative that has been reported in great detail since, a small crew from the Chicamacomico Coast Guard Station rescued 42 of *Mirlo*'s 51 crew. Despite having to launch a motor surfboat through 18-20 ft waves, transit nearly 10 miles offshore, navigate through towering flames as the tanker's volatile cargo spilled out around them, and then land the survivors back though the same pounding surf, they persisted. For this heroic effort, the rescuers received numerous awards and commendations (Marsh 1919:128-129; Skerrett 1919; McMaster 1920:26-27; Stick 1952:204-208; Bearss 1965a,1968; Johnson 1987:51-56; Gentile 1993:133-137; Larzelere 2003:151-154).

Despite this successful rescue, the tanker itself was a total loss. Following a series of explosions, the vessel's cargo of benzol and paraffin caught fire, resulting in several devastating explosions that broke *Mirlo* into two sections. None of those present, however, noted witnessing the vessel actually sink. In a statement issued immediately following the attack, *Mirlo*'s captain noted

> "The Mirlo was struck in two places, and the ship began to break. Both parts remained afloat for some time and I cannot say now that they have sunk completely. The ship, however, is virtually destroyed (McMaster 1920:26)."

The following day, as vessels arrived at Chicamacomico to load *Mirlo*'s crew, none of the tanker's remains were sighted.

Nearly a century later, its location remains a mystery. Likewise, a great deal of ambiguity surrounds the circumstances of its loss. At the time, German *U-117* was operating throughout the area and set a field of moored mines proximate to the Wimble Shoals buoy, the aid to navigation referenced by *Mirlo*'s captain just before the first explosion shook the tanker. Some accounts, including that of the tanker's captain, claim the loss was caused by a torpedo attack (Bearss 1968:387-389); others interpreted that *Mirlo* was the victim of the U-boat's minefield (Stick 1952:204; Gentile 1993:136). Review of *U-117*'s logbook, however, reveals that it was in the area and, in fact, attacked *Mirlo* with a torpedo. A careful study of primary sources chronicling the attack also reveal that *Mirlo* was equipped with a secret minesweeping device, the presence of which has important implications for how the vessel was lost.

Mirlo: Its Design, Construction, and Armament

British-built tanker *Mirlo* had a very brief service life. Laid down on 8 November 1916 by famed Sunderland shipbuilding company Sir James Laing & Sons Ltd, the vessel was completed on 23 August of the following year. *Mirlo*, derived from Latin *Merula*: a common Spanish blackbird, was one of three hulls ordered by prolific Norwegian shipping company Wilh. Wilhelmsen. Due to the shipping needs of the ongoing war effort, however, the British government requisitioned the completed tanker under wartime contract via Liverpool-based H.E. Moss & Co. Less than a year later, *Mirlo* was among hundreds of German U-boat causalities across the Atlantic Ocean (Lloyd's Register of Shipping 1918/1919: MIR-MIS; His Majesty's Stationary Office 1919:95; Marsh 1919:128-129; Smith and Holden 1947:1947:1-11; Stick 1952:204-207; Hocking 1969:475; Tennent 1990:171; Kolltveit 1994:103-298).

Despite its seemingly inconsequential career, however, *Mirlo* as a vessel represented the height of British shipbuilding owing to its Sunderland origins. Ever since the purpose-built oil tanker emerged as a profitable vessel design in the later part of the 19th century, one of the shipbuilders at the forefront of their production was *Mirlo*'s builder: Sir James Laing & Sons. The Laing family began constructing ships along the Wear River in 1793 and were, by the end of the Second World War, the longest operating shipbuilding company in the world. This reputation is even more impressive when one considers that Sunderland, during the 19th and 20th centuries, was considered the largest shipbuilding town in the world and home to dozens of prolific naval architects and engineers (Smith and Holden 1947:1-17).

With the emergence of a specialized class of oil-carrying ships, their company's focus shifted to producing these specialized craft as opposed to standard freighters. Smith and Holden described this transition:

Hugh Laing, son of Sir James, came into prominence with the birth of the oil tanker, and concentrated his efforts on the new production. The result was that Laing's attracted worldwide attention and received many orders for this new design. In the eighteen-nineties, they launched the oil carriers Turbo, Trocas, and Spondilus for Samuels, of London, and in addition several others for North-East coast owners (Smith and Holden 1947:16).

Less than 20 years later, during the height of the company's First World War production, Sir James Laing & Sons lead Sunderland shipbuilding by producing 18 merchant vessels totaling 109,924 gross tons, in addition to their naval vessel outputs. During this period, the company received the order to produce three 425-ft tanker hulls, those of *Mirlo*, *Mendocino*, and *Montana* (Smith and Holdern 1947:1-56; Kolltveit and Crowdy 1994:103-105).

The resulting vessels were 6,978 gross tons, 425 ft long, 57 ft in breadth, and 33 ft in depth of hold. The bows featured a 40 ft long forecastle, a 28 ft long bridge deck slightly forward of midships, and an aft deck 101 ft long. These vessels were patterned after the characteristic tanker design: all machinery placed aft and compartmentalized by means of a fireproof bulkhead. The cargo area was partitioned via a matrix of cofferdams and bulkheads, and networks of piping snaked over and within the decks to move and distribute the tanker's liquid cargo. Plans for these vessels are shown in Figure 1. The contemporary workhorse propulsion system, a triple-expansion steam engine, provided *Mirlo*'s motive power. This engine was supplied by four single-ended boilers and was capable of moving the tanker at a speed of 11-14 knots (Lloyd's Register of Shipping 1918/1919: MIR-MIS; Wild 1965:3; Kolltveit and Crowdy 1994:103-105).

Following *Mirlo*'s completion and subsequent requisition by the British government, the vessel was placed under management of H. E. Moss & Co. Captain W. R. Williams was placed in command of the tanker, and would remain so until the vessel's sinking. Fully intending to travel through hostile waters, the

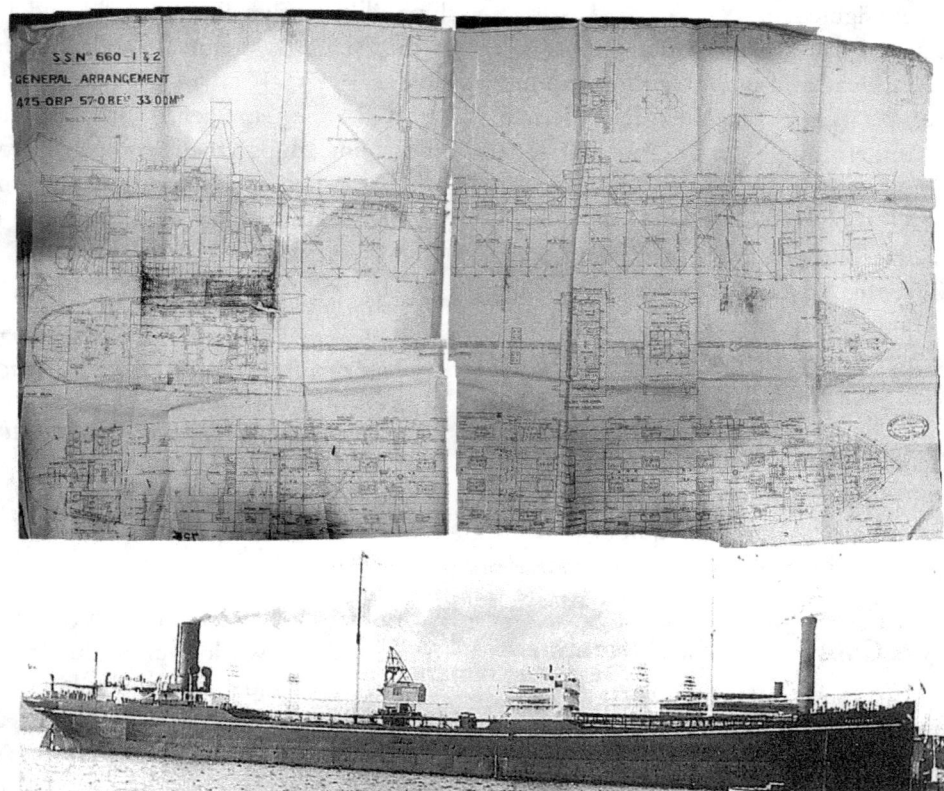

Figure 1. This set of vessel plans shows the general arrangement of hulls 660-662 by shipbuilder Sir James Laing & Sons Ltd., those of tankers Mirlo, Mendocino, and Montana. Inset underneath is a starboard profile image of Mendocino (Kollveit and Crowdy 1994:104), hull number 661, completed three months after Mirlo, hull number 660 (see Bearss 1965b for plans). Records retrieved by Marc Corbett and stitched into single image by the author.

British government installed defensive armaments on *Mirlo*. This included a single 4-inch breech-loading gun placed aft, and the assignment of a detachment of Royal Navy sailors to service the gun and serve as lookouts. The specific armament was most likely the British BL Mk IX, in a single mount weapon capable of firing a 311-lb charge 13,840 yards. The purpose of this weapon was to discourage any attempt by U-boats to surface and attack the vessel, a somewhat haphazardly heeded U-boat tactic during an era where traditional naval Prize Rules gave way to unrestricted submarine warfare tactics (His Majesty's Stationary Office 1919:95; Marsh 1919:128-129; Campbell 1985:41; Kolltveit and Crowdy 1994:103).

In addition to direct attack, another offensive tool employed by German U-boats was the use of moored mines deployed from the submarine while underwater. Once laid, the mines would extend upwards toward the surface of the water along a tether. The tether's length was less than the water's depth to keep the mines from breaching and thus remain concealed. Systematically placed along shipping lanes, these minefields constituted a prolific threat to allied vessels throughout the war.

Surface ships, however, were not completely defenseless against moored mines. In conjunction with regular minesweeping operations through important shipping lanes, a special device was developed in secret and fitted to individual ships. Invented by British Commander C. D. Burney in the early months of the war, paravanes became one of the most effective, and secretive, anti-mine devices of the First World War (Catlin 1919:1135).

Though shared with the American navy following their entry into the war, information about this technology remained highly guarded throughout the war. Described in an American post-war naval report, they operated as follows:

> From a special fitting attached to the forefoot of the vessel, a torpedo shaped body called a paravane is towed on each side. Vanes and rudders are fitted to the body, which cause it to tow some distance from the side of the ship, and at a fixed depth. A large slightly curved vertical vane, working like a kite, draws the paravane away from the ship. A horizontal rudder with suitable control gear regulates the depth of submergence....

two ropes leading aft and outboard from the stern, form a wedge which encounters mine moorings and deflects the mine away from the ship toward the paravane. The towing rope is attached to the paravane at what is called the cutter-head, in the jaws of which small saw tooth knives are fitted....The mine mooring slides into these jaw, where it is quickly severed, permitting the mine which is buoyant to come to the surface where it can be seen and destroyed (Catlin 1919:1137).

The British Admiralty observed marked success of these devices and by the fall of 1917 "the Admiralty had ordered all British naval vessels and all British merchant ships of 12 ft draft to be equipped with this device as soon as possible" (Catlin 1919:1140-1142). Analysis of Admiralty records reveals that, immediately following the implementation of this policy, numbers of British vessels lost to enemy mines dropped precipitously (see Table 1). In order to maintain the veil of secrecy surrounding these devices, the Admiralty decided not to refer to them by their technical name and instead opted for a pseudo code word: otter or otter gears (Catlin 1919:1134-1142).

This term(s) was borrowed from a commercial fishing trawl-gear component of the same name and similar function: both operated by setting a hydrodynamic board in such a position that moving water would force the board to fan outward and thus tension any line or net fixed between it and another rigid attachment. Within the commercial fishing application, two otter boards, fitted separately between the stern of a vessel and the opening of a net, would spread, thereby holding open an otherwise loose net (Engelbrektson 1975:179). Implemented as a minesweeping device the otter board principle involved two paravanes, each deployed from opposite sides of a vessel's bow, fixed with sturdy wire cables. With sufficient forward motion though the water, the paravanes would spread the cables away from the bow to create a wide snag capable of hooking moored mines. Once fouled, the mines would be directed, as described above, into a cutter head and allowed to drift safely away from the vessel (Figure 2).

Despite the sheer number of vessels on which this device was installed Lt. Catlin (1919:1142) reported that "this [code name] policy was followed out so rigidly in the British Paravane organization [that], in fact very few captains of merchant ships ever heard of the word

British Vessels Lost to Mines 1914-1918					
Month	Year				
	1914	1915	1916	1917	1918
January	0	1	3	8	0
Februar	0	2	14	12	1
March	0	0	7	12	3
April	0	0	6	14	1
May	0	0	8	14	1
June	0	2	4	4	2
July	0	1	5	11	0
August	1	7	1	6	0
September	2	8	7	9	0
October	4	7	7	5	0
November	1	9	6	8	1
December	5	4	12	8	0
Total	13	41	80	111	9

Table 1. Monthly totals of British-flagged merchant vessel lost to enemy mines. A dramatic reduction in vessel losses is apparent starting August of 1917, following an Admiralty order to install paravanes on all British merchant vessels with draft 12-feet or greater (Catlin 1919:1134-1142; His Majesty's Stationary Office 1919:1-99).

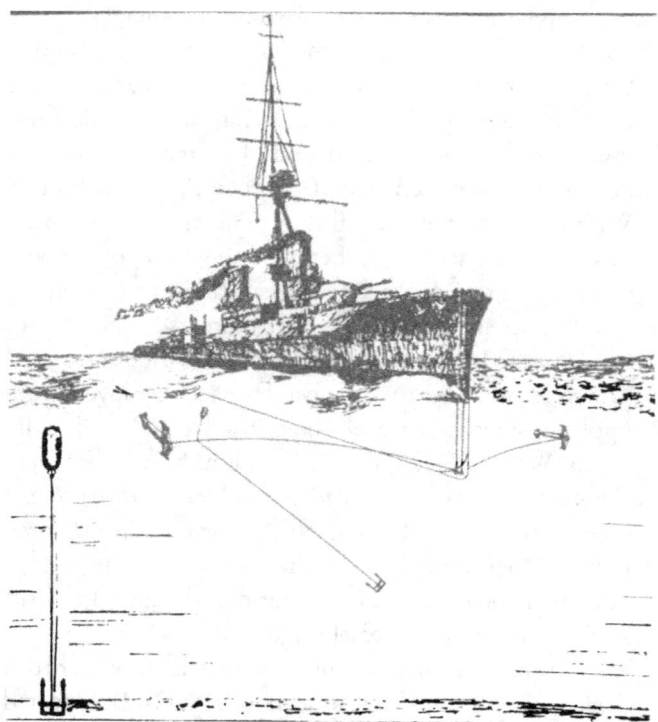

Figure 2. Diagram showing the operation of a paravane anti-mine device at use on a vessel. Drawing was created by Lt. George L. Catlin USNRF (1919:1134), for the US Naval Institute following the war.

paravane, always referring to the device by the name of otter, or otter gear." The Admiralty's 1917 decision to equip all British merchant vessels with a draught of 12 ft or greater with paravanes, took effect just as *Mirlo* was requisitioned for wartime use. Thus, in addition to its 4-inch gun, the tanker was equipped with another, top secret, armament to prepare it for the hostile waters in which it was soon to sail.

The War Patrol of U-*117* and the Sinking of *Mirlo*

In July of 1918, *Mirlo* departed England and travelled in ballast to the United States, destination New Orleans. Throughout the crossing, the tanker was unescorted but also keenly aware of the danger posed by German U-boats. The vessel followed Admiralty procedures for zig-zagging, its Royal Navy gun crew remained on watch, and the paravanes were deployed when necessary. For most of the journey, however, *Mirlo*'s crew occupied their time with normal shipboard tasks. This mainly involved cleaning the holding tanks in preparation for the cargo they would take on in New Orleans. (Bearss 1965a:Appendix II; Wild 1965:1-5).

Mirlo arrived safely and without incident. At New Orleans, they took on a mixed cargo of benzol and paraffin. The latter, an early type of aviation fuel, occupied the forward 12 cargo tanks, while the former was placed in the two aft-most cargo tanks. On 10 August 1918, the tanker departed New Orleans on a return voyage to London. Before crossing the North Atlantic, however, *Mirlo* planned stops in Norfolk and New York to replenish its coal supply (Ministry of Shipping 1918; Stick 1952:204-205; Wild 1965:5-6; Larzelere 2003:151). Meanwhile, a German U-boat operating along the Eastern Seaboard was setting a course for Wimble Shoals.

U-*117*, under command of Kapitänleutnant (Kplt.) Otto Dröscher, was one of a specialized class of mine-laying submarines: UE II type. Almost double the size of the UE I class minelayers, the UE II were 267 ft long, 24 ft in beam, and displaced a total of 1,512 tons when submerged. These boats could make 16.4 knots surfaced, and 8.4 while underwater on electrical propulsion. UE II boats had a range of 13,900 nautical miles and carried 12 torpedoes, 42 mines, and a single 5.9-in deck gun (Tarrant 1989:170-174; Williamson 2002).

In between sinking merchant vessels on 13 and 14 August, U-*117* laid its first minefield off Barnegat Light, which later claimed American freighter *San Saba*. Moving to the area off Fenwick Island, U-*117* placed another minefield later responsible for damaging USS Minnesota and sinking freighter Saetia. That same day, U-*117* sank Brazilian schooner *Madgruada* with gunfire. The following day, Dröscher transited to a small spit of sand off Rodanthe called Wimble Shoals to set up yet another minefield (Dröscher 1918:10; Marsh 1919:82-99).

Mirlo and U-*117* were soon to converge. Rounding Cape Hatteras in the morning, Captain Williams set a parallel course to land that would take the tanker northward to the next navigational waypoint: Wimble Shoals. A navigation buoy denoted the area and just as *Mirlo* passed this waypoint, Capt. Williams recalled the event that set in motion the vessel's loss and prompted the storied US Coast Guard Rescue:

On August 16, 1918, at 3.30 p.m. A.T.S. [4:30pm EST], when the steamer was steering a north course off Wimble Shoal Buoy, bearing north by west half a mile distance, she was struck on the starboard side aft by a torpedo, bursting No. 2 tank and blowing up the decks, which was immediately followed by another torpedo, which struck farther aft and set fire to the ship in stokehold and after end (Marsh 1919:128).

The vessel was hit in the aft tank containing the less volatile paraffin. Nevertheless, part of this cargo ignited and the force of the explosions knocked out the ship's dynamos and communication equipment, and put the engine room out of commission. Captain Williams gave the order to make ready the lifeboats, while attempting to steer his vessel towards shore (Marsh 1919:128-129; Bearss 1965a:252).

Observing from the Chicamacomico station, the guardsmen began putting their motor surfboat to sea as chaos ensued onboard *Mirlo*:

The tanker continued on her course for a few minutes, and then was seen to swing to port. Continuing to bear to port, she completed a circle around the buoy and headed offshore. Flames "shot up from the stern of the steamer," and a second explosion was clearly heard by the surfmen and villagers. All the while, the stricken tanker continued to bear to port; the smoke pouring out her side changed from white to black. Just as *Mirlo* was completing a third circle, there was another explosion. This time she broke in two, the bow drifting to the northeast and the stern to the southwest (Bearss 1968:391).

Captain Williams attempted to make the best of the situation throughout this ordeal. First, an attempt was made to run the vessel aground on the shoals, but damage to the stern of the vessel sent it circling in the manner described above. Seeing no other choice and engulfed in flames, the order was given to abandon ship (Marsh 1919:128-129; Skerrett 1919:511).

The View from the Periscope

Throughout 16 August U-*117* tracked along the waters off Wimble Shoals. In the morning, several vessels were spotted traveling south. The U-boat submerged and attempted to maneuver into an attack position, but the vessels' zig-zagging courses stymied Dröscher's efforts. By early afternoon, they were running on the surface and, upon sighting the Wimble Shoals buoy, began the day's planned mining operation (Dröscher 1918:10-11). As first reported by Bearss (1965a, 1968), one of the few historians studying the incident to obtain and translate Dröscher's logbook, it was at this time, while laying mines, that two merchant ships converged on Wimble Shoals from opposite directions. Ascertaining that one was a tanker, Kplt. Dröscher made the decision to target the same and broke from the mine laying to start a torpedo attack. It was noted in the logbook that, of the tanker's two masts, one was painted darkly and the other painted white; a practice which made determination of its course difficult for submarines (Dröscher 1918:10-11). This color scheme can be observed in Figure 1, with the same pattern shown for *Mendocino*, and in historical images of *Montana* (Kollveit and Crowdy 1994:104-105).

At a distance of only 400 m, U-*117* fired a single torpedo into *Mirlo*'s stern. Kptl. Dröscher noted that the vessel immediately caught fire. Heading south towards the buoy, U-*117* resumed station to continue laying mines as *Mirlo* burned (see Figure 3). A couple of hours later, after the completion of the Wimble Shoals minefield (see Marsh 1919), U-*117* surfaced and noted what it thought was a second steamer on fire. It was, in fact, a broken section of *Mirlo* drifting away. Throughout the night, Kplt. Dröscher continued to hunt for merchant vessels and, by the following morning, was making way northwards, back to the Chesapeake and Delaware areas (Dröscher 1918:10-12).

In retrospect, historians studying the loss of *Mirlo* without the benefit of U-*117*'s log as a primary source lacked an important data source to inform the ambiguity regarding the initial cause of explosion onboard *Mirlo*. Information from this log, which described details of *Mirlo*'s color scheme, conclusively places U-*117* and *Mirlo* together and that direct action, in the form of a torpedo attack, was the cause for the first explosion onboard the tanker. This contradicts and refutes the alternative claim that U-*117* was elsewhere at the time and *Mirlo* simply hit a mine previously left by the submarine (see Stick 1952:204). U-*117* was there, and by Kplt. Dröscher's account, fired a torpedo directly at *Mirlo*.

The Paravane as a Critical Element to *Mirlo*'s Sinking

Despite U-*117* firing a single torpedo into *Mirlo*'s stern, the demise of the vessel came after a series of three explosions. Accounts of the event described the first two explosions happening within rapid succession and assumed them separate torpedo strikes (Marsh 1919:128; Wild 1965:7). According to U-*117*'s logbook, only a single torpedo was fired, meaning the second explosion must have been internal, and resulted from secondary ignition of other flammable materials within the tanker as a result of the torpedo strike. More to the point, it was very unlikely that the second explosion was caused by a mine, since it occurred in stern of the vessel, near the first torpedo strike. Captain Williams noted:

The ship had been towing her otter gears from Florida Straits, and was towing them at the time of the accident. The ship was steering a straight course north, magnetic, and in my opinion it would have been impossible for these explosions to been caused by

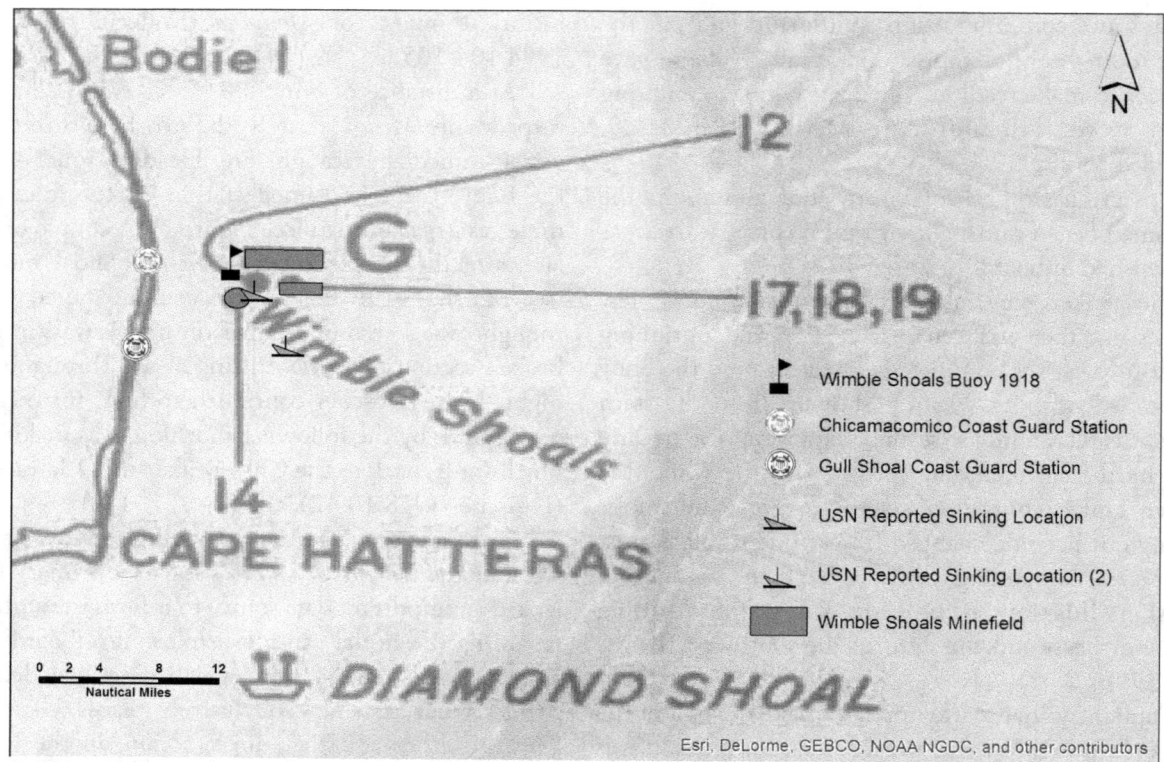

Figure 3. Using a digitized, georeferenced historical map, the location of the Wimble Shoals buoy, Chicamacomico and Gull Shoal Coast Guard Stations, two possible Mirlo sinking locations as reported in 1919 are represented over a map developed by the US Navy to depict German mining operations off the Eastern Seaboard during the war. The key for items 14, 17, 18, and 19 on the background map are locations of mines swept by USS Teal. Item G is the reported position of the minefield from U-117's logbook. Location 12 is a reported sinking location of Mirlo (Marsh 1919). Map by author, 2017.

mines- the explosions being 12-14 feet below the water line (Marsh 1991:29).

Several minutes later, after all three lifeboats were launched and all crew evacuated from the tanker, a third, massive explosion, broke *Mirlo* into two sections, setting the surrounding water alight (Marsh 1919:128-129; Wild 1965:7-8).

Most accounts assume the third and final explosion was the result of heat generated from fires in the aft paraffin holding tanks and engine room spreading to the more volatile benzol cargo in the remaining forward tanks. While there was little doubt that ignition of the benzol was responsible for a blast of sufficient force to break a 425-ft steel tanker into two parts, there is another possibility as to the source of that ignition.

After the first two explosions took *Mirlo*'s machinery out of commission, the captain attempted to steer the vessel towards land and close the distance between the lifeboats and shore, and possibly even ground the ship. Unable to control steerage, however, *Mirlo* was stuck turning to port and made a series of wide, concentric turns around the Wimble Shoals buoy prior to the third explosion, as shown in Figure 4 (Bearss 1968:391). During this time, lifeboats on the bridge of the vessel were being manned and lowered. Captain Williams, who was in the bridge and did not personally observe either port or starboard boats lowered, reported that the port boat's "...tiller fouled the after falls, causing the boat to shear off from the ship and capsize (Marsh 1919:129)." The third officer, however, did witness the portside lifeboat being lowered and offered an additional detail, that "...it had fouled the Paravane cords and capsized (Wild 1965:7)." Once capsized, the boat's occupants were cast out and left only to cling to the upturned hull. Surrounding flames prevented either of the remaining lifeboats from coming to their aid, and ultimately claimed nine crewmembers' lives.

When functioning normally, the paravane gear should spread perpendicularly away from the bow and not be in a position underneath the bridge deck, at the waterline, capable of fouling a lifeboat. Given, however, that *Mirlo* was making a series of wide sweeping turns to port, instead of a straight forward track, the paravane gear on the port side of the boat would have instead swung into the side of the hull, as evidenced by the fact it fouled the port lifeboat's tiller. As the vessel continued to swing to port, it was also passing through the string of mines previously laid by *U-117*. It is plausible that, during the final pass, the vessel actually struck a mine, which in turn detonated against the forward part of the hull, and set the benzol cargo on fire.

During the month following *Mirlo*'s sinking, the US Navy sent a minesweeper, USS *Teal*, to clear the Wimble Shoals area (Marsh 1919:138). They noted, as per the map in Figure 3, two separated areas of mines, arranged east-to-west, with a gap in between. This break corresponds with *Mirlo*'s approximate position at the time of attack, and could represent the area of a detonated mine.

Conclusion

The installation and use of a secret paravane system onboard *Mirlo*, by order of the Admiralty, was a detail not previously described within published historical research regarding the vessel's loss. Its deployment on the tanker at the time of its loss, along with corroborating primary source documentation of U-*117*'s torpedo attack, conclusively shows *Mirlo* was initially torpedoed by U-*117* and did not, as previously speculated by some historical accounts, accidentally hit a mine while passing Wimble Shoals. After being damaged and disabled, *Mirlo* began a series of wide-arching turns during which it most likely caught and fouled a mine placed earlier by U-*117*, the resulting detonation breaking the tanker in half and setting fire to the wreckage. Moreover, the paravane was a critical element in the fouling of *Mirlo*'s port lifeboat that, in turn, left its occupants stranded next to the burning tanker whereby nine of them drowned before the remainder were rescued.

Based on U-*117*'s logbook, only a single torpedo was fired at *Mirlo*. The second explosion, which occurred almost instantaneously after the first, must have resulted from secondary ignition of some flammable substance within the tanker's stern. Afterwards, in an attempt to steer the vessel to shore, Captain Williams began a slow turn towards port. Unable to correct, *Mirlo* continued to turn and completed a series of wide circles around the Wimble Shoals buoy. Following the third turn, a final explosion fueled by the tanker's benzol cargo, split the ship in half and set a large area of oil-laden water in the vicinity afire.

Review of these historical records will also propel future research needed to inform survey efforts to locate the vessel's remains. Awareness of the paravane system will assist in archaeological efforts to examine potential sites, which could yield additional information regarding the cause of the vessel's loss and its impact on the outcome for *Mirlo*'s crew.

Acknowledgments

Special thanks to Marc Corbett for sharing invaluable archival materials and also for his time to discuss many of the ideas in this paper. Many thanks to Joe Hoyt for encouragement to begin this project, draft review and editing, and brainstorming future directions for the project. Many years ago, William McDermott's enthusiasm and previous research efforts regarding *Mirlo* cemented my interest in the topic; thank you, Bill. Additional thanks to Dr. Nathan Richards for reviewing earlier versions of this draft and tirelessly insisting to publish.

References

Bearss, Edwin C.
1965a   Report on Chicamacomico Life Saving Station. Cape Hatteras National Seashore Resource Studies Project CAHA-H-1, Part 1-6. Cape Hatteras National Seashore, Southeast Region, National Park Service. Manuscript on file at Outer Banks History Center, Call Number 33MSS-58, Manteo, NC.

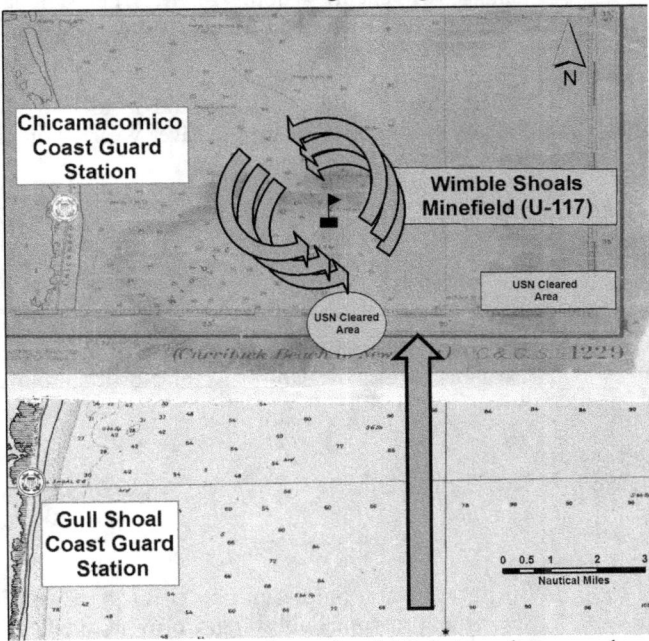

Figure 4. Map showing the path of *Mirlo* into the area where U-117 reported setting the Wimble Shoals minefield, adjacent to the Wimble Shoals buoy. After the first two explosions on the tanker, the vessel began a series of wide, slow turns to port around the buoy, shown by the circling arrows in the center. This path took it through the area where U-117 reported laying mines, and also where USS *Teal* cleared two remaining patches of mines in the weeks following. Note the gap between the two cleared areas, indicated a possible zone where *Mirlo* actually struck a mine, prompting the third, and final explosion (Map by author, 2017).

BEARSS, EDWIN C.
1965b General arrangement plans for hulls 660-662, Sir James Laing & Sons Ltd. Plans obtained by Edwin C. Bearss during the Report on Chicamacomico Life Saving Station. File S 17E, Chicamacomico Study Collection, Cape Hatteras National Seashore Archives, US National Park Service, Manteo, NC. Retrieved by Marc Corbett.

BEARSS, EDWIN C.
1968 The "*Mirlo*" Rescue. The North Carolina Historical Review 45(4):384-398.

BLAKE, SAMUEL
2006 A Comparative Study of the Effectiveness of German Submarine Warfare on the Eastern Seaboard of the United States in the World Wars. Master's Thesis. Program in Maritime Studies, Department of History, East Carolina University, Greenville, NC.

CAMPBELL, JOHN
1985 Naval Weapons of World War Two. Naval Institute Press, Anapolis, MD.

CATLIN, GEORGE L., LT. USNRF
1919 Paravanes. United States Naval Institute Proceedings, Vol 45(7):1134-1157

DRÖSCHER, OTTO KAPITÄNLEUTNANT
1917 Kriegstagbuch SM U-*117*. SM U *117* 11.06.18-22.09.18, SM U *117*, Recherche Kaiserliche Marine, German U-Boat Museum, Cuxhaven-Altenbruch, Germany.

ENGELBREKTSON, EINAR (EDITOR)
1975 The Lore of Ships. AB Nordbok, Gothenburg, Sweden.

GENTILE, GARY
1993 Shipwrecks of North Carolina from the Diamond Shoals North. Gary Gentile Productions, Philadelphia, PA.

HICKAM, HOMER H.
1989 Torpedo Junction. Naval Institute Press, Annapolis, MD.

HIS MAJESTY'S STATIONARY OFFICE
1919 British Vessels Lost at Sea, 1914-18. His Majesty's Stationary Office, reprinted 1979 Patrick Stevens Ltd, Cambridge.

HOCKING, CHARLES
1969 Dictionary of Disasters at Sea During the Age of Steam Including Sailing Ships and Ships of War Lost in Action: 1824-1962, Vol II M-Z.

JOHNSON, ROBERT ERWIN
1987 Guardians of the Sea: History of the United States Coast Guard 1915 to the Present. Naval Institute Press, Annapolis, MD.

KOLLTVEIT, BÅRD AND MICHAEL CROWDY
1994 Wilh. Wilhelmsen History and Fleet List 1861-1994. World Ship Society, Kendal, England.

LARZELERE, ALEX R.
2003 The Coast Guard in World War I: An Untold Story. Naval Institute Press, Annapolis, MD.

LLOYD'S REGISTER OF SHIPPING
1918/19 Steamers & Motorships. Lloyds Register of Shipping. Register Book. Register of Ships 1918/19. http://books.google.com. Accessed 15 January 2013.

MARSH, C. C. CAPT, USN (RET), (EDITOR)
1919 German Activities on the Atlantic Coast of the United States and Canada. Publication Number 1, Historical Section, Office of Naval Records and Library, Navy Department, Washington DC.

MCMASTER, JOHN BACH
1920 The United States in the World War (1918-1920). D. Appleton & Co. New York, NY.

MINISTRY OF SHIPPING
1918 British Merchant and Fishing Vessels Sunk or damaged by enemy action, Vol. III. Ministry of Shipping, 1917 - 1921: Correspondence and Papers. British Merchant and Fishing Vessels, sunk or damaged by enemy action. Vol. III. The National Archives, Kew, Richmond, Surrey, United Kingdom.

SMITH, J. W., AND T. S. HOLDEN
1947 Where Ships are Borne, Sunderland 1346-1946: A History of Shipbuilding on the River Wear. Thomas Reed and Co., Sunderland.

SKERRETT, ROBERT G.
1919 Our Senior Armed Sea Service. The Rudder Vol 35(11):507-513

STICK, DAVID
1952 Graveyard of the Atlantic: Shipwrecks of the North Carolina Coast. The University of North Carolina Press, Chapel Hill.

TARRANT, V. E.
1989 The U-Boat Offensive: 1914-1945. Cassell & Co, London.

TENNENT, A. J.
1990 British Merchant Ships Sunk by U-Boats in World War One. Periscope Publishing, Cornwall, England.

WILD, V. A., LT. RNVR (RET.)
[1965] Lt. V.A. Wild's Personal Notes Relating to *Mirlo*; Correspondence between *Mirlo* J. Wilby (daughter) and Mrs. Gray (researcher). Letter retrieved by Edwin C. Bearss during the Report on Chicamacomico Life Saving Station. File S 17E, Chicamacomico Study Collection, Cape Hatteras National Seashore Archives, US National Park Service, Manteo, NC. Retrieved by Marc Corbett.

WILLIAMSON, GORDON
2002   U-boats of the Kaiser's Navy. Osprey Publishing, Oxford.

John C. Bright
Research Coordinator, Maritime Archaeologist
Thunder Bay National Marine Sanctuary--NOAA
500 W. Fletcher St.
Alpena, MI 49707
Work Telephone: 989-884-6214
Home Telephone: 305-393-4652
John.Bright@noaa.gov

Carpeted with Ammunition: Investigations of the *Florence D* shipwreck site, Northern Territory, Australia

Jason T. Raupp, David Steinberg

On 19 February 1942, the merchant ship Florence D *disappeared in the murky waters of Australia's Northern Territory (NT) after being bombed and sunk by Japanese aircraft returning from their first air attack on Darwin. One of 59 merchant ships lost through enemy action around Australia during World War II (WWII) (Australian War Memorial Official Histories), the wreck was among northern Australia's great wartime mysteries. Located by a local fisherman in 2006, archaeological investigations confirmed the identity of the wreck. This paper provides an historical background for the ship, a description of archaeological research conducted at the site, and efforts to protect it through declaration as an historic shipwreck under the Commonwealth's* Historic Shipwreck Act 1976.

The Steamship *Florence D*: Manufacture and Merchant History

During World War I the United States (US) merchant fleet suffered tremendous losses. To supplement the fleet the United Shipping Board, through the Emergency Fleet Corporation, contracted the construction of hundreds of standard type merchant ships. The Great Lakes district would ultimately produce 331 ships (Dowling 1967:45). Known as "lakers", these vessels were built to basic design standards to expedite construction and to assure requirements, such as a high deadweight-to gross tonnage ratio and minimum cruising speeds. Among those constructed was the steel hulled screw steamer *Lake Farmingdale*, built by Superior Ship Building Company in Superior, Wisconsin. Officially given ship yard identification number 545, *Lake Farmingdale* was based on a variation of the basic design known as the 'Am. S.B. Co. [Superior Shipbuilders] modified' or design number 1099 (Dowling 1967:45,69). Figure 1 shows a construction plan for another Superior laker, *Lake Farlin*, which is very similar in design to *Lake Farmingdale*.

Completed in July 1919, *Lake Farmingdale* a single deck riveted steel ship, which measured 251 feet (ft.) (76.5 meters (m)) in length, 43.5 ft. (13.3 m) in breadth and 28.2 ft. (8.6 m) in depth with a registered gross tonnage of 2,618 tons (Lloyd's 1919-1920[I]:entry

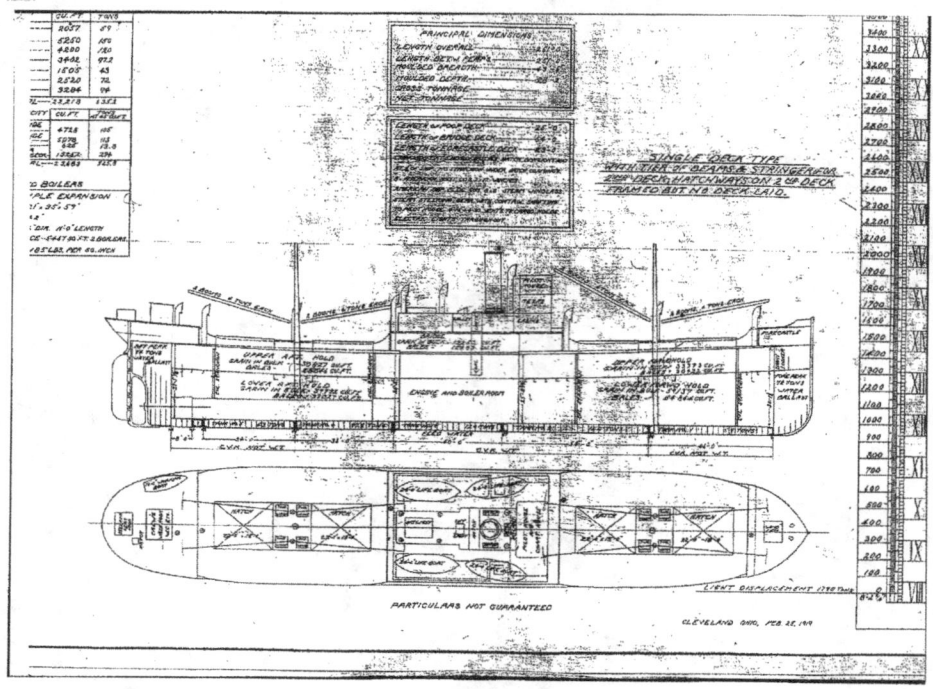

Figure 1. Construction plans for Lake Farlin (hull #544), another Superior built "laker" similar in design to Florence D (ex-Lake Farmingdale). (Courtesy of the Historical Collection of the Great Lakes, Bowling Green State University).

18573). After modifications the ship's final registered gross tonnage was 2,638 tons, with a length of 247.4 ft. (75.4 m) and a breadth of 43.3 ft. (13.2 m) (Lloyds 1944-45[I]:entry 74818). Initially registered in San Francisco, California to the Pacific Mail Steamship Company, *Lake Farmingdale* was operated by the United States Shipping Board and engaged in runs between Hong Kong and Calcutta every two months (*Pacific Marine Review* 1922:XVIII).

Around 1925, the ship was sold to the Cadwallader Gibson Lumber Co. in Manila, Philippines and its name was changed from *Lake Farmingdale* to *Florence D* (Lloyd's 1925-26[II]:323). The ship was to be used to transport timber from the company's forests to its mills, and for other services as required. Although Lloyd's entries continue to list the company as the owner, it is unclear whether the family maintained control of the vessel until the outbreak of WWII, since the timber company was closed following a series of setbacks.

Wartime Mission and Loss

With the outbreak of the WWII conflict in the Pacific region, allied forces required additional vessels to assist with the war effort. Flying from Darwin to Java (Indonesia) Colonel J. Robinson of the US Army was tasked to locate small, fast merchant ships capable of getting rations, ammunition, and other desperately needed supplies to General Douglas MacArthur's forces pinned down at Corregidor Island in the Philippines (Underbrink 1971:59). Though the role of *Florence D* in the war effort prior to its final mission is unknown, in February 1942 it entered into a contract with the US Army.

Loaded with cargos destined for Manila Bay, *Florence D* departed Surabaya (Indonesia) while another merchant ship, *Don Isidro*, also contracted by Robinson, departed Batavia (now Jakarta, Indonesia). The total cargo for both ships included: 500,000 rations; 10,000 rounds of 3 inch (in.) (76.2 millimeter (mm)) ammunition; 250,000 rounds of .50 caliber (12.7 mm) heavy machine gun ammunition; and 3,000,000 rounds of .30 caliber (7.62 mm) small arms ammunition. The cargo of *Florence D* also consisted of luxury items including canned fruits, jams, jellies, candies, cigarettes, and beer; that of *Don Isidro* included flour and dry rations (Underbrink 1971:76). According to Underbrink:

> *When the ship [Florence D] was nearly loaded, Colonel Robenson [sic] gave Captain Manzano a case of beer to be delivered to General M. Wainwright in the Philippines … Included with the package was a letter in which Robenson [sic] said '… This ship contains … practically all the 3" A.A. [anti-aircraft] ammunition there is in the Far East … (1971:75)*

Powell (1992:93) suggests that both ships may have abandoned their mission after coming under fire and were heading for the perceived safety of Darwin. For this reason, both were west of Bathurst Island on 19 February 1942. Unknown to the captains of *Florence D* and *Don Isidro*, however, Darwin was attacked on the same day by two massive waves of Japanese aircraft. This was the first time the Australian mainland had been attacked and the raids devastated the city, sinking most of the ships in the harbour including the destroyer USS *Peary*. Air attacks on the NT would continue for two years, with historians currently estimating the number at 64 raids (Alford 1991:78-79, Lockwood 2005:x). Thus, on that day the two merchant ships fled enemy fire, but were unwittingly steaming into a battlefield.

The first casualty of the Japanese attack force was a PatWing 10 PBY5 Catalina ("flying boat") based in Darwin and commanded by U.S. Navy (USN) Lieutenant Moorer (Lockwood 2005:58). Moorer's Catalina was shot down while conducting a routine patrol, but the crew made it into a life raft and were soon picked up by *Florence D* (Moorer 1942). Moorer described how, after observing the Japanese planes returning from its attack on Darwin, *Florence D* received and responded to a distress call from *Don Isidro* which was also under attack and on fire with many wounded. While underway to assist, *Florence D* itself was attacked multiple times taking direct bomb hits and was sunk. Though three Filipino crew and one USN airman were killed, the remaining crews made it to Bathurst Island on life-rafts. After some time on the island, the survivors were rescued by the corvette HMAS *Warrnambool* and taken to Darwin (Moorer 1942).

Site Discovery

Although the steamship *Don Isidro* was deliberately beached on Bathurst Island to avoid sinking in deep water, and its location has long been known, the whereabouts of Moorer's Catalina and *Florence D* became wartime mysteries. In 2006, however, local Darwin fisherman Wayne Keeping detected an anomaly on his depth sounder approximately 12 nautical miles from Bathurst Island. Although the target was distorted by an abundance of fish attracted to the structure, Keeping was able to determine that the structure was quite small and likely represented an aircraft wreck. In 2008, Keeping shared information about the anomaly with Jim Miles, a local diver and history enthusiast who had recently read *Ten Shipwrecks of the Northern Territory* (Clark 2008) and was most intrigued by the story of *Florence D*. Miles suggested that Keeping had discovered either the *Florence D* shipwreck or Moorer's Catalina. The pair later visited the site and Miles conducted three short bounce dives with visibility of less than .5 ft. (20-30 centimeters). On that dive he identified an iron rivet on an iron hull, suggesting it was the wreck of a ship rather than a plane. Miles also produced compelling (but ultimately inconclusive) remote sensing imagery, using a hull mounted Hummingbird side-scan that he had modified to tow in deep water (Miles 2008). Upon returning to Darwin, Miles and Keeping reported their findings and the location of the site to staff at the Museum and Art Gallery of the NT (MAGNT). MAGNT staff in turn informed officials at the NT Heritage Branch, who then organized an expedition to investigate the site in March 2009.

2009 Fieldwork

The aim of the 2009 NT Heritage Branch expedition was to determine whether the anomaly identified by Wayne Keeping represented the wreck of the steamship *Florence D*. Keeping joined the expedition as an observer, but Miles could not attend due to work commitments. Evidence supporting the identification included video from Miles' reconnaissance dives on the site which showed what appeared to be an iron sheet with rivet holes around its edges. Data relating to the techniques used in the construction of *Florence D* indicate that its hull was riveted (Report of Survey for Repairs, &c. 12 June 1919). The location of the anomaly was also seen as positive evidence since it corresponded with a survivor's recollection of the general geographic area for the ship's loss (Moorer 1942), and no other iron hulled vessels are historically known to have wrecked in the area. Despite these observations, questions about the small size of the anomaly from Keeping's depth sounder remained, since *Florence D* was a large ship with a known length of 251 ft. (76.5 m) and breadth of 43.7 ft. (13.3 m).

Due to the remote location of the site, the expedition platform was a 65 ft. (20 m) chartered fishing vessel equipped with living quarters and a large operations area, as well as sophisticated electronic navigation and sounding technologies. Among these was the MaxSea bottom profiling system which captures bathymetric data about the seabed while the vessel is underway. This system generated a detailed three-dimensional map of the seabed at the site and allowed for the identification of three distinct rises, which together measured approximately 230 ft. (70 m) in length. Since the known length of *Florence D* was 251 ft. (76.5 m), it was postulated that the three anomalies may represent the heavily reinforced bow, midships with engine and boilers, and stern sections of the ship. That the length of the wreckage was broken into three rises suggested that Keeping's depth sounder may have only identified one section, thus explaining his interpretation of the site as a much smaller wreck. To better understand the site prior to diving, a side scan sonar survey was conducted using an Imagenex Sport-Scan unit operated from the mothership's tender. The survey produced detailed imagery of a discreet wreck site and indicated a broken and twisted hull with features such as the bow and keel clearly visible.

The remote location of the site and regional environmental conditions make diving difficult and require a solid understanding of local tidal activity. Initial attempts to investigate the wreck through diver inspection were hampered by visibility. As predicted, however, visibility improved over the course of the fieldwork from approximately 1 ft. (0.3 m) to 5 ft. (1.5 m) in some areas, though the deeper sections of the wreck remained at near zero visibility. With the increased visibility diagnostic evidence was noted which included: a peeled back section of hull with rivet holes, a debris field of spilled cargo consisting predominately .30 and .50 calibre ammunition and 3 in. artillery shells, some provisions in bottles and jars, and the bow of the vessel with a visible hawse pipe (no chain). To optimize use of the limited dive time and brief windows of visibility provided by the neap tide, the crew was divided into two dive teams with one focused solely on collecting video and still photography of the exposed cargo, while the other further explored to better understand the disposition.

Using information obtained from both remote sensing and diver inspections, a general impression of the site was formed. The wreck rests on its starboard side with its bow to north in 36 to 60 ft. (11 to 18 m) of water. The three rises noted on the sounder coincide with the intact bow, an intact portion of the midships hull that is thought to be laying on the triple expansion steam engine, and the intact stern of the ship. With the identification of features associated with the ship's bow it was surmised that the exposed area of cargo originated from the lower reaches of the forward hold.

The results of the fieldwork confirm that the anomaly discovered by Wayne Keeping in 2006 is indeed the wreck of *Florence D*. This positive identification is based on a number of diagnostic features and data including: references to (or lack thereof) historic shipwrecks in the region, a general geographic location which corresponds with archival data and survivor accounts, the overall dimensions of the wreck, construction features such as the riveted steel hull, and the artifacts noted on the site. Conclusions about the wreck's morphology (general layout) suggest that the hull structure lies on its starboard side, broken into four main sections and that the turn of the hull obscures much of the deck features. The twisted and disarticulated nature of the wreck is consistent with those of a vessel sinking due to enemy bombing, as well as with post-depositional forces such as extreme cyclonic conditions which have also affected the wreck site. A ruptured forward cargo hold has created a cargo debris field that spreads across the lower forward hull area and the adjacent sandy seabed. Cargo predominately consists of .30 and .50 calibre ammunition and 3 in. artillery – much of which is unexploded – and some bottles and jars that once contained provisions. Since the wreck is a known war grave, and is an inherent danger to vessels attempting to anchor on it, recommendations included further archaeological investigation to better understand the wreck, declaration of the site as an historic shipwreck under the Commonwealth's *Historic Shipwrecks Act 1976*, and the designation of an exclusion zone around the wreck to protect it and the public from potential risks (Steinberg 2009).

2011 Fieldwork

In 2011, the NT Heritage Branch mounted another expedition to the *Florence D* shipwreck site (Steinberg 2012). Using the same vessel as a work platform, the investigation aims included further developing an understanding of the wreck's morphology; recording key diagnostic structural and engineering features such as the transom, propeller, and engine block; continuing the process of identifying and recording visible cargo; and conducting further side scan sonar surveys of the site to compare with previous data. A through-water communication system was employed to provide effective communication between the divers and the surface.

Diving operations during the entirety of the 2011 expedition were hampered by extremely poor visibility. The wreck sits in 60 ft. (18 m) of water, with the wreck's peaks rising to a depth of 36 ft. (11 m). Despite best efforts to plan dives to coincide with favourable seasons and tidal activity, unexpected environmental conditions prevented divers from visually inspecting the wreck. For the first half of the field operations, visibility was affected by turbidity – namely sediment consisting of fine sand, clay and silt stirred up from the seabed. As the expedition progressed, it was expected that the sediment would settle and visibility would improve, as was experienced in 2009. However, instead of clear visibility, a coral bloom then moved over the site and enveloped the wreck in a white cloud. Poor diving conditions persisted through the end of the optimum tidal period for dive operations. Despite these adverse conditions, efforts were made by divers to inspect anomalies identified from sonar data and to communicate what they felt with topside dive supervisors. Three main areas identified from 2009 sides scan imagery (Figure 2) were revisited in the 2011 fieldwork.

The first identified feature, referred to as Area A, includes a large rectangular structural object and was identified by the 2011 team as forward hatch coamings. The feature referred to as Area B appears to contain a boiler, although this was not verified in 2009. Confirmed as a boiler by divers in 2011, this was one of two "scotch

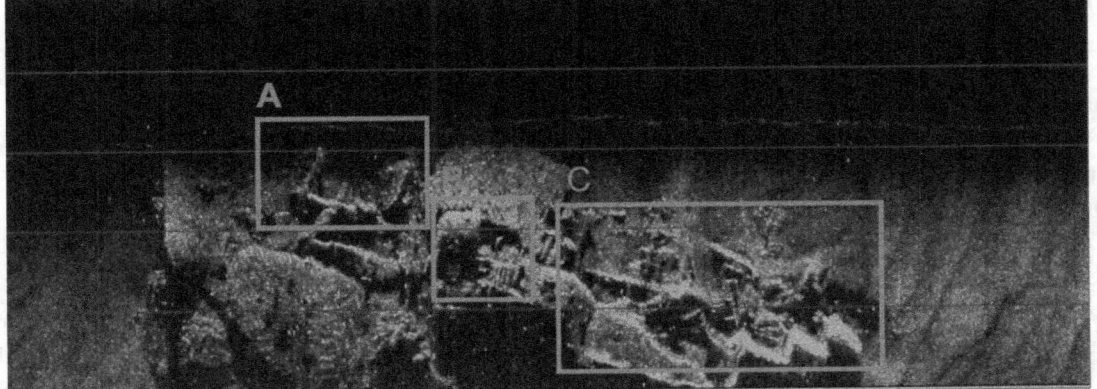

Figure 2. Sonar image of the Florence D site collected in 2009 with two distinctive areas highlighted. (Courtesy of NT Heritage Branch).

Figure 3. Sonar image of the Florence D site collected in 2011 with two distinctive areas highlighted. (Courtesy of the NT Heritage Branch).

type" boilers – each with three furnaces. Records indicate that the engine was converted for burning oil rather than coal, which only required an adaptation to the boilers rather than their replacement; hence, the relevance of the details of the original boilers (Lloyd's Vol.1 1919-1920: entry 18573). Although the poor visibility made determination difficult, divers reported that the boiler seemed to protrude out from broken hull debris with their faces remaining orientated bow to stern. Divers noted that the furnaces were arced across the top of the boiler, which indicates that the boiler has rolled from its original operational position; thus, it is clear that some movement has occurred either during the wrecking event or as a result of post-depositional change. Located approximately 115 ft. (35 m) from the bow, the boiler has moved only slightly from its original position. . The surveyed dimensions of the boiler are approximately 14.5 ft. (4.3 m) in diameter and 11.2 ft. (3.4 m) in length. The diameter of the exposed part of the boiler was measured at 10 ft. (3.1 m) and indicates that approximately only one-third of it is exposed above the surrounding hull debris. Area C appears to show steps of a substantial structure and likely reflects the staggered heights of the broken stern section structure. Diver inspection of this area indicated highly disarticulated and exposed detail rather than inverted hull plating.

Since poor tidal and visibility conditions limited divers' abilities to accurately record the site, the main focus of the fieldwork shifted to remote sensing. Again using an Imagenex Sport-Scan unit, sonar surveys were conducted to ensure that data was recovered from multiple directions of the site in order to assist in mapping this complex and disarticulated wreck. The multi-directional approach had the effect of changing the angle of shadows produced by features. Though some previously noted features were obscured, a much clearer impression of the large structural features was obtained.

The 2011 sonar surveys added valuable information about two sections of the site in particular (Figure 3). The first of these, referred to as Area A, highlights a section of the wreck at midships that was obscured in previous sonar imagery. Though this portion of the hull was considered to be intact, part of it appears to be ruptured and artifacts previously noted by divers in that area could represent spilled cargo that was once positioned at the lower levels of the ship. It is possible that remnants of the propulsion engine or the engine bed are intact; unfortunately, visibility was zero in this area of the wreck and prevented inspection. The other section of the wreck that yielded new data is referred to as Area B. This area appears to show the tapered end of the aft section of the hull and indicates that the extreme stern section is actually separated from the rest of the hull. Divers attempted to determine the nature of this end of the site, but poor visibility and heavy marine growth attached to the structure prohibited visual inspection.

Despite zero visibility conditions encountered at the site, the 2011 NT Heritage Branch expedition produced useful information and provided much insight into the wreck of *Florence D*. Combining data gleaned from both sonar survey and diver inspection, an updated sketch of the site was produced (Figure 4). Though the sketch has a considerable degree of error in terms of scale and distortion, it incorporates the major features visible in multiple sonar images and has been cross checked against diver observations to provide a working model that helps with site interpretation.

Personal Connections

After confirming the identity of the wreck as that of *Florence D*, the NT Heritage Branch sought to notify the families of the lost mariners and the USN airman. Consultation with the Filipino consul and with colleagues in the Philippines continues to date. Australian records on aliens residing in Australia have

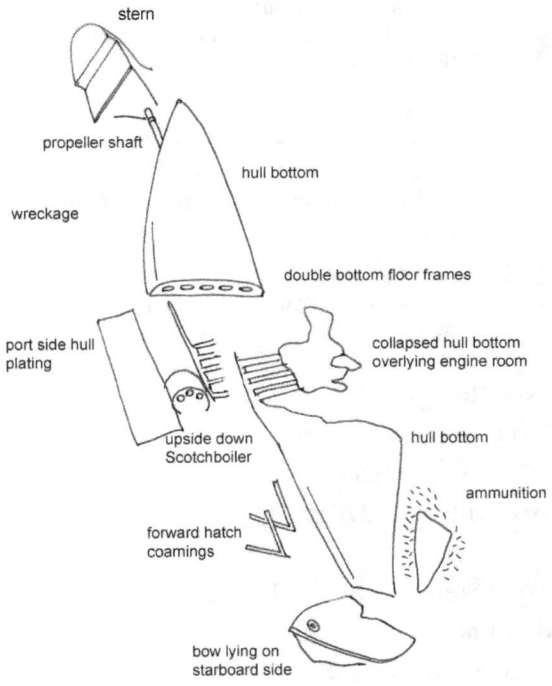

Figure 4. Sketch of the Florence D shipwreck site compiled from data collected during both expeditions to the site. (Sketch by Ross Anderson).

identified crew members that lived in Australia after surviving the sinking. The NT Heritage Branch was successful in locating a niece of Joseph Clifton Schuler (AM2c) of the USN -- an airman rescued by *Florence D* crew and who later died in the sinking of the ship. Although the brother of Airman Schuler had died some years previously, his niece shared the news of the wreck's discovery with a living cousin who had written to him during the war. In correspondence to Airman Schuler's niece, the Director of the NT Heritage Branch confirmed that:

I hope that the discovery of this wreck has provided you and your family some degree of closure and that you find our measures appropriate. I assure you that we have a great respect for the contribution your uncle made in the defence of Australia, and we protect this site accordingly.

Contact was also made with the Cadwallader family, who owned *Florence D* prior to its involvement in the Allied war effort. Through this correspondence we learned that the ship was named *Florence D* after a family matriarch. It was also discovered that during the Japanese occupation of Manila, the Cadwallader family were interned as prisoners of war and were rescued by commandos tasked by General Douglas MacArthur (David Steinberg, pers. comm. 9 April 2011).

Rewarding the Finders and Site Protection

In April 2009, *Florence D* was declared an historic shipwreck under the Commonwealth of Australia's *Historic Shipwrecks Act*. Minister for Environment Protection, Heritage and the Arts Heritage Peter Garrett also signed an instrument in April 2009 declaring a protected zone around the site thereby controlling access to the area. Then-NT Minister for Heritage Alison Anderson publicly thanked history enthusiast and diver Jim Miles and commercial fisherman Wayne Keeping for their discovery and for notifying authorities of the site, and awarded them each a memorial plaque.

The provisions enacted to protect the wreck were tested in 2011 when it was reported that a diver illegally removed a 3 in. artillery shell from the site. Following an investigation, the shell was retrieved and the guilty party prosecuted. The shell was ceremoniously handed to the US Ambassador to Australia by the NT Chief Minister, who then provided it to the Defence of Darwin Museum where it remains on display.

Conclusion

The discovery and positive identification of *Florence D* has laid to rest one of the great wartime mysteries of northern Australia. That this ship was contracted in Java, destined for Manila, and sunk outside Darwin waters in a Japanese attack demonstrates clearly how the story of northern Australia was interconnected with Allied campaigns to its north. Though archaeological investigations of the site were considerably limited by difficult diving conditions, remote sensing operations augmented data collection. The multi-directional side scan sonar survey approach, which allowed for the angle of shadows to change and reveal new features, proved to be an invaluable strategy. The discovery of spilled artillery shells and ammunition in the forward section of the site during dive operations led to the ship's definitive identification. The artifacts proved to be a poignant reminder of the ship's urgent mission and the fate of the Allied forces in Corregidor who desperately needed, but never received, those supplies.

Acknowledgments

The authors would like to thank Jim Miles and Wayne Keeping for their discovery of the site, research, and notification to authorities. Thanks also to Robert Neyland of Naval History and Heritage Command and Ken Terry of Casualty Assistance Division, USN for assisting in locating the family of Airman Schuler. Thanks are also extended to David Pearson of the Australian War Memorial for research into the ship's history and cargo. Final thanks to members of the 2009 and 2011 fieldwork teams: John Riley (R.I.P.), Sue Sultana, Greg Murdoch, John Armstrong, Ross Anderson, James Parkinson, Craig Garland, and Grant Treloar.

References

ALFORD, ROBERT
1992   Darwin's Air War 1942-1945: An Illustrated History. The Aviation Historical Society of the Northern Territory, Darwin, Northern Territory.

AUSTRALIAN WAR MEMORIAL
2017   Official Histories AWM 54 963/9/2 and AWM 54 81/4/141https://www.awm.gov.au/histories. Accessed 29 February 2017.

CLARK, PAUL (EDITOR)
2008   Ten shipwreck of the Northern Territory. Museums and Art Gallery of the Northern Territory, Darwin, Northern Territory.

DOWLING, EDWARD J
1967   The "Lakers" of World War I. University of Detroit Press, Ann Arbor, Michigan.

LOCKWOOD, DOUGLAS
2005   Australia Under Attack: The Bombing of Darwin 1942. New Holland, Frenchs Forrest, New South Wales.

MILES, JIM
2008   Searching for the SS Florence-D (*Lake Farmingdale*), Manuscript, Northern Territory Heritage Branch Report. Darwin, Northern Territory.

MOORER, THOMAS H.
1942   Account of Action Engaged in by Crew of PBY-5 Number 18 during Period 19-23 February. RAAF Historical Section, NW Area Interviews, NAA Item 7816, Combat Report 23 February 1942.

PACIFIC MARINE REVIEW
1921   "Pacific American Merchant Marine: Pacific Mail Steamship Company." *Pacific Marine Review* January 1921.

POWELL, ALAN
1992   The Shadows Edge's Australia's Northern War. Melbourne University Press, Melbourne, Victoria.

STEINBERG, DAVID
2009   The *Florence D* Shipwreck: A Wreck Inspection Report and Preliminary Assessment of the Site's Significance. Manuscript, Northern Territory Heritage Branch Report. Darwin, Northern Territory.

STEINBERG, DAVID
2012   The *Florence D* Shipwreck: A Report on the October 2011 Site Visit. Manuscript, Northern Territory Heritage Branch Report. Darwin, Northern Territory.

UNDERBRINK, ROBERT L
1971   Destination Corregidor. United States Naval Institute, Washington, DC.

Jason Raupp
East Carolina University
302 East 9th Street
Greenville, NC 27858

David Steinberg Senior Heritage Officer
Maritime Archaeologist
Heritage Branch
Department of Lands, Planning and the Environment
GPO Box 1680
Darwin NT 0801

Shipwrecks, Doghole Ports, and the Lumber Trade: Maritime Cultural Landscape Survey of California's Sonoma Coast

Tricia Dodds

Humans have interacted with California's Sonoma Coast for thousands of years; it has shaped their lives and they have left their mark on the landscape. During the mid-19th and early 20th century, the lumber trade affected the coastal environment as it contributed to the West Coast's economic development. In 2016, California State Parks and NOAA led a multi-partner effort that studied submerged and terrestrial archaeological resources to reveal the lumber trade's maritime cultural landscape. From lumbering operations to doghole ports and shipwrecks, the Sonoma Coast holds the physical traces of its role in building California and developing the nation's economy.

The Northern California coast and its adjacent ocean environment are intimately linked. In no other place in the world is there the right confluence of marine climatic conditions for the growth of Coastal Redwoods and their attendant ecosystems. Specifically on the Sonoma Coast, these magnificent trees form the stage for thousands of years of human interaction with the marine environment. Human activities have impacted this coastline and its resources as much as this environment has shaped the activities and culture of the people who lived there. In addition to physical remains in the form of archaeological sites, industrial structures, and settlements, these interactions have left cultural traces ranging from place names to no longer used ocean highways to form a maritime cultural landscape that is unique and nationally important. One of these interactions along the Sonoma Coast was the lumber trade. As a result of the California Gold Rush that drove Americans west, those Californians who explored the periphery of the San Francisco Bay area recognized the Sonoma Redwoods as another abundant, highly valuable natural resource (Delgado 2013). While the most cost effective way to ship the lumber was by water, the area's lack of navigable waterways meant that lumbering operations established sawmills at the few bluff-sided coves along the shoreline where it was possible to temporarily anchor a vessel. These small and exposed "doghole ports," so named because mariners quipped they were barely large enough for a dog to turn around, became centers of economic activity and allowed lumber to be efficiently transferred from shore to the waiting vessel below. In addition to the much in-demand lumber, vessels also carried other forest products such as bark used for tanning leather, railroad ties, cord

Figure 1. Trough lumber chute at Fort Ross Cove (Fort Ross Conservancy).

wood, and other produce from the farms and ranches that developed in the area (Marx and Lawrence 2016; Delgado 2013).

Vessels calling at the doghole ports found two varieties of transshipment infrastructure to load lumber and other commodities: trough chutes and wire chutes. Trough chutes were first used in the area during the 1860s and had a tall wooden A-frame set at the water's edge that supported a wooden slide held in place with cables and guy wires secured into the adjacent bluff. Beyond the A-frame was a long cantilevered arm known as a swing apron that extended out over the ocean. As lumber slid down the chute to awaiting vessels, a system of pulleys and wire cables raised and lowered the apron. A movable plank or clapper at the end of the chute controlled the speed that materials slid down the chute (Marx and Lawrence 2016; Jackson 1977). Figure 1 shows a trough chute in action at Fort Ross Cove.

During the 1870s, the wire chute came into existence, eventually replacing the trough chute, which was subject to being washed away by winter storms. Once a vessel had anchored at a port, chute operators stretched a thick wire rope wound around a large drum from shore to an anchor point beyond the vessel. Bunks of lumber or other cargo were then slung from a traveler pulley attached to the wire, with the load's weight moving the pulley down to the vessel. A braking system at the chute head controlled the traveler's speed, and returned the pulley either by a counter balance or by steam power allowing cargos to be transferred from vessel to shore as well. Another advantage of the wire chute was its ability to transfer packaged bundles of lumber, greatly speeding up the time it took to load a vessel.

The other critical infrastructure that made this operation possible was a series of mooring points spaced around the lumber chute's end to stabilize the vessel while loading and unloading cargo. Offshore of the anchorage, heavy anchors set on the seafloor were attached to lengths of chain buoyed by floating logs. Inshore, metal eye bolts set in the cliffs and littoral rocks secured the mooring lines resulting in a web of connections (Jackson 1977).

The lumber trade significantly influenced the local maritime cultural landscape. As the Pacific Coast and American settlements of the West became urbanized, the coastal and ultimately the international lumber trade grew in response. With its thick redwood forests, the Sonoma Coast was a part of California's coastline that sparked a lumber trade that lasted from the mid-19th to the 20th century. The Sonoma Coast's inhabitants adapted to the rugged maritime environment by creating these doghole ports and constructing small, maneuverable schooners that hugged the coast to transport the in-demand lumber to markets. That trade left behind not only place names and the physical remains of the doghole ports and those vessels unlucky enough to wreck off the coast, but also maritime communities such as Bodega Bay, Gualala, and Point Arena that still remain today (Delgado 2013; Marx and Lawrence 2016).

The Sonoma Coast and its lumber industry helped build not only California but the nation's economy and communities. People traveled from around the world to settle this place and established themselves and their families on these shores to engage in a lucrative trade with ports as close as San Francisco and San Diego or as far away as the Eastern Seaboard, Australia, and Asia (Delgado 2013).

During the summer of 2016, archaeologists, anthropologists, and historians initiated the Sonoma Coast Doghole Ports Project to survey the submerged and terrestrial archaeological resources associated with the lumber trade of the Sonoma Coast. This collaborative project included California State Parks (CSP) Maritime Heritage Program, the National Oceanic and Atmospheric Administration (NOAA) Office of National Marine Sanctuaries (ONMS), Sonoma State University, National Park Service, Greater Farallones Association, Fort Ross Conservancy, and California Department of Transportation (Figure 2). The Sonoma Coast Doghole Ports Project covered a thirty-mile long area of Northern California's coastline stretching from Duncan's Landing at the southern end to Gualala at the northern end. The survey team documented visible sites, features, structures, and artifacts to reveal aspects of the Sonoma Coast maritime cultural landscape and the doghole ports' role in the region's history. The project first focused on doghole ports within the CSP system, NOAA's Greater Farallones National Marine Sanctuary (GFNMS), and a number of California state designated marine protected areas with the goal of resource protection and interpretation of the historical and archaeological properties. The team also investigated several shipwrecks associated with the lumber trade as well as the larger Sonoma Coast's maritime transportation network. The team collected data and imagery for site assessments to help resource managers with baseline information for interpretation, monitoring, and enforcement.

A total of 11 doghole ports were surveyed for this project using non-disturbance archaeological survey techniques with no excavation or artifact collection.

The survey team recorded the resources associated with the doghole ports using photos and video, measured sketches, and Global Positioning System (GPS) equipment, and then compiled and imported the data into Geographic Information System (GIS) software to create a map of each doghole port's archaeological features. Initially, the project was divided into a land crew, which surveyed the cliffs, shoreline, and intertidal zone to locate archaeological features, and an underwater team based from the NOAA Research Vessel Fulmar. Divers conducted swim searches within the doghole ports to locate lumbering infrastructure artifacts as well as shipwrecks associated with the lumber trade. Project data analysis and mapping are ongoing; however, preliminary results from two doghole ports provide initial information on the variety of resources found. Future publications will elaborate on the larger Sonoma Coast maritime cultural landscape.

Fort Ross was the first doghole port visited during this survey. Most well-known for its Russian settlement, Fort Ross Cove also hold the remains of the SS Pomona, which has been the focus of much maritime archaeological research. In 1908, SS Pomona was traveling from San Francisco to Eureka when it struck an uncharted rock two miles from Fort Ross reef. Seeking to avoid loss of life as his vessel took on water, Captain Swanson decided to ground the steamer in the cove. Instead of reaching the targeted sandy beach, the ship rode up on a large rock that impaled its hull. Fortunately, the 147 passengers and crew safely escaped to shore with help from a nearby vessel (Smith and Breece 2002; Beeker 2005). While not specifically associated with the lumber industry, the Pomona is an integral part of the maritime cultural landscape, serving as an example of the effects of the coast's rugged topography, the involvement of the local ranching families in lifesaving, and vessel salvage activities.

Fort Ross Cove's northern shoreline was the central location of the port's lumber activities on land. James Dixon built the first trough lumber chute there in 1867. By 1873, the Call family had purchased the land, continuing to ship lumber and also expanding the area's farming and ranching activities. After strong winds blew down the trough chute in 1900, the Call family relocated the lumber loading facilities closer to the open sea in 1901 and reconfigured the trough chute as a wire chute. They rebuilt the wire chute in 1910 and eventually dismantled it in the early 1920s, ceasing lumber shipment from the port (Carlson et al. 1975; Kalani and Sweedler 2004).

Project archaeologists made many new discoveries this past summer within the lumbering transshipment area at Fort Ross, documenting numerous extant elements associated with the wharf and the two chutes, including mortared rebates that secured A-frame legs, stabilizing cables which held the chute in place, a timber

Figure 2. The project team consisted of archaeologists and researchers from California State Parks, ONMS, GFNMS, San Francisco Maritime National Historical Park, and Sonoma State University (Paul Veisze, California State Parks).

chute platform where the chute infrastructure was built, and mooring points for vessels docking under the chutes. The majority of artifacts were metal hardware such as pins, bolts, eye bolts, rings, and anchor points driven into surrounding rocks.

Near the southern mooring anchor at the chute end, the underwater survey crew found a small anchor on the cove's bottom. The anchor's small size precluded its use as a mooring. Most likely, it came from a small schooner, the J. Eppinger, which wrecked in the cove in 1901, as it closely resembled another anchor reportedly recovered from the J. Eppinger wreck by recreational divers in 1960 (San Francisco Chronicle 1901; Fort Ross Library 1960). Near the northern mooring location, divers located a diesel engine and other vessel remains. A likely candidate for this shipwreck's identity is the fishing vessel Riga that the Petaluma, California's Argus-Courier reported as burning and sinking in Fort Ross Cove on 11 May 1932. The survey team also relocated the SS Pomona, recorded the wreck's geographic orientation, captured imagery and assessed its site condition. Overall, the site remains in similar condition to when it was

Figure 3. Diver examining the Pomona's boiler (Matthew Lawrence, NOAA/ONMS).

mapped in the 1990s, although the boiler has degraded further as illustrated in Figure 3.

Gerstle Cove provides another example of the resources located during the doghole ports survey. Today, Gerstle Cove is part of Salt Point State Park, which is renowned for its natural beauty but has little interpretation of its cultural heritage for visitors. The cove's first lumber cargo, lowered laboriously down the cliffside, shipped out in 1854. In 1872, lumberman William Miller built the port's first chute, which operated until 1889. Funcke & Company built a second inner chute in 1876, which lasted considerably longer, only closing in 1917. Unlike other doghole ports in the area, Gerstle Cove also shipped out cargos of sandstone from a massive outcrop on the conveniently located adjacent marine terrace. Schooners carried the stone to San Francisco and the Mare Island Naval Shipyard in Vallejo (Rudy 2009). Mariners visiting Gerstle Cove used wire cables anchored to the rings in the cliffside to stabilize their vessels while loading cargo. These anchor points allowed them to position their vessels broadside at the end of the chute with as many as six mooring lines. Four mooring buoys also stabilized vessels farther out in the cove (Davidson 1889; Marx and Lawrence 2016). By the beginning of the twentieth century, there were few trees left, and the area was in economic decline. By 1909, the area was practically abandoned (Tittmann 1909).

The land survey team identified 15 features including an excavated footing for the chute structure, metal pins and eyebolts in an orientation that indicated the presence of more than one chute, steel bars, a metal rod, and quarried sandstone blocks abandoned on the slope above the former chute location. The dive team investigated three historically reported mooring locations, and at one of them found a large collapsible stock anchor and chain (Figure 4). Unfortunately, the team found that modifications to the landscape and its artifacts impacted the integrity of the lumbering landscape. In one case, a segment of old roadbed that led to one of the chutes was cut off by a modern paved road. Similarly, the team found an anchor behind the entrance booth at Gerstle Cove that likely originated from the mooring field before its removal by local divers.

Looking ahead to the future, NOAA and California State Parks have several goals for the Sonoma Coast Doghole Ports Project. By combining the results from the survey with historical maps and photos, archaeological resources will be placed into the larger historical context of the doghole ports and California's lumber industry. The team plans to make the project's results publicly accessible through geographically linked narrative text, photos, and video through an ArcGIS Story map. The agencies will also update Fort Ross' existing National Register of Historic Places nomination to add information on its role as a doghole port. Fort Ross will become a contributing property to a National Register of Historic Places Multiple Property nomination for Sonoma Coast's doghole ports that will include both terrestrial and underwater features as a maritime cultural landscape.

As a result of the successful partnerships developed during this project there are plans to expand the survey

Figure 4. Mooring anchor discovered at Gerstle Cove (Kenneth Kramer, California State Parks).

along California's coast to new areas. Using the same landscape-scale methodology, NOAA and California State Parks are preparing to conduct a similar survey of Monterey Bay National Marine Sanctuary and Point Lobos State Marine Reserve and State Marine Conservation Area as well as the Point Lobos State Natural Reserve. This investigation into co-located whaling, abalone fishing, quarrying, and coal mining will add another chapter to the maritime cultural landscape study of California's coast.

References

Beeker, Charles
2005   *S.S. Pomona* Shipwreck Project, Fort Ross State Historic Park, California. California State Parks, Sacramento, California.

Carlson, Earl V., Fred Meyer, and Norman L. Wilson
1975   Fort Ross State Historic Park Resource Management Plan and General Development Plan. California Department of Parks and Recreation, Sacramento, California.

Davidson, George
1889   United States Coast Pilot of California, Oregon, and Washington, 4th edition. Department of Commerce and Labor Coast and Geodetic Survey, Government Printing Office, Washington, DC.

Delgado, James P.
2013   The "Redwood Coast:" The Maritime Cultural Landscape of the Potential Expansion of Cordell Bank and Gulf of the Farallones National Marine Sanctuaries. National Oceanic and Atmospheric Administration Office of National Marine Sanctuaries Maritime Heritage Program, Washington DC.

Fort Ross Library
1960   Anchor from J. Eppinger. Historic photograph collection Fort Ross Library, Fort Ross, California.

Jackson, Walter A.
1977   The Doghole Schooners. Bear & Stebbins, Fort Bragg, California.

Kalani, Lyn and Sarah Sweedler
2004   Fort Ross and the Sonoma Coast. Arcadia Publishing, Charleston, South Carolina.

Marx, Deborah, and Matthew Lawrence
2016   Sonoma Coast Doghole Port Project Research Design. National Oceanic and Atmospheric Administration Office of National Marine Sanctuaries Maritime Heritage Program, Scituate, Massachusetts.

Rudy, Lyn H.
2009   The Old Salt Point Township. The Hay Press, Jenner, California.

San Francisco Chronicle
1901   Schooner J. Eppinger Wrecked. San Francisco Chronicle 4 January, San Francisco, California.

SMITH, SHELI O., AND LAUREL H. BREECE
2002 California State Marine Managed Areas: Cultural Resource Survey 2001/2002. Long Beach City College Maritime Archaeology Certificate Program, Long Beach, California.

TITTMANN, O.H.
1909 United States Coast Pilot of California, Oregon, and Washington, 2nd edition. Department of Commerce and Labor Coast and Geodetic Survey, Government Printing Office, Washington, DC.

Tricia Dodds
California State Parks
5172 Hwy 78 #10
Borrego Springs, CA 92004
tricia.dodds@parks.ca.gov

Second campaign of excavation on the *Saintes Bay Wreck*, Guadeloupe, FW

Jean-Sébastien Guibert, Franck Bigot, Magali Lachèvre, Jean-Jacques Maréchal, Marine Sadania, Noémie Tomadini, Magali Veyrat

This paper presents results from the July 2016 excavation of the Saintes Bay Wreck, *Guadeloupe, French West Indies (FWI). The wreck was hypothesized to be the* Anémone, *an 1823 French schooner built in Bayonne and used as a customs ship in Guadeloupe thanks to archival research (Guibert 2013). The 2015 campaign provided initial evidence confirming it (Guibert 2016). The 2016 excavation re-surveyed the site and excavated discreet trenches to understand the site's layout, evaluate the ship's structure, and to identify remaining material culture. Our goal was to definitively confirm or reject the* Saintes Bay Wreck's *identity as the* Anémone.

Introduction

In 2015, an initial archaeological campaign tentatively identified the *Saintes Bay Wreck* as the *Anémone*, a French schooner built in 1823 in Bayonne. The *Anémone* was used as a customs ship in Guadeloupe before it was lost in Saintes Bay in September 1824 during a hurricane (Guibert 2013). We returned in July 2016 as part of the French West Indies University research program. Our goal was to gain a thorough understanding of the site in hope of confirming the wreck's identity. The project involved fourteen professional and scientific divers, and nearly 170 hours of diving. Test trenches were opened with the intention of exposing the wreck structure to enable a more precise recording of the timbers and gain a better interpretation of shipbuilding techniques. Schooners were built following a specific type plan in 1823, thus we sought to determine if the *Saintes Bay Wreck* structure matched this plan. The work also sought to evaluate material cultural remains on the wreck and determine if they fit the context of items used aboard a 19th century, French West Indies customs ship. Both archival and archaeological records were used to provide insight on the ship's history, crew, and everyday life onboard.

Site location

The *Saintes Bay Wreck* is located in the middle of Saintes Bay, in line with and near the entrance of the Terre de Haut mooring. It is submerged in 24m of water. The site has been known to local divers since the 1990s, and has been partially looted. It wasn't until 2002 that scientific research was first conducted on site by the Département des Recherches Archéologiques Subaquatiques et Sous-Marines (DRASSM) (L'Hour and Massy 2002). The site appears as a mound or sand tumulus, with visible but unidentified metal structural elements. Fragments of copper sheathing and probable pig iron are scattered around the site.

The 2015 and 2016 Campaigns

The *Anémone* is well documented through archives and bibliographies; however, until 2015, researchers had no theories as to its final whereabouts (ANOM SG/GUA/CORR/68 25/3/1825; Lacour 1855; Boudriot 1989). Our findings in the 2015 campaign led us to believe the *Saintes Bay Wreck* site was the *Anémone*. We reached this hypothesis through the discovery of an 1818-type 12 pounder carronade, 19th century ceramic and glass artifacts, and structural features matching the *Anémone*'s 1823 plan type (Guibert et al. 2015; Guibert 2016). However, our findings were nonconclusive. Thus, the 2016 project was carried out to gather more evidence.

The 2016 campaign brought us a better understanding of the site layout, and we were able to locate the stern and bow (Figure 1). Both the material culture and the frame structure analysis supported the identification hypothesis. Items found on the sea bottom in close proximity to the wreck site have been identified as a cooking oven and marmites.

Survey and excavation methods consisted of probing the seafloor in the area of the wreck, in situ observation, test trench dredging, artifact and structure sampling, and structure marking and mapping. At the end of the campaign, both trench tests were back filled. Project personnel also took the opportunity to contact the discoverer of the site to study artifacts he plundered in the 1990s.

Building on historical research undertaken in 2015, our 2016 efforts focused on the chronology and history of the *Anémone*, as well as the crew. We also reviewed Bayonne's shipbuilding techniques, examining the records of the five other schooners built according to the

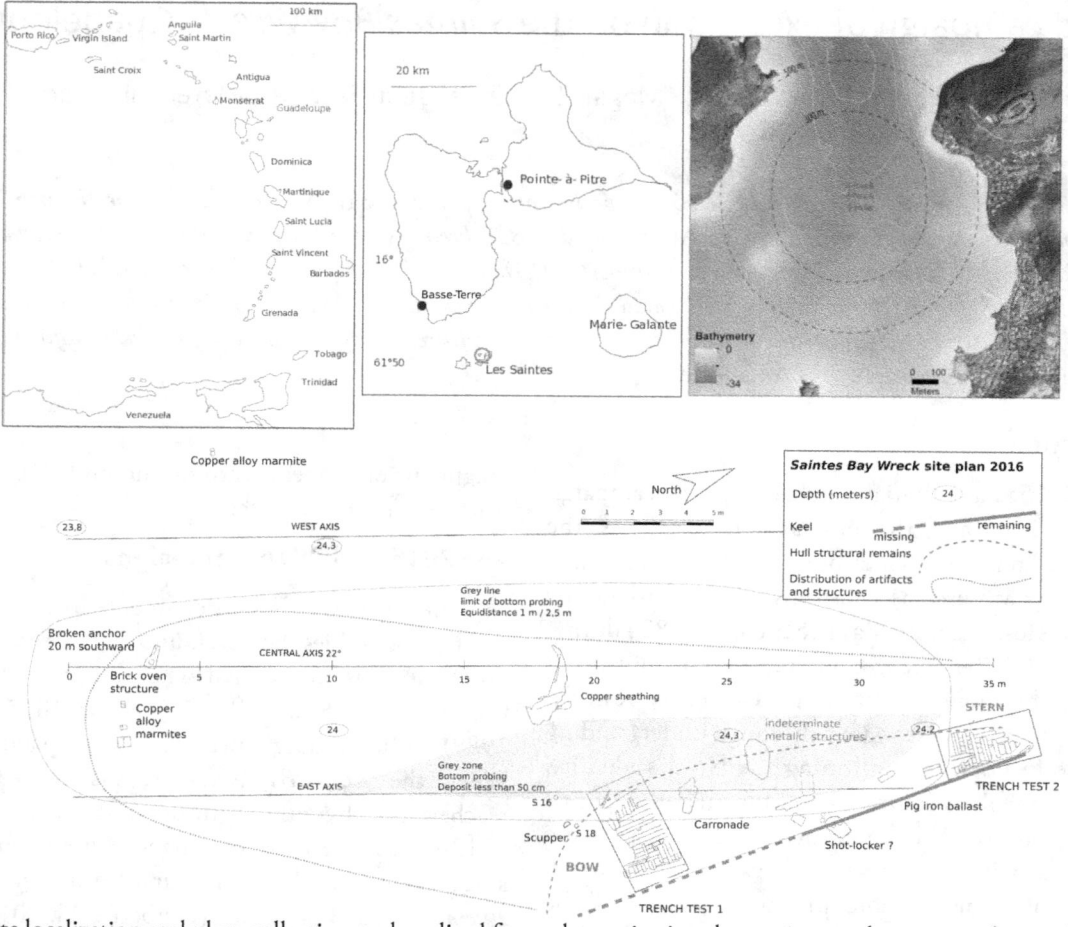

Figure 1. Site localization and plan, collective work realized from photos, in situ observations and measures, digitized by author / site localization by Émilie Lagahé.

same plan type. Through our research, we developed a comprehensive overview of the history of the *Anémone*. She participated in the Spain war in 1823 before being sent to the West Indies, where she was involved in customs missions such as fighting against the illegal slave trade. She was lost in Saintes Bay in September 1824 during a hurricane (Guibert 2015).

Anémone and its sister ship, Rose, were built within five months in Bayonne. The archives give us *Anémone*'s characteristics: she was copper sheathed, had filling frames, and was built with 24 frames (type plans mention 20 frames) (SHD Rochefort 2G21/71). Archival data on others schooners built to the same plan type (mainly Émeraude and Topaze, built in Cherbourg and Jacinthe and Jonquille in Toulon) show that they were built to uniform size specifications (21m long × 5.8m in beam × 2.36m depth-of-hold) (Figure 2). Records also corroborate the precise internal layout of the ship, the presence of a Kersaint's galley, the use of 13 tons of pig iron ballast, as well as the ship's general layout and ordnance: 2 carronades, 2 swivel-guns and 2 blunderbusses (SHD Cherbourg 2G5 214).

Studying the muster roll found in the archives cast light on the *Anémone*'s crew. It was composed of 29 members: two officers, Captain Louis Guillotin and Surgeon Jean-Sébastien Peychaud; six noncommissioned officer; 17 seamen; three apprentice sailors (all from France - mainly the South-West region); and one pilot from Saint-Martin (FWI). Seven additional seamen had disembarked or had deserted during the ongoing campaign (SHD Rochefort 3E2 1224). The 29 members of the crew died during the loss of the ship. Most of their corpses were discovered the day after the wreck, drowned and floating in the vicinity of Cabrit Islet, by a Saintes fisherman (ANOM État civil Guadeloupe Terre-de-haut 1824 20-48).

Site Layout

Structures at the sea bottom

A broken anchor located 20m south of the site (and 45m from the hull remains) has been studied to determine if it belonged to the *Saintes Bay Wreck*. It is

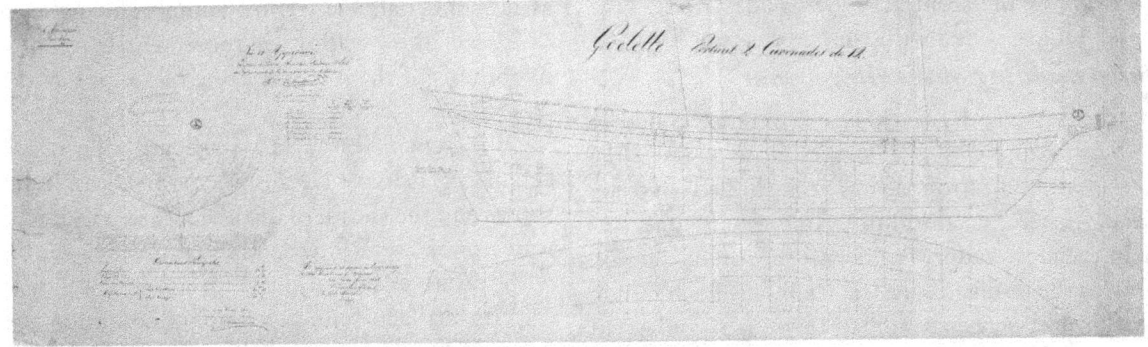

Figure 2. Schooner Anémone plan type, 1823, (SHD Vincennes 8 DD1 97).

broken on its shaft and measures 3.1m long × 2.6m wide. The estimated weight of it could be more than 1,000 pounds (452 Kg) according to late 18th century proportions. This is larger than the schooner anchors mentioned in archival data (Sadania 2015).

A bread oven has been identified 15m south-west of the hull remains (Figure 1 and 3). The structure is 1m long × 0.5m wide. The hearth comprises half the structure, and it includes a vault built with bricks and mortar; the floor is built with tiles. The oven is located nearby four brass galley elements, which were identified as marmites and were surely attached to a Kersaint's galley. Kersaint's galleys were in use in the beginning of 19th century (Figures 1 and 3). Three marmite sizes have been identified that could match with this kind of Kersaint Galley structure. The marmite studied in 2016 is 335 mm (L) × 265 mm (W) × 491 mm (H), with an estimated capacity of 40L. The one studied in 2015 is 210 mm (L) × 144 (W) × 310 mm (H), with an estimated capacity of 9L. It is possible the marmites were linked with the oven structure.

Unfortunately, it is difficult to assess if all these structures are linked with the wreck for two reasons. First, they are located in a secondary position far from the hull structure. Secondly, the archives mention that the *Anémone* had a Kersaint's galley, which is usually built with metal, but do not mention a bread oven. However, given their proximity, it is difficult to explain these structures' presence in any way other than belonging to the *Saintes Bay Wreck*. It is possible that mooring ships in the area may have dragged those elements away from the primary wreck structure with their anchors.

Several copper alloy sheets have also been found (some still attached to the hull, some unattached) and have been studied either while still attached to the hull, or when dismantled from it (Figure 1). This discovery

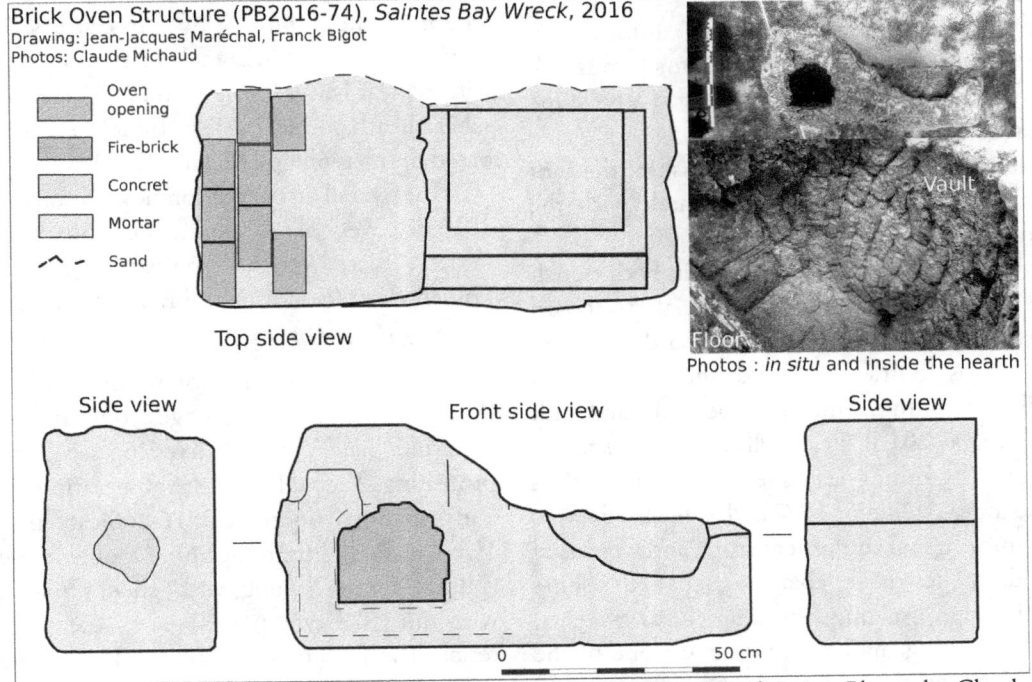

Figure 3. Brick oven structure, Drawing by Jean-Jacques Maréchal, digitized by Franck Bigot, Photos by Claude Michaud.

is consistent with archival records describing the Anemone's hull as plated with copper sheeting.

Understanding of the site's layout

Trench Test 1 and Trench Test 2 were excavated in 2016. The first one was located very close to the 2015 trench test (where a carronade has been studied) in order to observe structural continuity. The second one was located in the area comprising the aft section of the ship according to the results of the Trench Test 1. Each trench was 3m x 2m and were excavated to between 30 and 45cm depths. Trench Test 1 exposed the forward starboard side of the *Saintes Bay Wreck*, while Trench Test 2 uncovered the ship's aft starboard side (Figure 1). In Trench Test 1, a deck-clamp with a notch for a lower deck beam was discovered and studied in situ. The portion of the wreck uncovered in Trench Test 1 would have been below the waterline while the ship was still afloat, and includes structural elements such as sheathing, planking, frames and ceiling. In 2015, we had hypothesized that the keel and keelson were located under the carronade. In 2016 we abandoned this hypothesis and suspected these structures would have been situated along the eastern limit of Trench Test 1 (Figure 4). However, our team was unable to locate or identify these structures, leading us to believe that they no longer exist.

In Trench Test 2, we identified copper sheathing, planking, and frames, and the sternpost knee as well as the keelson and keel. We believe these represent structural elements of the stern, according to their characteristics and the site's layout.

Our trench tests provided ample information leading to a better understanding of the site's layout. We were able to identify and interpret many of the ship's lower hull structures. The galley elements we were able to locate match with the front part of the ship; the shot lockers location and pig-iron ballast match with the middle holds of the hull.

Cultural material and artifacts found in both trench tests match the location of the fore and aft starboard side: In Trench Test 1 (the fore starboard side test trench), nails, glass bottles, ceramics, sheave axes, and two lead rolls were found, which may be associated with keelhauling (Veyrat 2016). Lead rolls are called such as they are formed by rolling lead sheets onto themselves for compact storage (Diderot 1777). The lead rolls were part of the ship's original equipment store, and were used to create lead patches or to replace or repair the ship's equipment (i.e., aprons, lamps, sounding leads, weights, ammunition). Cutting marks are visible on one of the lead rolls, supporting the hypothesis that it functioned as raw material. Only three faunal remains were found in 2016. The position of those remains confirms the hypothesis of the discovery of a barrel of salted meat in 2015.

In Trench Test 2 (aft starboard side test trench), ceramic, glass wine bottles, weaponry (lead bullets, flint stones and the sheath of an officer's saber), and a draught water mark were found. These artifacts may be linked with the aft section of the ship.

The artifacts found are in poor condition and sparse in number, however, and this may be explained by the looting the site has suffered. It seems likely that collectors had already removed many of the diagnostic or better-preserve artifacts. One of site's discoverers let us have a glance at his collection from the site. It included an 1812 carronade firing lock, forged in a Bringol workshop (Paris) that was active from 1800 to 1816; thus the firing lock fits well within the chronological range to support our hypothesis (Buigné and Jarlier 2001); coins dating from 1788 to 1818; and gudgeons. The looted coin collection included an 1818 five francs' silver coin representing Louis the 18th, making it a post quem artefact. This coin is an interesting find on account of this post quem date, despite it having been removed from its context.

All of these artifacts corroborate a chronology that supports the identification of the *Saintes Bay Wreck* as the *Anémone*. Ceramic samples collected during the 2016 campaign originated from France (Biot, Vallauris, Beauvais and Creil workshops) (Moussette 1981) and date from the beginning of 19th century. The two glass wine bottles found in Trench Test 2 are Bordelaise bottles with typical 1820s forms (Serra 2011; Losier 2012). The saber sheath found in Test Trench 2 dates from 1802 based on its typology (Pétard 2006).

The overall artifact chronology is consistent with the 2015 discovery of a 12 pounder carronade manufactured in 1818, based on the typology of Jean Boudriot and Hubert Berti (Boudriot and Berti 1992 ; Guibert 2015).

Shipbuilding

Though the examination of the vessel's construction is still in its beginning stages, our findings on frame structure have been interesting so far and prove promising. The hull structure observations made in 2015 and expanded upon in 2016 indicate the *Saintes Bay Wreck* had a lightly-built hull. Double frames and single (filling) frames, along with chocks placed consistent with the 1823 type pattern, are present in both trench tests. The pattern is as follows: Double frame; chock; single frame; chock; single frame; chock; double frame.

Figure 4. Diver working in test trench 1, Photo by author.

In Trench Test 1, the chocks are located on the sides of the central axis. In Trench Test 2, they are located on the keel axis. Double frames are 24cm wide, with chocks that are 17cm wide and 11cm wide single frames.

Measurements of each double frame observed on site match with the distance of each double frame observed on plan. The sternpost knee, stern, keelson, and keel were also located in Trench Test 2. Because of the depth of the deposits in this area, however, the keel was unable to be studied thoroughly. The entire area needs to be reopened in order to accurately define all observations.

The above information matches the hull plan type of 1823. However, internal construction seems to differ from the hull plan. Archaeological observations have provided critical details regarding the vessel's constructions, including the use of chocks, frame sizes, and which types of wood were used. All wooden samples (keelson, planking, frame and ceiling samples) are oak, except a foot waling sample which is pine.

Perspectives

To date archaeological study matches with the identification of the *Saintes Bay Wreck* as the *Anémone*. Material culture chronology and typology, as structural element characteristics, represent a coherent whole that can be associated with a lightly-built French Navy ship dating from the end of the first quarter of the 19th century. Several archaeological evidences correspond with archival sources recording the *Anémone*'s loss. Those first evidence reinforce the identification of the *Saintes Bay Wreck* to the *Anémone*. The site has been chosen for study to expand our knowledge on the naval construction and material culture of early 19th century French navy schooners. Future research will further focus on the ship's construction, and on its material culture (faunal and ceramic remains etc.)- that of a French naval ship engaged on a custom mission in the West Indies. To date it is the only identified and known site of such a ship type, and one on such a mission. The fact that it was engaged against the illegal slave trade gives the *Anémone* site a patrimonial element that is quite unusual and both historically and archaeologically significant.

Archival Sources

Archives Nationales d'Outre-mer (Aix-en-Provence) [ANOM]: Série SG Série Géographique Guadeloupe 1815–1900. Correspondance 1815-1845, Généralités 1815–1859 ; Série État civil Guadeloupe Terre-de-haut 1824 20-48

Service Historique de la Défense (Rochefort) [SHD]: Série 2G21 Situation des constructions, refonte radoubs et réparations ; Série 3 E2 Revues et armements

Service Historique de la Défense (Cherbourg) [SHD]: Série 2G5 Plans de bâtiments mixtes

Service Historique de la Défense (Vincennes) [SHD]: Série DD Service général, Sous série 8DD1 Plans de navires

References

Lacour, Auguste
1855   Histoire de la Guadeloupe. E. Kolodziej, Paris, France.

BOUDRIOT, JEAN
1989   La Jacinthe Goélette 1823 Monographie Étude historique. Paris, France.

BUIGNÉ, JEAN-JACQUES AND JARLIER, PIERRE
2001   Le qui est qui de l'arme en France de 1350 à 1970. Répertoire des arquebusiers, armuriers, inventeurs, fourbisseurs, couteliers. éd. du Portail, La Tour-du-Pin, France.

BOUDRIOT, JEAN AND BERTI, HUBERT
1992   Artillerie de mer France 1650-1850 Étude historique et technique, Ancre, Nice, France.

GUIBERT, JEAN-SÉBASTIEN
2013   Mémoire de mer Océan de papiers Naufrage, risque et fait maritime à la Guadeloupe (fin XVII-mi XIXe siècles). Doctoral dissertation, Université des Antilles et de la Guyane, Guadeloupe, France.

2016   Results from the first excavation on the Saintes Bay's Shipwreck, Guadeloupe, FWI. 2016 ACUA Proceedings, Paul F. Johnston editor, p. 65-70, Advisory Council on Underwater Archaeology Publication.

GUIBERT, JEAN-SÉBASTIEN, FRANCK BIGOT, JEAN-JACQUES MARÉCHAL AND NOÉMIE TOMADINI
2015   Navigation antillaise site de la Passe de la Baleine, Les Saintes Guadeloupe, Ouacabou Université des Antilles, Schoelcher, France.

L'HOUR, MICHEL AND MASSY, JEAN-LUC
2002   Bilan scientifique du Drassm. Ministère de la culture, Paris, France.

LOSIER, CATHERINE
2012   Bouteilles et flacons : les contenants utilitaires français du début du XVIIIème siècle au début du XIXème siècle. Aspects techniques et sociaux, in Journal of glass studies, Volume 54, New-York.

MOUSSETTE, MARCEL
1981   Les terres cuites grossières des latrines des maisons Estèbe et Boisseau, Les collections archéologiques de la Place Royale, Québec, Canada.

PÉTARD, MICHEL
2006   Le sabre d'abordage : histoire du sabre de bord de la Marine française, de Louis XIV à la Troisième République, éd. du canonnier, Nantes, France.

SADANIA, MARINE
2015   Les ancres à jas de la façade atlantique maritime française de l'Antiquité au milieu du XXe siècle. Doctoral dissertation, Université de Nantes, France.

SERRA, LAURENCE
2011   Le verre comme mode d'emballage en Provence à l'époque moderne et contemporaine. Industrie, productions, commerce (1720–1920), Doctoral dissertation, Université d'Aix-Marseille, France.

VEYRAT, MAGALI
2016   le mobilier en plomb dans la marine en bois (XVIe-XIXe siècles). Le cas du littoral français. Doctoral Dissertation, Université de Nantes, France.

Acknowledgments:

The authors would like to express their gratefulness to editors John Albertson and Frederick Hanselmann for their precious help in translation.

Jean-Sébastien Guibert, PhD
AIHP-GÉODE EA 929 Université des Antilles
UFR Lettres et Sciences Humaines
Campus de Schoelcher
BP 7207 97275 Schoelcher Cedex, France.
059 (0)5 90 57 02 59
059 (0)6 90 65 77 31
jsebguibert2@hotmail.com / jean-sebastien.guibert@antilles-univ.fr

Franck Bigot
AIHP-GÉODE EA 929 Université des Antilles UFR Lettres et Sciences Humaines
Campus de Schoelcher
BP 7207 97275 Schoelcher Cedex, France.
059 (0)5 90 57 02 59
059 (0)6 90 65 77 31

Magali Lachèvre
Curator
Ministère de la Défense
Service historique de la Défense de Cherbourg
57 rue de l'Abbaye – CC314 – 50115
Cherbourg-en-Cotentin Cedex, France.
00 33 (0)2 33 92 65 07
00 33 (0)2 33 92 46 48
magali-a.lachevre@intradef.gouv.fr

Noémie Tomadini
MNHN-CNRS, Sorbonne Universités
55 rue Buffon, CP56 (Anatomie Comparée), 75005 Paris, France
33 (0)1 40 79 32 92
33 (0)6 51 64 00 51
noemie.tomadini@gmail.com / noemie.tomadini@mnhn.fr

Marine Sadania ,PhD
UMR 6566 CReAAH
263, Avenue du général Leclerc
Campus de Beaulieubâtiment 24-25
Université de Rennes 1 CS74205
35042 Rennes Cedex

www.ingramcontent.com/pod-product-compliance
Lightning Source LLC
Chambersburg PA
CBHW081459070526
44586CB00019B/2426